For Antoni Domènech (1952–2017),
teacher and,
even more important,
friend.

PRAISE FOR *AGAINST CHARITY*

"This book is a gift. Daniel Raventós and Julie Wark present a rich analysis of charity from the perspectives of philosophy, history, religion, and anthropology. They then argue that charity is an unequal relationship, presupposing the persistence of poverty and serving as a prop for capitalism. They offer many telling examples from contemporary philanthropy and international humanitarianism. Raventós and Wark conclude that a basic income for all is a necessary move toward social justice, and give us both a philosophical justification and practical suggestions for its implementation

— Joan Roelofs, author *Foundations and Public Policy*

This book promises to transform our understanding of contemporary capitalist society. In exploring "the kindness scam" embodied in charity today, it is for one thing, highly informative. Raventós and Wark remind us that when Princess Diana, that paragon of aristocratic kindness, was asked why she engaged in charitable work, she giggled and said, "I've got nothing else to do." They also show how inter-related are charity, luxury and celebrity… At the end of the day, they state, "our notions of altruism" are embedded in a wide field of history where the bearers of charity are not too different from old missionaries brandishing the gift of the Bible. Poverty and the suffering of others are depicted as problems to be ameliorated not abolished. Today's large-scale refugee movements, and rampant inequalities in the capitalist heartlands, are not seen as problems of the victims, but as threats to the safety of the rich.

— Kenneth Good, honorary fellow, global studies, RMIT University

In this impressive book, Wark and Raventós offer a searing indictment of the business of charity and its role in sustaining and whitewashing a neoliberal system of brutal inequality. Charity, at the end of the day, is not about helping people out; it's about keeping the have-nots in place and the powerful in power—something Wark and Raventós drive home with profound analysis and sarcastic wit. Particularly gratifying is the section on celebrity philanthropy, which gloriously makes asses out of everyone from human rights lawyer Amal Clooney and her human rights-obliterating wardrobe to Mother Teresa, patron saint of dictators, to football hero David Beckham—whose charity-based pursuit of knighthood was sadly thwarted by, as he graciously put it, "a bunch of cunts." *Against Charity* is a most refreshing and necessary antidote in an era in which the likes of Bill Gates, the Clintons, the United Nations, and a bazillion other undeserving outfits have been elevated to the realm of humanitarian superstardom. I won't implicate Wark and Raventós in the charity industry, but I will say they've given us a great gift.

— Belén Fernandez, author *The Imperial Messenger*

OTHER WORKS

Daniel Raventós
Basic Income: The Material Conditions of Freedom
Pluto Press, 2007

Julie Southwood (neé Wark) and Patrick Flanagan
Indonesia: Law Propaganda and Terror
Zed Press, 1983

Julie Wark
The Human Rights Manifesto
Zero Books, 2013

AGAINST CHARITY

First published by *CounterPunch* 2018.

AK Press
370 Ryan Avenue #100
Chico, CA 95973
www.akpress.org

CounterPunch
PO Box 228
Petrolia, CA 95558

ISBN-13: 978-1849353045
e-book ISBN: 978-1-849353052
Library of Congress Control Number: 2017936240

Typography and design by Tiffany Wardle.

Typeset in Minion Pro, designed by
Robert Slimbach for Adobe Systems Inc.
and Founders Grotesk, designed by Kris
Sowersby for Klim Type Foundry.

AGAINST CHARITY

Daniel Raventós & Julie Wark

TABLE OF CONTENTS

PART I
PROBLEMS

PREFACE
IN PRAISE OF KINDNESS

The word *kind*, in Old English *cynd(e)*, is of Germanic origin and related to *kin*. The original sense was nature or innate character so it came to mean a class distinguished by inherent characteristics and, by the fourteen century, courtesy or noble deeds expressing the feeling that relatives have for each other. There is a sense of equality built into this word. Fraternity too. And respect.

Charity, at least in its institutional form, has all but left behind its very early meanings of "disposition to do good," and "good feelings, good will and kindness" to take on its present form of a relationship between giver and receiver which is unequal because the receiver is in no position to reciprocate. But it is still usually presented as kindness, often as a way of masking the unkind disparity built into the relationship and sometimes, perhaps, expressing a wish that it had never relinquished its more kindly past. So, for example, Jack London wrote, "A bone to the dog is not charity. Charity is the bone shared with the dog, when you are just as hungry as the dog." The "charity" he describes harks back to origins and is more like kindness than charity as we now know it because it suggests equality, a kinship in hunger between the giver and the dog. And perhaps the dog can reciprocate by giving warmth to the man.

The more usual kind of charity, the one that has become institutionalized, is the one Chinua Achebe speaks of in his *Anthills of the Savannah*: "While we do our good works let us not forget that the real solution lies in a world in which charity will have become unnecessary." This is, unfortunately, the sort of charity that has become almost sacrosanct, that sort that draws attention to difference, and masquerades as kindness when it's usually benefitting the giver more than the receiver. One of the less salacious revelations of the recently released Lady Di tapes is that, when asked why she engaged in charity work, she giggles and says, "I've got nothing else to do!" So much for the recipients.

Since, in its oldest sense, kindness is attending to the good of kin and community, Aristotle tells us in the very first paragraph of *Politics*, "Every state is a community of some kind, and every community is established with a view to some good [...] But if all communities aim at some good, the state or political community, which is the highest of all, and which embraces all the rest, aims at good in a higher degree than any other, and at the highest good." Nowadays, however, the operative word in politics is "divide," the great chasm between the very rich and the many poor, the divide between men and women, citizens and refugees, blacks and whites, the pitting of one ethnic group against another, one religion against others, "progress" against the planet, private against public, and so on. Government, and especially the Trump Administration, is inciting division for the benefit of a few power holders in what amounts to an outright war against the public sphere, the public itself, and the public good. Institutional charity, further enriching tax-relieved millionaires and billionaires as they dole out their philanthropy to their pet projects, only upholds this division.

History, of course, and psychological studies—the Milgram experiment being one of the more notorious—have shown how in an authoritarian, egocentric setting apparently reasonable human beings can become desensitized to the suffering of others and act cruelly towards each other. The psychological toll taken by this desensitization on perpetrators or human instruments of *unkindness* (where *kind* is taken as both adjective and noun) doesn't get much press but, to give one example, the RAND Center for Military Health Policy Research estimates that 20% of the veterans who served in Iraq or Afghanistan suffer from major depression or post-traumatic stress disorder. Being unkind and thus acting against your own kind isn't good for humans. Yet the concerted misanthropy of political leaders for whom ordinary people have scant value, and billionaires who are not people like us but strut around as pampered freakish characters making outlandish utterances in their unreality shows are desensitizing whole nations to the plight of others leading, on the individual level, to hate crimes, racist attacks, a resurgent far right and, at the national level, to imposers of austerity policies who knowingly (you only need to read Yanis Varoufakis' recent memoir, *Adults in the Room* to know how knowingly) destroy millions of lives, to governments that are spending billions of dollars to harm refugees and immigrants, and to the shaming and distress of many citizens with this treatment of our fellows.

The awful inane drivenness of capitalist life is, in the name of freedom, hedging in our life-choice options and strangling our capacity to appreciate the beauty of our planet and to learn from other humbler species to such an extent we're mindlessly killing everything for the sake of unnecessary consumer goods and idiotic distractions. Scientists are speaking of a Sixth Extinction. If we are unable to recognize and respect each other, reclaim our kind, our humanity, recognize all humans as our kin, and practice kindness to our kind and other kinds of species, the alternative towards which we are already heading is truly terrifying.

Our title is *Against Charity* but it could equally be "For Kindness" (also in the kin sense of properly recognizing all, every one, of our kind), which would in fact be a call for universal human rights and their three great principles of freedom, justice and dignity. Almost any human being will say that he or she aspires to have and enjoy them. But they can't be given by charity because equality and fraternity are their other two essential qualities. They can only come when we recognize that we are all kin. And act in kind. So, in writing this book, we have not just limited ourselves to revealing charity as the "kindness" scam that it is, but we have also described the means by which we might be kinder to each other as creatures sharing the same planet.

Such a measure would have to be universal. Nobody can be excluded or treated as different. A universal basic income is not a pipe dream. In economic terms it is perfectly feasible. And it could guarantee the right to exist of absolutely everyone. Poverty could be abolished and the violence of what Pankaj Mishra describes in his recent book *The Age of Anger* as a global pandemic of rage might at least be attenuated. With a universal basic income, it would be possible to share the values of freedom, justice and dignity with all our human kind by the simple fact of respecting the basic right of material existence. If only we could achieve it, charity would be unnecessary and it could lay the groundwork for kindness to prevail.

Barcelona
August 2017

CHAPTER 1
DEPICTIONS

CHARITY IS FREQUENTLY REPRESENTED IN ART AS A SAINTLY activity, incarnated by people of exalted virtue like St. Elizabeth of Hungary, St. Lawrence and St. Nicholas with their bags of money ready to be doled out among the poor, or St. Martin of Tours who cut his cloak in two so he could give half of it to a beggar (and in one version his half—not the beggar's—was made whole again). More interestingly, in works by such painters as Andrea del Sarto (1486–1530), Lucas Cranach the Elder (1472–1553), Michele Tosini (1503–1577), and Anthony van Dyck (1599–1641) charity, the milk of human kindness, is personified in the form of a beautiful and sometimes voluptuous woman with a clutch of young children and, often, an actively suckling baby. Many *Virgo lactans* images suggest that, by feeding her child, the Virgin's breast feeds all humanity (*Mater Omnium, Nutrix Omnium*).[1] And, after all, the first bounty humans usually receive is the flow of life from a nourishing breast which, if it respects the baby's personhood, allows him or her to grow, free and autonomous, although it can also nurture stifling dependence.

In his *De factis dictisque memorabilibus (Memorable Deeds and Sayings)*, the historian and moralist Valerius Maximus (c. 30 CE) tells the pagan tale of how a young woman, Pero, suckled her father, Cimon, who was imprisoned and condemned to death by starvation. Her devotion moves the authorities who release Cimon. However, in Pliny the Elder's retelling of the story—perhaps trying to get around the incestuous subtext—"a plebeian woman of low position" nurses her imprisoned mother. Whatever the case, this is a story of family *pietas* in which kinship takes precedence over and breaks society's laws. But the transgressive element was soon erased. The story was taken over by Christianity and has been referred to as *Caritas Romana* ever since. There are many fascinating paintings[2] depicting Pero's generous daring, including, "The Seven Works of Mercy" (1607) by Michelangelo Merisi da Caravaggio, the "antichrist of painting."

At the end of John Steinbeck's *The Grapes of Wrath* the stillborn baby of Rose of Sharon Rivers (née Joad) is put in an apple box and released into a stream. Her uncle tells the dead child to float down to the town, rot and, by its stink, tell them that it died of injustice: "That's the way you can talk." In the book's last paragraph, Rose of Sharon breastfeeds a starving man they find in a barn. She takes command of the situation, but not from any lofty social position or sense of superiority. And in this case, in this written scene, unlike the paintings of charity in which the benefactress is shown as literally superior, always occupying the upper plane and foreground of the composition, Rose of Sharon lies down beside the man she suckles: she is on the same level as the receiver. The scene upset Steinbeck's publishers and a lot of other people too, apparently more for its sexual connotations than this subversive turning of Roman Charity into an act of simple, humane giving, from one victim to another. Or was seditious solidarity the real problem?

In painting, this sense of generous comradeship between vulnerable equals rarely appears because charity is a power relationship governed by divine or earthly predominance. And, also perhaps, because the great sponsors, benefactors and collectors of painting were the richest people of the times who could pay to project their own image of charity (and how they related with it). One unusual exception, explicitly drawn from Peter Paul Rubens' Roman Charity paintings, is "Partisan Ballad" (1969) by the Belarusian artist Mai Volfovich Dantsig. This depicts a partisan woman suckling a comrade on the Eastern Front during the Second World War. Both are armed. The work was withdrawn from at least one exhibition in Russia when local authorities found it "incestuous" (sic: was this because they saw "Roman Charity" and the original story of Pero and her father/mother in this work?), and it was eventually shown in 2015 as part of the exhibition "Exploring the Legacy of WWII in Russian Art" at the Saatchi Gallery in London[3] but, in this context of violence and suffering, the theme of charity was probably lost. Finally, this sensitive matter of lactating charity reached a high point of arid decorum with a faceless Mother Teresa of Calcutta, depicted by M. F. Husain (1915–2011), waving a bony hand over a brown baby whose head seems to be turned away from her breast which, painted black like the face, looks like a void.[4] This brings us closer to another view, that of the emotional emptiness of charity.

The milk of human kindness had risky or risqué connotations and artists strove to show the abundance of charity in a more or less chaste form, especially after the nineteenth century. Prior to this, in social life, exposed breasts, seen as a sort of homage to classical Greek nude sculptures, were acceptable in upper-class and aristocratic circles, while bare shoulders, legs and ankles were not. However, unlike the charitable variety and like the marble breasts, these pearly orbs on courtly display were rarely working breasts as their owners usually employed wet nurses. When the charitable breast belonged to the Madonna, artistic representations tended to follow social dictates, at times with strange results. In some images, anatomy is overridden and the mammary accoutrements are placed in strange positions, for example almost level with the collarbones, as in Paolo di Giovanni Fei's "Madonna and Child" (1370s)—in which mother and infant look very bored—and Hans Memling's more sensual "The Virgin Nursing the Christ Child" (c. 1487–1490). Then there are many images of the Virgin's milk being more widely shared, sprinkled on unhappy looking souls in purgatory, under a layer of surly cherubs in Pedro Machuca's "The Virgin and the Souls of Purgatory" (1517), or in Jean Thenaud's "The Triumph of Fortitude and Prudence" (c. 1522–1525), where lactic abundance pours from both breasts of a slightly demented-looking Virgin into a two-tiered container at which cherubs are washing their hands, and thence into a circular river. And in the *Lactatio Bernadi* paintings the Virgin accurately squirts her milk, sometimes from quite a long distance, into the mouth or onto the diseased eyes of St. Bernard of Clairvaux. However, after the Council of Trent (1545–1563)—or the Vatican's counterreformation—nudity in religious iconography was frowned upon and the Madonna Lactans was pastured out, although there are exceptions, for example William-Adolphe Bouguereau's quite decorous "Charity" (1878) in which a beautiful young woman seems to have been suckling no less than five chubby cherubs while gold coins spill from a large pot on which she rests one of her feet. But perhaps, here, the money outshines the milk.

Another ancient charity-giving breast was that of the pelican. In his *Etymologies* (Book 12, 7:32) Isidore of Seville (7th century CE) describes how the mother pelican killed her unruly offspring after being struck by their beaks, whereupon she grieved for three days. She then opens her own breast and sheds her blood to revive her children.[5] Six centuries later, the Franciscan monk, Bartholomaeus Anglicus, in his *De proprietatibus rerum*, (Book 12), embroiders the story to make it a clear Christian allegory, and cites the ultimate charitable act of spilling one's blood for another.

> [...] then for great bleeding the mother waxeth feeble, and the birds are compelled to pass out of the nest to get themselves meat. And some of them for kind love feed the mother that is feeble, and some are unkind and care not for the mother, and the mother taketh good heed thereto, and when she cometh to her strength, she nourisheth and loveth those birds that fed her in her need, and putteth away her other birds, as unworthy and unkind, and suffereth them not to dwell nor live with her.

The mother bird is now Christ, wounded by sinful humanity, cut open on the cross to shed his blood and save God's children. Nowadays, images of maternal abundance are not exactly crowd pleasers, as scandalized reactions to the "shocking" *Time Magazine* cover (May 21, 2012) attest. The picture shows a good-looking young woman who, instead of stalking down a catwalk, is looking defiantly at the camera with a protective arm around her three-year-old son (who seems somewhat wary) as he sucks on her breast. The issue is ostensibly "attachment parenting" (well, it's literally that). The photographer, Martin Schoeller, said he was using images of the Madonna and Child as his reference[6] but this didn't stop the cries of outrage against "*that cover*," that "notorious" cover in which charity somehow got lost.

Goya gave another view of charity. In Plate 49 of his "Disasters of War" prints, he shows, from downside up, "A Woman's Charity" (*Caridad de una mugger*, 1812–1814)[7] in the form of a cloaked woman who, hunched over and with her back to the viewer, is offering food to two larger-than-life figures sprawling on the ground. One of them, a woman, is scowling and scratching her face. She isn't looking at her benefactress. To the right, two dark-clad respectable people are lurking but trying not to get involved in this scene. The dominant figures here are the recipients and Goya has witheringly humbled the giver. In another plate of the series, number 27, titled *Caridad*,[8] he goes still further, this time showing people stripping dead bodies and unceremoniously dumping them into a pit. Where is the charity here? Is it from the dead giving their last rags to the living? Or is it the living giving this brutal burial to the dead? Charity for the receiver is no abundant breast, no shining cloak cleanly cut in two by a knight's sword, and neither does it take the form of gold coins carefully ministered like a sacrament from a saint's white hand. For Goya it is a cruel, dirty business which degrades everyone.

Today's imagery of charity is poor and childish compared with the lavishness and technical sophistication of yore. A Google search shows that hands in bright colors tend to clasp in circles, or make heart shapes, or pray (and Mother Teresa, too, is prominent as an icon of modern charity), or drop a few coins but they don't give actual sustenance. There's not much warmth in these images, and sometimes it's hard to tell if empty outstretched hands are begging or giving. There are also slogans urging us to "give the gift of charity." But charity is not a gift. This naïve misapprehension or cynical confusion needs clarifying but, before turning to this in the next chapter and, in particular, to Marcel Mauss's masterly anti-utilitarian treatise on forms of exchange and social structure in *The Gift*,[9] we shall take an excursion into etymology in an attempt to shed some more light on what charity might be.

Since around the 1150s, the word charity has meant "benevolence for the poor" (Old French, *charité*), the disposition to do good (Old French, *benevolence*), and also good feelings, good will and kindness (Latin, *benevolentia*). This then took on hues of mercy, compassion, alms and charitable foundations (because if poverty becomes institutionalized then there will also be institutions for the poor, mainly established by the church which has a firm grip on the monopoly of the "disposition to do good"). In the Latin nominative form, *caritas*, it gets more interesting, gnarly even. *Caritas* was often used in Vulgate to translate the Greek *agape* or Christian love of one's fellows, rather than *amor* which is somewhat too close to carnal matters. But after passing through costliness, esteem and affection it heads, etymologically at least, to whore, with the Latin cognate *carus* meaning "beloved" or "dear": the (illusion of) love not given but paid for. This *caritas* meaning "dear" or "valued" goes back to the Proto-Indo-European *ka-* ("like," "desire") which evolves into *hore*, prostitute or harlot in Middle English, and the Gothic *hōrs*, meaning adulterer, as well as similar words in other languages, including "lover" and "desire" from Old Persian *kama*, and the same word in Sanskrit for the Hindu god of love (hence the title *Kama Sutra* where *sutra* means a collection of aphorisms in the form of a manual). Metaphorically, at least, the connection between charity and whoring is suggestive if charity is seen as one kind of false love.

Another intriguing concept, now in the world of charity management, is "stewardship" going back to the idea implied in the Gospels that we are responsible for the care and management of that which belongs to another (God). The Apostle Paul asks "What do you have that you did not receive?" (1 Corinthians 4:7). Matthew's parables (24–25) urge the faithful to be stewards of God's kingdom through charitable acts like feeding the hungry, clothing the unclothed, and succoring those who are in prison. In today's philanthropic language stewardship supposedly refers to ethical accountability and responsibility in the use of charitably contributed resources. But, however much the word "ethical" is uttered, charity management is a fine playground for corrupt practices, as we shall discuss later.

Perhaps the Spanish translations of "stewardship," *custodia, tutela, dirección, conducción, gobierno, mandato*, come closer to the reality of today's philanthropy since all of them refer to a relationship in which the caretaker of someone else's property exercises power. This situation of inequality, or absence of rights, is repeated in the common expressions *dame una caridad* (as a beggar says: give me something I lack), *hacer una caridad* (what a philanthropic person does—*a* selected act of charity but not benevolence in general), and *por caridad* (asking for clemency, understanding or benevolence from some more powerful person). In Greek translations of the Gospels, "stewardship" is rendered as οικονομία (*oikonomía)*, literally meaning "good management of the household" from which "economics" is derived. But the associated, more egalitarian senses of one human family—kin, being an equal member of one human*kind*—were lost long ago.

Then again, statutory definitions of charity seem to recognize its status as a socioeconomic phenomenon with legal, religious and moral dimensions, and not something to be left to normal folk. In sub-section 1 of the UK Charities Act 2011,[10] charity has moved a long way from the lactating breast and is defined as an institution: "For the purposes of the law of England and Wales, 'charity' means an institution," which is established for charitable purposes only, and is subject to the control of the High Court. Said "charitable purposes" cover quite a mélange of altruistic and state-entrenching projects: prevention or relief of poverty; advancement of education; advancement of religion; advancement of health or saving of lives; advancement of citizenship or community development; advancement of the arts, culture, heritage or science; advancement of amateur sport; advancement of human rights, conflict resolution or reconciliation or the promotion of religious or racial harmony or equality and diversity; advancement of environmental protection or improvement; relief for those in need because of youth, age, ill-health, disability, financial hardship or other disadvantage; advancement of animal welfare; promotion of the efficiency of the armed forces of the Crown, or of the efficiency of the police, fire and rescue services or ambulance services.

There are plenty of contradictions here. To begin with, one should be very leery of the state's interest in advancing human rights when, for example, in the words of David Cameron,[11] it sells "brilliant things" like Eurofighter Typhoons to Saudi Arabia on the very day that the European parliament voted for an arms embargo on the country because of widespread airstrikes against civilian targets in Yemen,[12] in violation of international law. A war crime, to be precise. On the domestic scene, promoting the armed forces of the Crown is difficult to imagine as a charitable activity, while advancement of human rights and environmental protection have become more revolutionary than benevolent in recent years. To sum up, charity is dubious, even as a concept. It depends very much on who is mouthing the word.

It's not so much the charitable act itself that's important but the relationship between the parties involved. It might feel uplifting for a paragon of society, busy with the Christmas shopping, to drop a buck in a beggar's bowl. But the beggar sees the brightly wrapped parcels, compared to which a crumpled greenback looks quite meager, to put it nicely. Surely it's an affront to be handed the crumbs from the rich man's table when you can never aspire to the caviar, oysters, and all the other goodies piled on that table, especially when the rich man preens and prides himself on his generosity, gets tax deductions, gives his little homilies and gets some wonderful advertising to brush up his image if he's a celebrity. Oscar Wilde was right. The best among the poor are ungrateful and rebellious.[13] Thomas Szasz was also right: "The proverb warns that 'You should not bite the hand that feeds you.' But maybe you should, if it prevents you from feeding yourself."[14] However you look at it, charity's a one-way relationship. In general, the poor can't be benevolent. They are disbarred from this brand of good will, munificence and offering the milk of human kindness: *Quod licet Jovi, non licet bovi* (What is permitted to Jove is not permitted to the cow). Charity makes babies of its recipients, infants at an all-powerful breast, a kind of archaic superego. You have to feed now, when I say. You have to stay in that position. You have to depend on me. Omniscience: I know what you need. If charity is the opium of the privileged, as Chinua Achebe remarked in *Anthills of the Savannah*,[15] they won't be keen to renounce it. No wonder Rose of Sharon smiled mysteriously as the starving man in the barn drank at her breast for she had broken the rules and literally offered the milk of human kindness. Her milk was not charity but a gift, a gift in true solidarity.

CHAPTER 2
CHARITY IS NOT A GIFT

SIR THOMAS BROWNE POINTED OUT LONG AGO IN HIS *RELIGIO Medici* (1645), that, "It is as erroneous a conceit to redresse other Mens misfortunes upon the common considerations of mercifull natures, that it may be one day our own case, for this is a sinister & politick kind of charity, whereby we seem to bespeake the pities of men in the like occasions: and truely I have observed that those professed Eleemosynaries, though in a croud or multitude, doe yet direct and place their petitions on a few and selected persons."[16] It was ever thus: the "few and selected." Charity, which is not the lot of all men, tends to be discriminating. This means that it needs to be institutionalized in order to distinguish between the worthy and unworthy needy in accordance with the ruling values and ideology of the place and day. Some people (the cherubic little babies in art) are eligible for this love of "humankind" and others aren't. This situation bears some resemblance to that of human rights which, although avowedly universal, are certainly not that and are therefore the prerogative of some. As such, they too have become institutionalized in unequal societies which dole out privileges and call them rights.

Charity is generally deemed to be a good thing because many people harbor at least subliminal feelings of love and kindness towards other members of the species. Indeed, there is a large area of research in psychology in which scholars are trying to prove that altruism is innate. If the values of love and kindness—combined as decency, or conformity to the standard of treating all others well—were put into practice on a universal scale, it would be reasonable to assume that exploitation of humans by other humans wouldn't happen, wars would end, poverty wouldn't exist, and society would be very different. This raises the essential difference between charity as an institution and individual acts of kindness. There are many examples of disinterested acts of magnanimity by individuals and some charitable institutions (usually small) so, if this book is a criticism of "charity," it is not inveighing against all acts of charity but specifically denouncing a particular institutionalized form which both shores up and, inadvertently or actively, participates in and benefits from the unjust systems that make charity necessary and, in all likelihood, not only discourage disinterested, independent manifestations of love of humankind but make them dangerous. An extreme example of this, but certainly not the only one, is the assassination in 2016 of Berta Isabel Cáceres Flores, the Honduran environmental and indigenous rights activist.

To rephrase the old saying, the way things are, charity begins in the mansion, tends to stay in the mansion, to benefit mainly those who live in the mansion, and to such an extent that it becomes antisocial. If we see this "charitable" behavior, not as expressing universal love of humanity but as destroying society and even the charitable person's own milieu, by condoning and reproducing the misery and conflict brought about by great inequality, perhaps the question posed by Sir Thomas Browne should give pause for thought: "But how shall we expect charity towards others, when we are uncharitable to ourselves? 'Charity begins at home,' is the voice of the world; yet is every man his greatest enemy, and, as it were, his own executioner." Yet, one of the most enduring clichés of charity is that it is about disinterested, humanity-loving gift giving.

Gift giving is far more complex than it may first appear. A gift, not given and accepted freely and in conditions of possible reciprocity, can be a poisoned chalice or, at least, an affront to the dignity of the receiver. Economic exchanges, including gift giving and receiving, are usually made in accordance with a clear understanding of the conditions of the deal, for example, time factors, interest and repayment. In gift economies a gift is presented in more or less equal, well recognized conditions, and the obligation is not individually burdensome but part of a social exchange in which the community is strengthened. Property, here, is not an alienable thing but signifies a relationship between people. In unequal relationships the gift can be crushing and, in the case of charity, wrongly understood as a gift, humiliating. Without some kind of debt relationship, reciprocity is ruled out. If gift-giving, unlike a commodity transaction, binds the members of a society or societies together, charity is a false, divisive gift, not least because the receiver, unable to reciprocate, cannot willingly enter into any socially binding relationship with the giver. In her Foreword to Marcel Mauss's classic work *The Gift*,[17] Mary Douglas sums up his main thesis: nothing is given freely:

> [...] the idea of a pure gift is a contradiction. By ignoring the universal custom of compulsory gifts we make our own record incomprehensible to ourselves: right across the globe and as far as we can go in the history of human civilization, the major transfer of goods has been by cycles of obligatory returns of gifts (p. viii).

The idea of the free gift is antisocial, because, "it is the donor's intention to be exempt from return gifts coming from the recipient. Refusing requital puts the act of giving outside any mutual ties" (p. vii). This raises two questions. Who is excluded? Who excludes? If charity means exclusion from reciprocal exchange, then it tells us a lot more about class structure than the goodness of givers. It is no wonder, then, that a wide range of august charities—including, for example the Dana-Farber Cancer Institute, John F. Kennedy Centre for the Performing Arts, and the United States Holocaust Memorial Museum[18]—for all their prattle about embracing and succoring suffering humanity, are not exactly famous for their transparency. Like Mauss, Mary Douglas argues that, "Class structure would be clearly revealed in information about giving within and exclusion from reciprocal voluntary cycles of exchange [...]. If we persist in thinking that gifts ought to be free and pure, we will always fail to recognize our own grand cycles of exchanges, which categories get to be included and which get to be excluded from our hospitality" (p. xv). Unsurprisingly, this kind of information is not included in census or most survey records.

This insight about inclusion and exclusion in exchange cycles is all the more striking when considered in the context of today's exclusive, global-reach, socially and politically agglutinating "cycle of exchanges," which is basically limited (at least in terms of influence) to a handful of immensely rich people who own more than half the world's wealth. This small circle of powerful exchangers, claiming to be "delegates" or representatives of the rest of us, has shrunk so dramatically that the "community" welded together by equal-basis exchanges in the neoliberal world, fits snugly into the mountain stronghold of Davos.

Then again, re-creating what Mauss calls the "bond of commonality" forged by the gift, there are new "grand cycles of exchanges" emerging mainly in resistance to the power of the Davos coven, most notably the commons movement, which is expressly seen by many of its supporters as a new gift economy. Expanding rapidly, it has many areas of activity, including resistance to the biopiracy of multinationals privatizing traditional skills and knowledge of natural resources; protecting commons assets like air, water, forests and minerals; land trusts; reclaiming public space; the movement for a more equitable, eco-friendly society aiming to keep political and socioeconomic excesses in check; copyleft; and a new "gift economy" in which the giving relationship rejects money as an unacceptable alienable currency and takes place within a community of shared purpose whose members give time and creativity to the community and reap benefits in return; free, open software communities, wikis and other websites, crowdfunding the collaborative and creative commons, blood donation systems and exchanges in scientific and academic research.

The Gift is an eloquent rebuttal of the assumptions behind today's economic theory because, with his account of exchange systems in non-Western societies, Mauss demonstrates that the "free market" is not an inevitable product of human nature and that, in many parts of the world, stable social life is seen as a much more important goal than capital accumulation. Mary Douglas takes up cudgels in joining Mauss's onslaught (as a revolutionary socialist but not Marxist) against utilitarianism, setting his work squarely in the framework of the French political philosophers' animus towards the English utilitarians, mainly because of their attempts to water down key Marxist principles in their impoverished conception of the person as an individual rather than as a social being, their shying away from the fact that social relations change with shifts in the mode of production, their negative concept of liberty and, hence, their overlooking of the moral role of political participation, and their failure to explain the importance of social norms. In a nutshell, the main problem is individualism (pp. x–xi). And charity, being antisocial and egoistical, beyond the bounds of reciprocity, is an eloquent expression of that. In 1990, when Douglas was writing, utilitarianism was still alive and well as social theory, now safely cocooned in the respectability of a carefully trimmed, narrow, specialist discipline of economics.

> Utilitarianism is not just a technique of econometrics, nor a faded philosophy of the eighteenth century. [...]. Social Darwinism walks again and the survival of the fittest is openly invoked. Philosophically creaking but technically shining, unified and powerful, utility theory is the main analytical tool for policy decisions (p. xvi).

These policy decisions, now that economics has been severed from its roots in political economy, are not remotely concerned to—or, rather, desperately anxious not to—inquire into the inner workings of social structure as expressed in facts like who is included and who is not included in cycles of exchange. A glance at the World Economic Forum reports after 2012 shows that the Davos clique has abandoned its concerns about disaster prevention and is now focused on "resilience," its euphemism for survival of the fittest.

Some writers, for example Jonathan Parry,[19] have pointed out how, in the form of charitable alms-giving, for example in India (*Dāna*), the "pure" so-called gift of charity can be "poisonous." He criticizes conventional interpretations of *The Gift* and, following Mauss, notes that "an ideology of the 'pure' gift is shown to be inseparable from the ideology of the purely interested individual pursuit of utility" (p. 543). Alms-giving precludes mutuality and, if you pass the same beggar every day, he or she will keep asking for handouts so the cold-bloodedness of inequality becomes increasingly entrenched as dropping the dollar in the box becomes a mechanical action with minimal human contact. On the large scale, this is basically what happens with humanitarian or development "aid."

Today, twenty-seven years after Mary Douglas wrote her Foreword, utilitarianism still hasn't gone away. One of its foremost proponents, Peter Singer, has quite a lot to say about it in relation with charity. What he cares about is utility, the "bang for the buck,"[20] so he believes that, in terms of human welfare, it is better to help those in extreme poverty in developing countries because the buck bangs better there. He calls this "effective altruism." Since the social aspect of reciprocity doesn't enter his equation, he seems to believe that the bucks supposedly helping poverty-stricken people in other countries actually remain there and do some good. In fact, charity bucks bang best at home, usually in the pockets of the donors. *Irin News*[21] shows with compelling graphics how little of the relief aid economy, worth about US$156 billion, actually reaches the supposed beneficiaries. If you follow the money, it doesn't take much research to discover that official emergency aid money mainly flows back to source, to UN agencies, large western-based charities, the Red Cross or Red Crescent Movement, the arms industry and big western construction companies, for example. Only a minute fraction is channeled directly to frontline charities in affected countries.

Charity is inconceivable in a gift-based society. The gift may be an economic factor but, in particular, it is also based on the notion of honor. Marcel Mauss, combining history, sociology and ethnography in analyzing his anthropological data, calls it a "total social fact." It is religious, mythological, shamanic, juridical, economic, and also a mainstay of a large social structure since it brings together tribes, clans, families and even groups from different territories. The gift is political inasmuch as it functions as a form of power, advancing personal and community interests, but this power is tempered because it entails three basic obligations: to give, to receive and to reciprocate. It is the third condition, reciprocity, which implies a relationship between more-or-less equals and disqualifies charity as a gift. Gift exchange, where gifts are continually circulating, is a feature of clan-based but not class-based societies in which commodities are fungible and alienated.

In the gift-exchange system—which is basically in the male realm (at least in the literature, which tends to ignore the economic role of women) as opposed to that of the abundant female breast of Roman Charity—one shouldn't refuse a gift because, assumed to be given to a more or less equal recipient, it entails obligations. Indeed, it underpins the social system as a form of commitment, a covenant understood by everyone. Rejection, showing an unwillingness to participate, is viewed as an antisocial act, affecting the whole group. In Mauss's words, "To refuse to give, to fail to invite, just as to refuse to accept, is tantamount to declaring war; it is to reject the bond of alliance and commonality." The giver is obliged to give because, "the recipient possesses some kind of property right over anything that belongs to the donor," an ownership expressed and understood as a "spiritual bond" (p. 13). Unlike commodity exchange which, dealing in alienated objects, entails the setting of prices and rules for buying and selling, the gift exchange establishes a relation between subjects in the form of gift-and-return-gift, in a perpetual cycle in which the idea of conservation is key. The gift is inalienable from the society.

In the economic system known as potlatch—from Chinook Jargon, originally derived from the Nuu-chah-nulth word *pała·č* meaning "to give away"—characterizing some societies, for example the Kwakiutl, the Haïda, and the Tsimshian of the Pacific Northwest Coast, "The punishment for failure to reciprocate is slavery for debt," says Mauss (p. 42). This seems to suggest the inverse of the charitable relationship in which having to depend on charity is a form of subjugation while, in these societies, when a person can't or won't give, thus breaking the bonds of reciprocity, it is the recalcitrant giver who is enslaved and thus removed from the realm of social life among more or less equals. Yet it was not all equal because, essentially, the gift increased the power of the giver who could then acquire dependents, or what Chris Gregory[22] calls "gift-debtors" The individual unable to repay the loan or reciprocate the potlatch loses rank and even status as a free man. Among the Kwakiutl, when an individual whose credit is poor must borrow he is said to sell a slave.

Before the Europeans reached the Pacific Northwest in 1774 the diseases they had imported elsewhere in North America had already arrived and infected local Indian groups, thus bringing about a massive decline in the population. This led to fiercer competition among chieftains trying to uphold the threatened social hierarchy, not based on accumulation but wealth for giving or destroying. Eventually, the introduction of western manufactured goods in the late 18th and early 19th centuries caused massive inflation in the gifting economy.

Uninterested and unable to understand anything of this complex principle of social structure and, worse, scandalized by a practice that was so antithetical to the parsimony of Christian charity, missionaries saw it as a terrible, profligate obstacle to conversion and civilization. The lawmakers agreed. In 1884, the "Indian Act" outlawed it and the associated dances, and anyone found engaging in them was liable to imprisonment. However, the tradition was deeply entrenched as the very foundation of society, and the settlements were so numerous that even converted tribes were able to continue the potlatch. Contrary to expectations, it did not die out as younger, educated, more "civilized" people supplanted the old leaders, and the law was finally repealed in 1951. Indigenous people today still organize potlatches as a way of reaffirming their birthright and abiding social values.

Another, not dissimilar system is the Kula (Ring), the complex gift exchange system of the Trobriand Islands of Papua New Guinea, which was studied by Bronislaw Malinowski.[23] In his suggestively titled work *Argonauts of the Western Pacific* he sets out to understand why people undertook the arduous, risky journey across the sea if it was only to exchange "trinkets," mainly necklaces, bracelets, and armbands. He found that this was an intricate exchange system which, reserved for chiefs, was clearly linked to political authority, a trading partnership understood as noble and entailing mutual obligations like solemnity of presentation, hospitality, protection and assistance. There was an "opening" gift and, later, a reciprocating gift or, in Malinowski's words a "clinching gift" to seal the transaction. This is the *kudu*, the tooth that "bites through, and liberates" (Mauss: p. 26). Malinowski's account has been criticized by subsequent anthropologists like Annette Weiner[24] who points out that Trobriand Island society is matrilineal and Malinowski overlooked the exchanges between women, who hold great political and economic power, but her contribution only makes the question of the social and reproductive bonds of gift giving more intriguing without affecting the contrast between these dynamic exchange cycles and the cold comfort of charity. Weiner also develops Mauss's ideas of inalienability by discussing his notion of the "spirit of the gift" in terms of reciprocity, the standpoint from which she addresses the paradox of keeping while giving. This notion would seem to be corroborated by the fact that, once a person is in the system, it is impossible to leave it because gifts always have to be returned. Knowing this, the person keeps the gift or at least its spirit.

Elsewhere in Papua New Guinea, in the highlands around Mount Hagen, the "big man" system known as Moka, which is mainly based on pigs, is all about debt (*moka*). If a man returns an amount equivalent to what he has received that is the end of the relationship. In order to keep the exchange going, he has to pay *moka*, the extra, which increases his prestige and makes the receiver indebted. It is deemed best to give a gift to a big man because, once equipped with that partner's *moka*, a man can pass on the extra, increase the number of his exchange partners, and thereby improve his chances of repaying a gift. As the network expands, the most active members become big men who strive to give the biggest gift to a competitor. Anyone who pays back only what has been received or is unable to do even that is a *rabisman* (rubbish man), but the prestige of the big man is also in danger because, without enough followers to look after his growing herd of pigs, he runs the risk of being unable to pay the *moka*. And the big man who out-gifts him can then no longer count on the necessary surplus to keep his followers happy, so the system breaks down and new big men start to emerge.

The important difference between the potlatch, Kula and Moka, and commodity exchange is that, in the first three systems, the object given by one person to the other is an integral part of the system and not alienated. A commodity has a use value (its intrinsic property) and, in particular, an exchange or extrinsic value, which is the "quantitative proportion in which use-values of one sort are exchanged for those of another sort," in the words of Chris Gregory.[25] Taking the approach of political economy Karl Marx, unlike Adam Smith and David Ricardo, distinguished between commodity and non-commodity economies, understanding that the exchange value of a commodity was a historically specific property requiring certain social conditions for its existence. Hence,

> [...] the exchange of commodities evolves originally not within primitive communities, but on their margins, on their borders, the few points where they come into contact with other communities. This is where barter begins and moves thence into the interior of the community, exerting a disintegrating influence upon it. The particular use-values which, as a result of barter between different communities, become commodities, e.g., slaves, cattle, metals, usually serve also as the first money within these communities.[26]

To sum up, commodity exchange is a quantitative relationship involving alienable objects between people who are in a position of mutual independence, while objects exchanged as gifts are inalienable and the relationship between transactors is then a qualitative one governed by the rules of communality and mutual benefit. So Marx pointed out that if alienation marks the transfer of private property, it "has no existence in a primitive society based on property in common."[27] Chris Gregory identifies five criteria which distinguish commodity from gift exchanges: 1) immediate versus delayed exchange; 2) alienable versus inalienable goods; 3) independent versus dependent agents; 4) quantitative versus qualitative relationship; and 5) exchange of objects versus exchange between people. The nature of the gift economy constitutes one of the foundational debates of anthropology, and the question of market and non-market exchange is by no means settled so this brief account of the nature of the gift makes no pretension to being exhaustive. The sharp distinction between the gift and the commodity has been challenged by several writers with objections citing western ethnocentrism, romanticization of the gift (for example, Arjun Appadurai, James D. Carrier), false conceptions of the gift economy (John Frow), and the ways in which objects can flow through spheres of exchange, becoming gifts and then being turned back into commodities, and so on. Perhaps the distinctions are blurred at times but this would not deny the crucial points made by Mauss, Douglas and Gregory, in particular concerning reciprocity, social ties and alienation, which are aspects that are especially germane to the question of charity.

Writers who want to blur the distinctions between the gift and the commodity or the alienable and inalienable items of exchange must explain the proscription in some societies of capital goods. Among the Uduk people from the borderland of Sudan and Ethiopia a gift cannot be invested but must be consumed. Some writers locate the origin of the gift economy in food sharing, giving rise to the idea that the gift is something that must perish. But it is much more than that. The Pirahã people of Brazil (people whose language does not include numbers) put it nicely. One man, explaining the fact that a successful hunter will invite others to a feast instead of conserving the food for a time of scarcity said, "I store meat in the belly of my brother."[28] In other words, the generous feast is a safeguard against possible failure in the individual's future search for food. This is not so far from the precept of the Trobriand islanders of Papua New Guinea: a gift cannot be hoarded but must keep moving (socially).

The gift economy can take many forms and certainly can't be pigeonholed merely as primitive and a feature of societies that are about to become extinct. These forms can range widely, from religious tithing, the Theravada Buddhist "feasts of merit" in Southeast Asia, which bear certain similarities with the potlatch, Wikipedia (except for some operational aspects of its website), free schools, Creative Commons, open-source software development, and peer-to peer file-sharing (P2P).

In contrast, charity is static and socially arid however often the charitable act is repeated because it is one-way, unequal and does its bit towards ensconcing a discriminating status quo. A Kashmiri cautionary tale tells of two Brahmin women who tried to confine their obligatory alms-giving to their own caste by giving only back and forth to each other. When they died they were turned into poisoned wells, a fitting metaphor for their barren notion of giving. The bottom line of charity is that it is an assault on the three basic principles of human rights: justice, freedom and human dignity. Imposing a gift on someone who can't reciprocate is an offence against dignity. The donor's exemption from receiving a gift in return together with the obligations it entails is an affirmation of his or her freedom and social standing and a denial of those of the recipient. The supposed beneficiary is dependent on the will of the donor and is thus—as recognized by very different social thinkers ranging from Aristotle to the Kwak'wala speaking peoples—unfree. The unfreedom is unjustly perpetuated and consolidated by the political institutionalization, the religious overtones, and the mindless respectability of the unequal relationship of charity.

In the words of Mary Douglas in her Foreword to *The Gift* (p. x), "A gift that does nothing to enhance solidarity is a contradiction." And Mauss concludes that, "The unreciprocated gift [...] makes the person who has accepted it inferior" (like the "Rubbish Men" who are unable to reciprocate in the Moka system), and hence, "Charity is [...] wounding for him who has accepted it, and the whole tendency of our morality is to strive to do away with the unconscious and injurious patronage of the rich almsgiver." (p. 65).

Marcel Mauss's colossal work in the form of a small book examines reciprocal gift-giving in societies as far-flung as those of American Indians, Eskimos, Melanesians, and Australian

Aborigines, and also finds the same basic principles in ancient legal systems—Roman, Germanic, Indo-European and classical Hindu—all of whose laws incorporate the basic principle that there are no free gifts. On the basis of this wide-ranging evidence, he argues that a great part of human society is based on collective exchange practices. His theory of the gift is one of "human solidarity" but he also lays bare power relationships in the economic structure of society—"all dues, gifts, fines, inheritances and successions, tributes, fees and payments" (p. xii)—showing that these mechanisms make it possible to know who is excluded and who benefits. But unlike capitalism and its secrecy, even or especially in charitable operations, the gift economy is public by nature and these factors are known to the participants.

The revealing mechanisms of economic structures which Mauss describes are not confined to faraway places but would seem to be intrinsic, albeit to different extents and in different forms, to all human societies. The often systematic confusion between charity and the gift is also indicative of who is excluded and who benefits, as can be illustrated much closer to home, for example by attempts in eighteenth-century England to present increasingly harsh anti-pauper laws as Christian magnanimity. Here, charity became prominent as an ideology of benevolence which, regulated by a plethora of laws, regulations and institutions—and, in the case of upper-class women who have fallen on hard times, moral tutelage, as Sarah Scott's novels *A Description of Millenium Hall and the Country Adjacent, Together with the Characters of the Inhabitants and such Historical Anecdotes and Reflections as May Excite in the Reader Proper Sentiments of Humanity, and Lead the Mind to the Love of Virtue* (1762) and *The History of Sir George Ellison* (1766) describe—underpinned a social and economic system which worked in favor of the gentry and inflicted silk-glove-sheathed violence on the underclasses. Charity and benevolence served not only to mask the brutality of agrarian capitalism but were also essential in constructing and maintaining the relations of dominance as industrial capitalism was consolidating and being institutionalized.

Raymond Williams[29] identifies one of the key economic elements of this charitable underpinning of the most uncharitable enterprise of pauperizing a very large proportion of society, quoting Rosa Luxemburg when pointing out that the Christian tradition of benevolence was a paralyzing "charity of consumption" only:

> The Roman proletarians did not live by working, but from the alms which the government doled out. So the demands of the Christians for collective property did not relate to the means of production but the means of consumption.

Any notion of charity of production in which people might have worked together "in loving relations" was all but absent. Feeding on the structural inequalities of feudalism, incipient industrialization was not going to tolerate any worker's claims to the benefits of his or her own labor. No doubt John Locke's insight about the earth's bounty was too close to the bone.

> [...] all the Fruits it naturally produces, and Beasts it feeds, belong to Mankind in common, as they are produced by the spontaneous hand of Nature; and no body has originally a private Dominion, exclusive of the rest of Mankind, in any of them, as they are thus in their natural state: yet being given for the use of Men, there must of necessity be a means to *appropriate* them some way or other before they can be of any use, or at all beneficial to any particular Man. [...] Though the Earth, and all inferior Creatures be common to all Men, yet every Man has a *Property* in his own *Person*. This no Body has any Right to but himself. The *Labour* of his Body, and the *Work* of his Hands, we may say, are properly his.[30]

References to charity signaled doling out food and, sometimes, the rich and poor breaking bread at the same table like loving members of the same family, but the relations of production were entirely bereft of love, an absence that was occasionally disguised by full bellies granted by a temporarily beneficent master, cloaked in the symbolism of bread and god. And as Williams concludes, "In the complex of feeling and reference derived from this tradition, it matters very much, moreover, that the name of the god and the name of the master are significantly single—our Lord" (p. 31).

Humanitarianism today has elements of these old ideas of charity in accepting catastrophe as established, basically something that happens to the wretched of the earth, and rushing to remedy supposedly natural disasters with consumer goods without a thought to the causes of said disasters, a viewpoint that harks back to the Middle Ages: "In the scarce medieval economy, poverty could be seen as the natural consequence of what seemed natural calamities: famine, sickness and plague" (p. 83). In theory, the response was "natural" charity, which all good men were expected to practice as a duty to God, their creator. Grinding everyday poverty of was part of the established order and, with the transition to the post-feudal, more abundant society, old ideas of the compulsory poor-rate, a tax to help the "deserving poor" (in which "deserving" can be read in two ways) levied on landowners, and the sixteenth-century Poor Laws were organized into a new administrative machinery because paupers had to be systematized as part of the system that produced them. So, from the early eighteenth century there were "charity schools," sometimes more honestly called "industrial schools" for the "Promotion of Christian Knowledge," the development of a parish-based workhouse system whereby the able-bodied were put to work and some of the sick and elderly received care. By 1780, London workhouse children were being sent to the spinning mills of Lancashire and Yorkshire.

In charity's arbitrariness, a legal distinction between "criminal vagrants" and the "deserving poor" had long been made. In early modern England, twenty-eight statutes on vagrancy were passed between 1700 and 1828. In its inception, the modern state was draconian and only the meekest of paupers received charity. Vagrancy or vagabondism—etymologically related with the Old French *walcrer*, "to wander"—one of the few ways in which a poor person could exercise a modicum of freedom, was an intolerable crime in a society wherein the Christian values of work and orderliness were paramount for the overlords and, when embraced by the poor and with a bit of luck, were rewarded by some crumbs of charity. Roaming or itinerancy meant lack of control, bore the seeds of unruly, dangerous crowds and their hunger marches and, in the background, the potentially incendiary effects of landlessness and social dislocation in the countryside. A vagrant was a masterless man, a dreadful anomaly, and could be enslaved, hung, imprisoned or transported. The point here is that, in their inception, the vagrancy laws were part and parcel of the official approach to charity in changing times. It is difficult to find a clearer example of the fact that charity means control and domination.

When the social structure of gift-based societies is broken down by "free" markets, and the degree of equality which enables reciprocity or Mauss's "human solidarity" disappears when wealth and power are concentrated in the hands of a few, charity steps in, wearing the garb of a gift. In recent years it has become a secretive, highly lucrative business known as philanthrocapitalism. Charity, with its static utilitarian features and wretched conception of the human being as an isolated, alienated individual is just another prop of the capitalist and neoliberal systems. Ignoring changes in the mode of production (and, especially, those related with disaster-causing environmental destruction and global warming) this system now produces oligarchic forms of charity, for example the Bill Gates Foundation, in its particular version of utilitarianism. But the commons are resurgent in politics today, as are smaller political units, for example municipal administrations, which are much more visible. There is a new emphasis on "horizontality"[31] which is described by the cultural anthropologist Marianne Maeckelbergh of the news site *Global Uprisings* as, "a fiercely egalitarian, decentralized, networked, form of democratic decision-making," rejecting "fixed representation as a political structure," and saying no to the geographically delineated space of the nation state and uniformity as the guiding principle of democratic deliberation. Instead, each member of the networked polity "has to take active responsibility," which means that "participants are continuously challenging (with varying degrees of success) inequalities and discriminations as they arise within their own structures of governing."

This kind of structure requires reciprocity.

Charity has no place here.

In some quarters at least, the gift culture is renascent.

CHAPTER 3
RELIGION: LOVE AND PROPERTY

SHIFTING FROM GIFT-GIVING ECONOMIES—FROM THE RELATIONSHIP between approximately equal givers and receivers and, ultimately, exchangers in a circular economy that was conservationist and respecting cyclical time—to notions of charity in early civilizations involves adopting another time frame, one that is a surmise of past (already gone), present (little understood) and future (imagined/hoped for), exemplified by the metaphor of the destructive "arrow" and its built-in idea of "progress" implying constant obliteration of what belongs to the past to make way for an ever-more abundant future, based on exploitative commerce and consumption of alienated goods. Today, things have reached such a pass that, in an antihuman neoliberal system, nearly everything, including human beings, is commodified. And if human beings are commodified, old religious ideas of loving our fellows through charity are increasingly ideological, justifying, for example, why so many charitable foundations make so much money out of the plight of the wretched of the earth.

If the female breast once represented charity, it was only as a metaphor and the flow was from a privileged woman or the denatured but definitely superior Holy Virgin to the inferior deserving poor. The old female deities had long ago been cut down to size and reduced to unsullied maidens, wives and chattels, a plummeting in the status of women summed up in around 700 BCE by Hesiod's fable of Pandora's jar. After Prometheus stole the secret of fire, the purportedly feckless, foolish wife of his brother Epimetheus (also described as none too bright in some accounts), Pandora ("all gifts") opened the forbidden jar and unleashed the banes of sickness, decrepitude and vice on humanity. And she, the first woman, created by Hephaestus and Athena in accordance with Zeus' instructions, who had started out as an incarnation of the Earth Goddess, the Creatrix, ended up as a mere instrument for punishing humankind, reviled for the rest of history. Just like Eve. In the Jewish tradition Yahweh punished Eve for the Fall of Man[32] but it is not so well known that she had been preceded by Adam's first partner, Lilith, who was made of filth and sediment instead of "pure" dust as Adam was. The almost totally censored story goes that she refused to obey this man or adopt the recumbent posture in intercourse and, after being expelled from paradise, she went off to copulate with demons on the shores of the Red Sea while Adam's newly designed helpmeet went through various incarnations in Judaism and Christianity to become docile, holy, virginal and, above all, dependent and submissive. Whether in the form of Lilith or Eve, Adam's helpmeet was not a product of the "first fine careless rapture" of divine creativity but an afterthought in response to Adam's gripe that, unlike the animals, he had not been given a female counterpart.

The God of the Bible is unequivocally male and the Holy Trinity consists of three males, the Father, the Son, and the Holy Ghost. The Bible gives Adam and Eve three male children, Cain, Abel, and Seth. In the long list of Adam's descendants, not one female is named. Women embody evil and weakness and, under Mosaic Law are much more vulnerable than men. Indeed, Israelite men gave thanks for not having been born a woman. To all intents and purposes, the subsidiary role of women in the Old Testament carries through to the New. The apostle Paul, one of the main sources on Christian charity decreed that no woman could presume to teach or tell a man what to do because Adam was created before Eve. The biological reality is inverted in a very early example of alt-truth: "For man did not come from woman, but woman from man" (Corinthians 11:8). However, woman will be saved through bearing children (Timothy 2:15) but she must also be constant in holiness. So the "all-giving" Pandora, and Eve, the "mother of all the living" (Genesis 3:20) ended up in Christian depictions of charity as an asexual bodily function, a squirting breast surrounded by harmless chubby cherubs because a woman had no independent powers for, as Paul decrees, "the husband is head of the wife" (Ephesians 5:23).

In charity, the twofold question of who gives and to whom also enfolds a gender question, now on the giving side. This relegation of women to charity minions or accessories has continued through the centuries. Hence, for example, in the United States where at the end of the nineteenth century new charity programs dealing with poverty and provision of alms were striving to put charity on a scientific basis for purposes of monitoring and coordinating aid, the members of 55 groups reporting to the national conference of charities in 1892 numbered 453 men and 3,534 women among their active members. The women were the foot soldiers of charity, "visitors" who went to the homes of the poor to "uplift" them, while the men held nearly all of the officer positions.[33] Today, since nearly all billionaires are male, most of the biggest philanthropic foundations are headed by individuals called Bill, Mark, Howard, Garfield, Henry, Mohammed, Josiah, Paul, David, Andrew, Sulaiman, and so on. It's clear that a large part of humankind is excluded from the more flamboyant kind of charitable activity because of poverty, but less attention is given to the fact that most of the once "all-giving" female half of humanity is essentially excluded from autonomous charity (unless she is making cakes for fairs) as a result of being dependent on male largesse. Melinda, after all, is first and foremost Bill's wife… and his name, of course, appears first in their foundation.

In his materialist anthropological account of family economics, *Origin of Family, Private Property and the State,*[34] Friedrich Engels quotes the work *Ancient Society; or, Researches in the Lines of Human Progress from Savagery, Through Barbarism to Civilization* by the anthropologist Lewis H. Morgan, who describes how the rise of alienable property led to a change from the matrilineal system to patrilocal residence and patrilineal descent and, thus, the disempowerment of women. Engels details men's increasing control of the sphere of production, when "household management no longer concerned society," when "the wife became the head servant, excluded from all participation in social production" (p. 39), and the rise of private property brought increasing inequality. The monogamous family was the institution through which property could be passed down from generation to generation so marriage took on the attributes of a property relationship. Now that men controlled production and property, charity basically became a male thing except for the limited "female" functions now allocated to women in the domain of giving.

Ending his study, Engels makes the link between alienated, male-controlled property and charity:

> Therefore the more civilization advances, the more it is compelled to cover the evils it necessarily creates with the cloak of love and charity, to palliate them or to deny them—in short, to introduce a conventional hypocrisy which was unknown to earlier forms of society and even to the first stages of civilization and which culminates in the pronouncement: the exploitation of the oppressed class is carried on by the exploiting class simply and solely in the interests of the exploited class itself; and if the exploited class cannot see it and even grows rebellious, that is the basest ingratitude to its benefactors, the exploiters (pp. 95–96).

He then quotes Morgan, whose judgment of civilization ends with a warning which should be well-heeded now that the Sixth Extinction is underway: "The dissolution of society bids fair to become the termination of a career of which property is the end and aim; because such a career contains the elements of self-destruction." More than thirty years before Mauss's *The Gift* appeared, Morgan ends on an optimistic note venturing that the new society "will be a revival, in a higher form, of the liberty, equality and fraternity of the ancient gentes," a society in which charity was unnecessary.

Among the earliest charitable foundations were temples caring for the sick in ancient Egypt. In the fourth century BCE King Pandukabhaya of Anuradhapura (in what is now Sri Lanka) set up an early form of the hospital, as did King Ashoka in India in the third century BCE. Documents from ancient Mesopotamia and Egypt seem to suggest that charity, as "social justice," is a sacred principle. Some tenets of charity, later to be declared as essential by Islam, Judaism and Christianity, appear in very ancient political systems as notions of justice in the public sphere, based on *righteousness* (a principle deemed to be the very essence of the ancient Jewish concept of charity, *tzedakah*). "Righteous law" is among the legal principles inscribed in the Code of King Urukagina (24th century BCE), ruler of the Sumerian city-state Lagash. This is perhaps the first recorded example of government reform, aiming explicitly to achieve a higher level of freedom and equality by limiting the powers of the priesthood and large property owners and taking measures against usury, hunger, and seizure of property and persons. "The widow and the orphan were no longer at the mercy of the powerful man." Following suit, Hammurabi, King of Babylon from 1792–1750 BCE, had inscribed on large stone tablets his decree that widows and orphans were to be protected by the state. Women, once all-bountiful goddesses, had become a specific object of charity. The dual purpose of obeying divine order and easing human suffering (or quelling social unrest) was almost always evident in these early edicts. In ancient Egypt, for example, charity was a means to immortality by way of propitiating the gods and also showing a kindly disposition towards one's fellow human beings.

Much later, in the East, Confucius (551–479 BCE) called upon rulers to give an example to the people by showing respect, tolerance and generosity towards others. With his great respect for hierarchy, Confucius rejects the idea of universal love and devises a scheme of obligatory devotion spreading out from one's father, through one's family to members of one's society. For him, the public good was the responsibility of "benevolent government." About a century later, his anti-authoritarian critic Zhuang Zi (otherwise called Chuang Tzu—fourth or third century BCE) celebrated the dignity of society's outcasts in his marvelous defense of justice and freedom, the *Zhuangzi*, in which he warns of the divisive nature of authoritarian charity: "But when philosophers and prophets appeared, tripping up people over charity and fettering them with duty to their neighbor, doubt found its way into the world. And then, with their preoccupation with the performance of music, and their fussing over ceremony, the empire became divided against itself."[35] Questioned by Tang, a high official of Sung, Zhuang Zi explains his humanist, universalist view of charity. For him, it does not stand alone and cannot be institutionalized for it is part of a virtuous whole. "Filial piety, fraternal love, charity, duty to one's neighbour, loyalty, truth, chastity, and honesty, these are all studied efforts, designed to aid the development of virtue. They are only parts of a whole."[36] This "virtuous whole" could be subsumed under "kindness" in its fullest etymological senses.

In India, the *Arthashastra* (c. 300 BCE) of the thinker Kautilya (or Chanakaya) would seem to have influenced the Buddhist convert Ashoka (300–232 BCE), after his violent beginnings, to practice humane treatment and magnanimity towards all his subjects. Buddhists tend not to see wealth as intrinsically evil as long as it is attained by honest means and used for the benefit of the wider society. Giving without seeking anything in return brings spiritual wealth and discourages acquisitive impulses which lead to suffering. Charity to the monastic community is particularly valued as is discreet compassionate giving to the poor and the sick. This is an essential step on the path to enlightenment. In Hinduism giving is encouraged and, as part of Dharma—behavior, including laws, duties, virtues and correct living respecting *rta*, the order that makes life and the universe possible—is concerned with obligations rather than rights and, in practice, underpins an unequal system by being rigorously encoded as different levels of caste obligations.

The oldest accounts of justice in European natural law are difficult to disentangle from the early notions of charity because descriptions of natural right and God-given right sometimes seem to flow together. They both posit inherent moral standards that are independent of, and above the positivity of existing conditions and are based on models ranging from physical nature, to God, to human nature and reason. In this framework, practicing benevolence was more a right than an obligation, part of a natural system. Cicero wrote in his *De Legibus* that justice and law are derived from what nature has given to man. He ponders the function of man, how to unite humanity and concludes that we are obliged by natural law to contribute to the general good of society. Positive laws were the means of providing for the "the safety of citizens, the preservation of states, and the tranquility and happiness of human life,"[37] and were therefore an incentive to virtue. But virtues were also self-serving so, in the First Book of *De Legibus*, Cicero describes laws enhancing our own happiness and, in the case of charity, cultivating mutual benefits. But with the consolidation of increasingly unequal political systems and their self-preserving laws, the principles of natural justice and charity parted ways.

The Romans saw their *philanthropia* as a form of display sustaining a clearly vertical social structure. And, like the Greeks, Roman philanthropists expected some form of public recognition in return for their manifest benevolence. According to Seneca (4 BCE–56 CE), the gratitude generated by elite giving would hold society together, which meant that charity had to be carefully calculated. Both gifts and beneficiaries were to be chosen with the maximum benefits to the donor in mind, showing his power and largesse in the best possible light to society at large. Emperors, of course, had the advantage since they were able to endow society with the most sumptuous gifts. One of the great Roman donors was Gaius Maecenas (70–8 BCE) whose name lives on as synonymous with patronage of the arts, in Spanish as *mecenas* and French as *mecene*. A supporter of Virgil and Horace, Maecenas was an ideologist who believed that art and literature could ease public opinion through the political transition from Republic to Empire. A more populist donor was another ally of Caesar Augustus, the general Marcus Vipsanius Agrippa whose specialties were repair of public buildings, cleaning sewers, and distributing salt and olive oil to the masses. Differences in donor priorities led Cicero to argue there were two kinds of benefactors, those who flaunted their wealth by putting on feasts and games seeking to win popularity (the "prodigal") and the "generous" ones who were kind and did good deeds like ransoming captives. His warning about the former kind (perhaps presently reincarnated as owners of football clubs, or baseball teams, not to mention throwers of glitzy charity parties, for example) is pertinent today. "Now there are many—and especially those who are ambitious for eminence and glory—who rob one to enrich another; and they expect to be thought generous towards their friends if they put them in the way of getting rich, no matter by what means. [...N]othing is generous if it is not at the same time just."[38]

The reforming Emperor Julian (The Apostate, 331/332–363), a man of anti-Christian sentiment, but also Pontifex Maximus, Chief Priest of the State Religion, spelt out the benefits to the state of Christian and Jewish notions of charity in his Letter to Arsacius,[39] High Priest of Galatia (in central Anatolia). He saw that governmental reforms were not sufficient, asking "[why do] we think that this is sufficient and do not observe how the kindness of Christians to strangers, their care for the burial of their dead, and the sobriety of their lifestyle has done the most to advance their cause?" He orders that grain and wine must be distributed in Galatia, eighty per cent to the helpers of priests and the rest to "... strangers and beggars. For it is disgraceful when no Jew is a beggar and the impious Galileans support our poor in addition to their own; everyone is able to see that our coreligionists are in want of aid from us." He echoes his almost-contemporary St. Augustine in wanting to bar priests, purportedly the personification of charity and its distributors, from entertaining people in "vile" professions (chariot drivers, dancers, and mimes). Quoting from *The Odyssey*, he urges Arsacius to remind those of the "Greek religion" that "all strangers and beggars are from Zeus." In the end, it is a matter of appearances, of making a better showing than the opposition. "Do not let others outdo us in good deeds while we ourselves are disgraced by laziness."

Roman law made a niche for less exalted donors who could work discreetly through legally recognized societies but there was little comfort in all this for the poor in the imperial cities, and still less for the hapless inhabitants of foreign lands absorbed into the empire and seen as the fortunate recipients of the superior bounty of Roman civilization. This isn't all that different from the charity borne to foreign parts by nineteenth-century missionaries spreading their message to the furthest reaches of Africa and Asia in the name of the British Empire.

In early Greek society the notions of charity and philanthropy (as "love of humanity") enjoyed considerable status. After all, Prometheus, cruelly punished by Zeus, justified his action by claiming that he had stolen fire prompted by *philanthropos* for mankind. In Mycenaean and archaic Greek society (1400–700 BCE) Zeus Xenios (Philoxenon or Hospites) was the patron of hospitality (*xenia*), protector of strangers and avenger of any wrong done to them. Hospitality, or lack thereof, is one of the main themes in Homer's *The Odyssey*. Odysseus, when he finally returns home, reminds Penelope's impertinent opportunist suitor Antinous that gods and Furies exist for beggars, and that his rudeness to a stranger will bring death, not marriage upon him, a prophecy he soon fulfills with a well-aimed arrow through Antinous' neck.

Basically, the uses of charity were a matter of politics, in the best tradition of political economy because the concern was to shore up the class system. By the fifth and fourth centuries BCE, charity was more grounded in society than in the realm of the gods because evil was now seen as earthly matter or, as Plato put it, "the cause of evil we must look for in other things and not in God"[40] Aristotle, the pragmatist, is concerned about the destabilizing effects of poverty, "for the weaker are always asking for equality and justice, but the stronger care for none of these things."[41] In the seventh, sixth and fifth centuries BCE a growing number of citizens had attained more political rights but, by the Hellenistic period, after 323 BCE, the upper classes, understanding that the legal enforcement of political rights was not going to work in their favor, offered the *hoi polloi* the sop of a certain amount of charity, "to be granted or withheld at their own pleasure," as G. E. M. de Ste. Croix puts it.[42] After all, if the times got tough, it was easier to cut down on charity than to repeal laws. Poverty was a god-given reality, according to Hesiod in around 700 BCE, and those who did not help others in need were cursed. Yet the poor were far from being the chief concern of ancient Greek philanthropy. Rich citizens conspicuously contributed to the costs of temples, expeditions, theatre productions and municipal projects, as well as liturgy and sports, in an early form of the much-flaunted celebrity-style charity we have today. Charity, as in Rome, was a form of display and, in some senses, perhaps, not unlike the vying for prominence in the gift cycles of elders in Papua New Guinea or among the Kwakiutl. But there was one essential difference, which is that the system in which rich Greeks were striving to conserve a considerable degree of individual economic predominance was essentially an unequal one.

In any case, these performances were also an obligation because rich men were expected to give direct support to state security, for example by buying ships for the navy. So "charity" became a kind of tax payment and the gentlemen of Athens were not immune from the temptations of evasion or demanding state honors when they deemed the public demands to be too great. By the sixth century CE, "philanthropy" referred in Greek to the tax exemptions which the Byzantium emperors—for centuries endowed with the title "Your Philanthropy"—granted to charities like orphanages and schools. And herein, probably, lies the origin of tax exemption/avoidance/evasion for modern charities.

Ste. Croix points out that by the fourth century of the Christian era, slavery was universally and uncritically accepted as part of the natural order. Christianity, he says, made no difference to the situation, "except to strengthen the position of the governing Few and increase the acquiescence of the exploited Many, even if it did encourage individual acts of charity" (p. 209). Charity, like going to war, was something men did. If a lady entered the scene it was better if she was lactating and virginal and hence not interfering with any husband's property or the general political structure. Or she could discreetly give to Christ personified in the needy, as St. Jerome (c. 347–420) exhorts the highborn Demetrias in Epistle 130:14, "It is yours to clothe Christ in the poor..."

Early Hebrew ideas of charity seem to have been influenced by those of the Babylonians, Egyptians and other peoples of the ancient Middle East and combined with their own religious and social thought as laid out in the scriptures, especially the Hebrew Bible. The root *aheb* (to love) united the terrestrial and divine in charity by citing God's love for mankind, and mankind's love for God, expressed through love for the other people God created. However, the now prevalent idea of using charity to underpin the established order, fix hierarchies of status and highlight property ownership, was a constant. At root, the idea of philanthropy was about civic responsibility: giving was an obligation of noble or privileged status rather than a right and duty of common humanity.

In ideological terms, Christianity shifted from the "public figure" or civic type of charity to adopting, in accordance with the teachings of Christ, a more universal value of "love" (aheb) or "charity" (ἀγάπη, agápē in Greek), as set out in Saint Paul's letter to the Corinthians: a Christian was obliged to provide help, not just to a fellow citizen but to any person in need. Philanthropy was now shifting from public munificence to a more private beneficence although the privileges of the property system remained intact, partly because the rewards promised in the New Testament were not just earthly, as Luke (12.33) made clear: "Sell your possessions and give to charity; make yourselves money belts which do not wear out, an unfailing treasure in heaven, where no thief comes near nor moth destroys." But heavenly reward was not enough and it was generally agreed, with a little tweaking of Christ's injunctions in the Gospels, that a Christian could own property but not in excess. He could use it but not abuse it and was a kind of "trustee" for the poor on whom he had to bestow his charity.[43]

But who were these deserving "poor?" The distribution of charity was regulated not by consideration of a person's need but by his or her morality. According to Saint Augustine (354–430), no alms should be given to practitioners of such "reprehensible professions as fortunetellers, gladiators, actors and actresses, and prostitutes" for, "Those who give to gladiators give not to the man but to his evil art. For if he was only a man and not a gladiator, you would not give…"[44] By the Middle Ages, Bronislaw Geremek concludes, "The Christian doctrine of poverty had little to do with social reality; poverty was treated as a purely spiritual value. The medieval exaltation of poverty did not alter the fact, however, that the pauper was treated not as a subject but as an object of the Christian community."[45]

Ancient Judaism had presented a single male God as the essence of beneficence, protector of the weak, the widowed, the orphaned and homeless. Jehovah was the lord and master of all creation and he had given safe haven and hospitality to the Israelites in the form of the Promised Land. They were refugees, strangers but "sojourners with me" (Leviticus 25:23). In this capacity, Jews were obliged to "Love the stranger therefore, for you were strangers in the land of Egypt" (Deuteronomy 10:19) under pain of committing apostasy if they did not obey. This meant that charity—institutionalized in prescribed rituals of giving organizing the Hebrew calendar—became a form of worship. Helping the poor was more than benevolence. It was what God expected, a matter of divine (rather than earthly) justice or, in other words, more righteousness (*tzedakah*) and less love (*aheb*). *Tzedakah* is mandated by law because it is a repayment of a debt to God. Sentiment does not enter the picture. Since, it is assumed that all wealth belongs to God, any goods given to the poor are really God's gifts and humans are only the agents (or stewards) who ensure they are distributed.

One of the most influential texts on these old ideas is a treatise on *tzedakah*[46] written by the Sephardic philosopher, astronomer, physician, and one of the leading Torah scholars of his times, Rabbi Moses ben Maimon (Maimonades–1135 or 1138–1204). This was basically a compilation of existing rabbinic laws, emphasizing the philosophy underpinning them and, in particular, the idea that God considers the poor to be close to Him. But the established unequal social order always goes unchallenged: "For there will never cease to be needy ones in your land" (Deuteronomy, 15:11).

Maimomedes drew *inter alia* on Leviticus ("You shall not pick your vineyard bare, or gather the fallen fruit of your vineyard; you shall leave them for the poor and the stranger—19:10) and Deuteronomy as well as other parts of the Torah. He discusses the biblical laws regarding agricultural gifts for the poor, including those pertaining to the "edge" of crops, "overlooked gleanings," "separated fruit," malformed bunches of grapes, and "ownerless property"; "the tithe for the poor"; how much, from whom, and to whom; donations to the Jewish community and relations with the Gentile community; the redemption of captives; charity institutions, rules for *tzedakah* collectors; motivations for giving, and even an eight-level charity hierarchy: 1) supporting a fellow Jew so that he no longer needs to be dependent on others and thus eliminating the need for alien charity; 2) giving to unknown poor people anonymously and respecting their dignity; 3) giving to known poor people anonymously; 4) giving—for example, by dropping coins behind one's back—to an unknown person who knows the benefactor; 5) giving directly before being asked; 6) giving after being asked; 7) giving inadequately but willingly, with a smile; and 8) giving unwillingly.

Charity was nothing less than an integral part of the people of Israel. Generosity and Jewish identity were inseparable, so much so that Maimomedes affirmed that one cannot be Jewish without being charitable, and that the throne of Israel stands on *tzedakah* (Isaiah 54:14) and is only established on *tzedek* (righteousness). There can be no redemption without the practice of charity. But, for all the hints of universality, charity was firmly based on a fairly limited notion of kinship for a highly pragmatic reason. The Chosen People were alone and had to be self-sufficient because no one else was going to take care of them. Deuteronomy (14:1) asks, "And if a brother does not show compassion for another brother, then who will have compassion for him? And to whom can the poor of Israel look?" Without the (same) *kind*ness of kinship they were doomed. According to *tzedakah* law, relatives took precedence but widows and orphans were also to be embraced as kin. And kinship brought obligations of empathy. Maimomedes (10:5) warns that, "[I]t is forbidden to speak harshly to a poor person or to raise your voice in a shout, for his heart is broken and crushed." Nevertheless, the reality is that, by the advent of the Common Era, charity in Jewish communities had, in many cases, become a means of signifying social status and guaranteeing priestly privilege. As Zhuang Zi had predicted long before in China, selective charitable acts gave rise to sectarianism and, out of the resulting social strife, emerged disaffected Jews who, like Jesus of Galilee, kept preaching the old values of humble, empathetic charity.

The conception of alms-giving passed almost unchanged from Judaism to Christianity, although the notion of atonement for sin was usually associated with it in the latter tradition. In the fourth century St. Optatus, justifying his support for the social order, claimed by way of citing Proverbs XXII: 2 that God had created rich and poor so that the sinner could atone for his faults. After all, did not Ecclesiasticus 3:30 say that "Water will quench a flaming fire; and alms maketh atonement for sins?" Clement of Alexandria (c. 150–215), in his treatise upholding Christian property ownership, rejoices in the fact that almsgiving can buy salvation and sets charity in the realm of business: "What a splendid commerce! What a divine trading!"[47] Gregory Nazianzen, a fourth-century Archbishop of Constantinople, theologian and rhetorical stylist (*Carmina Theologica*, II: xxxiii, 113–116), salved whatever conscience a rich man may have had: "Cast away all and possess God alone, for you are the dispenser of riches that do not belong to you. But if you do not wish to give all, give the greater part; and if not even that, then make a pious use of your superfluity." This is starting to sound a little like Peter Singer's altruism.

Charity, an ideological pillar and source of prestige, had to be more than a freely determined individual act. It needed to be codified and regulated by the church. Thomas Aquinas (1225–1274) listed seven obligatory good works, which were more in the category of "superfluous" (later known as supererogatory) than a great onus on the rich: clothing the unclothed; offering water; giving food; redeeming from prison; giving shelter; nursing the sick and aged; and burying the dead. Aquinas returned the

Christian tradition to ancient Greek notions of charity when he grappled with the question raised by Aristotle: could giving be virtuous if it was self-interested in expecting rewards? He got around the matter by using the old Hebrew argument that charity is an act of love for God, indirectly expressed in the form of beneficence towards one's fellow men. It was the greatest of the three Christian virtues, faith, hope and charity. After all, it was written (1 John 4:8) that God is charity (*deus caritas est*, or in the Greek *θεὸς ἀγάπη ἐστίν (Theos agape estin)*) although this is more usually translated as God is "love" (back to *aheb* again).

In the Muslim tradition, charity is codified as an obligation, the third pillar of Islam (*zakat* which has the senses of to strengthen and to purify) and, as a voluntary act (*sadaqah*), seen as a virtuous deed. The root, *s-d-q* refers to righteousness and truth and, in the Quran signifies moral excellence when used to describe the prophet Joseph (*al-siddiq* – truthful) or to denote a trusted friend (*sadiq*). Attempts have been made to find etymological links with the Hebrew *tzedakah* and some scholars see *sadaqah* as a loan word. In any case, the differences between the rules of charity in Judaism and Islam are not great. Both religions set out who must give what, maximum and minimum donations, charitable preferences and distribution, with special attention to orphans and widows, rules about crops, the spirit in which one must give (and specifically ungrudgingly and anonymously) and rewards.[48] *Zakat* lists eight kinds of "good" beneficiaries: the poor with no means to support themselves, those with insufficient means, collectors of *zakat*, converts to Islam, slaves, debtors, jihadists, and stranded travellers.

In the Middle Ages, charity was increasingly institutionalized. The Church, funded by the tithe and supported by the Crown, provided social care. As early as 511, the Council of Orleans had named bishops "fathers of the poor" and, accordingly, one quarter of church revenues had to be distributed among them. But the rich still wanted something for their money and tended to offer more for the afterlife insurance of prayers for their departed souls than for the daily needs of bodies struggling to survive on earth. By late medieval times, philanthropy aiming at social reform was almost non-existent. As urban centers grew, finance and trade were displacing landed wealth. Able-bodied, reasonably well-fed serfs were not the asset they had once been. However, with the Enlightenment, philanthropy started to appear in its modern form with an expanding civil society, and voluntary and mutual associations. In 1741, Captain Thomas Coram established the London Foundling Hospital for abandoned children and orphans. This was the first initiative of its kind and would act as a precedent for future charities in the western world.

Now culture has taken over the role of religion, conserving many of its precepts regarding empathy, altruism and charity, albeit in new guises like philanthrocapitalism, humanitarianism, foundations, the exhibitionist rich and film stars who jet around cuddling and adopting little babies from poor countries. One striking example of modern-day altruism is the kind that springs, not from a sense of guilt but from entitlement, from the self-righteousness of benevolence. Andrew Carnegie felt so entitled to his wealth that he saw his acquisitiveness as a moral value of the highest order and therefore he had the duty to get richer. As his biographer David Nasaw puts it, "Recognizing that the more money he earned, the more he would have to give away, he pushed his partners and his employees relentlessly forward in pursuit of larger and larger profits, crushed the workingmen's unions he had once praised, increased the steelworkers' workday from eight to twelve hours, and drove down wages."[49] This form of charity spawned the infamy of the armed Pinkerton mercenaries and the dead and wounded of the Homestead massacre.

Throughout the entire history of these concepts, one complex of ideas has remained more or less constant. Poverty or social inequality is taken for granted, discussion of justice (and human rights) is absent, and property is always protected. It's all about an individualized yet highly institutionalized culture of apparent (and often self-serving) giving and, of course, has nothing to do with what the established order takes away from people.

CHAPTER 4
~~EFFECTIVE~~ USEFUL ALTRUISM

DIFFERENT DISCIPLINES USE A VARIETY OF TERMS LIKE "ALTRUISM," "empathy," "cooperation," "generosity," "charitable behavior," and "pro-social behavior" for actions that benefit others at a cost to oneself. This costs-benefits framework is not free of an assumption that an act shouldn't be undertaken unless its benefits outweigh its costs, whatever moral arguments are presented to the contrary. Altruism has evolutionary explanations based on animal behavior and, in evolutionary psychology, is applied to charity, political and environmental causes, and general niceness to others. It has branched out into studies including evolutionary game theory, kinship ties, in-group behavior, strategies for protecting vested interests, costly signaling, reciprocity (in which some charities include small gifts with their solicitation letters, hoping to induce reciprocity in a somewhat larger size, just as supermarkets try to entice buyers with free samples—in something not unlike a slot-machine version of the Papua New Guinea highlanders' Moka), competitiveness (often behind announcements that someone has made a large donation, fishing for an even larger one), and it is hoped that understanding altruism will eventually lead to finding ways of making people more charitable. In a nutshell, the whole field is inward-looking.

Altruism and utilitarianism seem at first sight to differ because the latter is concerned with maximizing good results for society as a whole while (effective) altruism is professedly about maximizing good results for everyone but the actor. However, in *The Principles of Ethics* (1879) Herbert Spencer squared the circle, arguing that if the rest of society outnumbers the utilitarian, then a true utilitarian must end up practicing some form of altruism.

And, for John Stuart Mill, utilitarianism was a form of ethical altruism, although he also believed that a commitment to the general happiness was compatible with each individual enjoying some gratification of "egoistic propensities" because this was necessary for a happy life, and even favorable to the development of benevolent behavior toward others.

A whole slew of studies has shown that if philanthropic behavior is made public, benefactors feel they are more likely to gain. This would seem to be confirmed by celebrity charity antics, although the extent to which they support their charities, why, and the results for the beneficiaries of their altruism tend to be skipped over. There are always more details given about what A-listers are wearing at a gala ball than about the real conditions of people they are supposed to be helping. Signaling theory tries to understand altruism as being a little more complex than a simple form of "I'll scratch your back and you scratch mine" but, basically, it's about individual benefits for donors in publicly displayed altruism. Hence, "costly signaling" is about behavior that refers to the donor in three out of four points (that said, if the donor wants to signal something, he needs at least one beneficiary, so the first point also refers to him, at least partially): 1) beneficial to others, 2) observable to others, 3) costly to the signaler in ways that can't be reciprocated, and 4) associated with the signaler's wealth, aptitude, strength and fitness. This theory, taking inequality for granted, is pressed into service to explain apparently wasteful altruistic behavior in situations where delayed reciprocity is unlikely to occur. But why it's unlikely to occur is usually not explored.

It has been well noted that in pre-capitalist societies, good hunters who risk killing large game may get no more meat than anyone else after publicly sharing their bounty. But their generosity boosts their reputation and signals important phenotypic information. A man who is a high-quality signaler tends to be more successful in building alliances and finding a mate. The theory of costly signaling is not far from Thorstein Veblen's account in *The Theory of the Leisure Class* where giving "of valuable presents and expensive feasts and entertainments"—far from laying the foundations for a circulating fund creating trust, stability and esteem as happens in a gift exchange society—is about individual competition. For Veblen, profligate consumption by leisure class was a display of power: "Conspicuous consumption of valuable goods is a means of reputability to the gentleman of leisure."[50] He immediately makes a connection between the "costly entertainments" of the potlatch and throwing a society ball, although, in fact, there is a big difference between the two because the former is community-oriented and the latter an individual form of self-promotion and, what is more, potlatch organizers were not exactly gentlemen of leisure. The important point here is that once the benefits of ostentation are understood, it is a short, and not only a linguistic step, to "conspicuous compassion," as Patrick West observes in his *Conspicuous Compassion: Why Sometimes It Really Is Cruel to Be Kind.*[51]

In group terms, the costly devotional practices of religion may seem maladaptive but they bind a community together through conspicuous ritual, often performed publicly in order to demonstrate loyalty to the group whose members then respond by further investment in the group. However, this is quite an exclusive community and the costlier the contributions to the group, the less likelihood there is of free riders. In general, according to the theory of costly signaling, only an individual of elevated status has the resources to behave altruistically, and the more altruistic he is, the higher his status will be ("he" and "his" because patriarchal selection has determined, through property rules, that large-scale "conspicuous compassion" is generally a male pursuit).

The explanation for altruistic signaling is sought in evolutionary theory. Natural selection might mean that the genes of thriving individuals have evolved to ensure that relatives with similar genes benefit from "inclusive fitness," which several scholars believe is why altruism is directed first to family members. But some individuals extend their altruism beyond the family, which "reciprocal" altruism then seeks to explain by suggesting that allies, thus created, will eventually return the favor.

Focused on individual (or, at most, in-group) behavior rather than on the social setting of this behavior, altruism is regarded by scholars in the field as a great mystery because altruistic individuals apparently sacrifice their personal interests, money or time and, seem thereby to reduce their chances of surviving or reproducing and, according to the theory of natural selection, this kind of behavior should eventually disappear. But altruism has hung in, to the extent that it is booming in academia as a self-referencing specialization, and practiced among celebrities who understand its perks very well. To give one example, David Beckham, with a family (Brand Beckham) fortune of nearly half a billion pounds (which makes him richer than the queen[52]) says in a recent interview that he hopes to be remembered "for his charity work as much as for his football."[53] And it turns out that he was doing his charity work because he was really hoping for a knighthood (but the "bunch of cunts" in the honors committee overlooked him because of concerns over his tax affairs).[54] Obviously, the "bunch of cunts" didn't understand what Beckham knew: almost every act of altruism constitutes some kind of tradeoff.

The gender transaction appears in some altruism research which suggests that women looking for a long-term partner find kind men more attractive as someone who might be willing to share resources with her and her children. Men tend to be more altruistic in the early stages of a romantic relationship, or when showing off for an attractive woman, while women are less likely to signal altruism to an attractive man (after all, she can't go squandering his resources). Both sexes, but especially women, usually state that kindness is the most desirable trait in a partner.

So, "[…] if you're a man looking for a committed relationship with a woman, you shouldn't hesitate to flaunt the fact that you're an unpaid mentor for elementary-school kids or that you help your elderly neighbor buy groceries every week."[55] Although it is theorized that evolution has shaped psychological mechanisms like emotions which promote altruistic behavior, the evolutionary approach basically focuses on the social utility of altruism. Selective investment theory hypothesizes that close social bonds and emotional and cognitive mechanisms evolved to ensure survival and reproductive success by means of long-term, high-cost altruism among people depending on one another. Often the aim is to discover how to promote it through "[…] research to create situations in which charitable behaviour pays off in the long run."[56]

Altruism—this behavior in which, by all accounts, an agent incurs a personal cost while enhancing the well-being of another—seems at first sight to be counter-intuitive, at odds with the basic tenets of Darwinian evolution. Darwin himself recognized that altruism represented a challenge to his theory of evolution: "[…] he who was ready to sacrifice his life, as many a savage has been, rather than betray his comrades, would often leave no offspring to inherit his noble nature."[57] At this point, the neurobiologists weigh in, looking for the neural bases of altruistic behavior using functional magnetic resonance imaging. They have found, for example,[58] that the mesolimbic reward pathway, which tends to light up in response to sex or food, and the subgenual cortex/sextal region are activated by charitable activity, and these structures are closely related to social attachment and bonding in other species. The conclusion is that altruism, rather than being a superior moral faculty in some individuals is hardwired in the brain and associated with pleasurable sensations.

One influential study, *The Altruistic Brain: How We Are Naturally Good*, by Donald Pfaff,[59] takes issue with the Christian notion of original sin and the capitalist notion of human self-interest as the motivating force behind kindly acts, and hypothesizes that human beings are "wired" to be good, just as we are "wired" to acquire natural language(s). Pfaff presents and interprets evidence in favor of Wilhelm von Humboldt's idea, raised in his treatise on freedom and human responsibility,[60] that humankind is intrinsically more inclined to philanthropic than to self-serving actions (as if philanthropy was free of suspicion of being self-serving). Since humans are born at a stage of development in which they need a great deal of looking after, Pfaff argues that evolutionary survival depends on caring mothers, fathers and other relatives. The human brain, he says (p. 58) overlaps and blurs images of other people with our own self-image by means of "an increase in the excitability of cortical neurons, such that when the nerve cells representing the other are firing signals, the nerve cells representing self are also firing." There is an "ethical switch" in the brain which is activated before we carry out an act so "instead of literally seeing the consequences of the act for another person, we automatically envision the consequences as pertaining to our own self!" (p. 60).

Pfaff's arguments may not necessarily support wiring for altruism or innate goodness but they would suggest the social nature of humans. But what kind of social? The Golden Rule or law of reciprocity, "Do unto others," can lead to contradictory and violent results. Who knows what a person would like? A sadist is not a masochist. Most of us would like to be treated well but does this mean that we should treat violent white supremacists well? Or do we think of their victims, side with them and make life miserable for the abusers? Social questions tend to be overlooked in respectful accounts of all the religions that urge one or other version of the Golden Rule.

There is a danger in Pfaff's theory, especially when he claims that his research on altruism can be "deployed to help bring antisocial individuals into the mainstream" (p. 221). Into what "mainstream" fold does he want to bring these individuals? This is a cultural and political issue and can frequently be used, as we know from all kinds of terrible experiments in social engineering, to discriminate, attack freedom and difference, destroy identities, and do harm in general. One only needs to think of "treatments" given to homosexuals and difficult women who were very kindly locked up—James Joyce's daughter Lucia (with the help of Joyce's benevolent rich fans), to cite just one awful case. Pfaff is basically concerned with social initiatives designed to encourage altruistic brain functions even if social conditions including poverty and great inequality appear to be intractable. But, in those circumstances, the dispossessed are more likely to be "antisocial." Surely it is natural to express anger against a society that harms you. So should angry rebels be made "mainstream" with a bit of altruism? It's not so long ago that lobotomy was seen as well-intentioned. Pfaff's altruism isn't far from the old religious precepts which accept injustice and try, at most, to fiddle with the status quo (with a view to its furtherance).

Richard Dawkins in his scientific game-changer, the best-seller *The Selfish Gene*, examines the "biology of selfishness and altruism" and concludes that gene selfishness usually results in egocentric behavior in an individual, although there are circumstances when, among individual animals, a gene's interests are best fulfilled by fostering a certain level of altruism. He offers a gene-centered account of evolution, explaining, for example, that a bird or insect takes risks when reproducing, not to help itself or the species but to ensure that its genes live on, surviving at the expense of other genes. The title of the book led to speculation that Dawkins was advocating individual selfishness (endowing genes with mental traits and abilities like egoism and intentionality). He often said he wished he had called his book "The Immortal Gene."

Another biological approach to altruism comes from David Sloan Wilson, SUNY Distinguished Professor of Biology and Anthropology at Binghamton University,[61] who argues in his book *Does Altruism Exist? Culture, Genes, and the Welfare of Others* that multilevel selection—a version of group selection in which natural selection can occur simultaneously at many levels in the biological hierarchy, from genes, to individuals, populations, and species—explains altruism and this suggests a way of guiding the evolution of human social institutions, for instance the economy. In Wilson's view, evolutionary theory can pinpoint altruistic group interests and social arrangements that favor them: "If we want to solve the most pressing problems of our age, such as world peace and global environmental sustainability, then more cultural evolution is required and it must be guided by a sophisticated knowledge of evolution…" (p. 88). Given that the problems of our age are extremely pressing and millions of people are dying or living in great distress because of them, and evolution is somewhat impaired when whole species are disappearing by the minute, "cultural evolution" might be fun to play with but rather slow in bringing improvement.

Moving from neurobiology to psychology, one goes from a sophisticated discussion of the neocortex to a description in the *International Encyclopedia of the Social Sciences* (2007) which seems merely to have added the word "motivational" to run-of-the-mill descriptions in order to make it "psychological" so, here, altruism is "a motivational state with the goal of increasing another's welfare." "Motivational" doesn't help much if we know nothing about the motives, let alone the needs of the beneficiary. Altruism seems to thrive in a social vacuum. In sociology, too, signaling yet again abandonment of the emancipatory Enlightenment principles that once prevailed in the humanities, a commonly used definition of altruism is vague and value-laden: a "principle of unselfish regard for the needs and interests of others." But this unselfish regard doesn't seem to extend as far as, for example, Rakhine State in Myanmar where the Rohingya people have long been subjected to genocidal persecution.[62] This well-documented tragedy is so little known that Google spell check objects to the words "Rakhine" and "Rohingya." Although many studies ponder the relationship between altruism and the common good, there is hardly ever any mention of the material conditions giving rise to the socially based need for altruism.

In today's secular societies, normative discussion of charity or philanthropy tends to focus on altruism and empathy which appear, at least to some degree, in all the ancient views on charity, but now brushed up for modern times. If in the long-ago past, the different concepts were marked by the relationship between divinities and good deeds on earth, today's debate would revolve more around individual (and sometimes social or state) responsibility for suffering people. The word altruism ("otherism") was coined by Auguste Comte (1798–1857) as an antonym for egoism. Coming fairly close to what is now called "evolutionary ethics," Comte saw mutual aid among between men as a continuation of phenomena of cooperative behavior which abound in biology. Credited with founding the discipline of Sociology, "positive philosophy" and "social evolutionism," and also described as devising a post-theist "religion of humanity," Comte was influential in the nineteenth century, at a time when "charity was the bedrock of poor relief."[63] With the growing popularity of the relatively new ideas of *laissez-faire, laissez-passer* (let do, let pass)—attributed to Vicente de Gourney (1712–1759)—sometimes with the flourish of "*le monde va de lui-même*" (the world goes on by itself), it was soon understood that this version of individualism needed to be tempered with some altruism, which was eventually formulated by Auguste Comte.

But six decades after the onset of the Thermidorian Reaction, there is no longer talk of rights. Indeed, in his *Catechisme positiviste*,[64] Comte consciously removes rights from his framework. "[The] social point of view cannot tolerate the notion of rights, for such notion rests on individualism. We are born under a load of obligations of every kind, to our predecessors, to our successors, to our contemporaries. [...To live for others], the definitive formula of human morality, gives a direct sanction exclusively to our instincts of benevolence, the common source of happiness and duty. [Man must serve] Humanity, whose we are entirely." At this point, it is instructive to return to the kind of rights that nineteenth-century French thinkers were reacting against with their notions of altruism. The essential right, first formulated by Robespierre in his speech on subsistence of 2 December 1792, flew in the face of all the previous religious and secular doctrines of charity: "What is the first object of society? It is to maintain the inviolable rights of man. What is the first of these rights? The right to exist. The first social law is thus that which guarantees to all society's members the means of existence; all others are subordinated to it." This is the right which, with its radical implications for societies devastated by ever-widening inequality, is still loftily ignored in altruism theory today.

In an early article of enduring influence,[65] Peter Singer discusses the commonly accepted distinction between duty and charity. A rich man, he says, is expected to obey the law as a matter of obligation (but the fact that he often gets rich by breaking the law isn't mentioned). However, giving money for disaster relief is more a praiseworthy act than a duty. The man who gives nothing is not condemned, for it is considered that he has no obligation to give (though the law works in his favor and makes the poor poorer). The rich man's charity, Singer tells us, is the kind of action that philosophers and theologians call supererogatory (one that is good to do but not wrong not to do). But doesn't this version of the charity of privilege recall Comte's fears about the individualism that would arise from rights?

The word supererogation comes from the Latin *super-erogare* (paying out more than is due). The term first appears in the Latin version of the New Testament with the parable of the Good Samaritan. Since his action is said to be at once praiseworthy and non-obligatory, philosophers logic-chop about whether there can be any morally good actions that are not morally required, if such actions exist and, if they do, how come they are optional or supererogatory. It might be more fruitful to reflect on Margaret Thatcher's insight when she went straight to the heart of the question: "No-one would remember the Good Samaritan if he'd only had good intentions; he had money as well."[66] She was not only nailing the fact that indulging in charity belongs to the realm of the privileged but, along the way, doing some realistic political economy.

The Catholic Church Fathers put a moralizing spin on supererogatory charity, adding two more virtues: chastity and obedience. Hence, in 1 Corinthians 7, St Paul gives as an example the fact that a man may be free to marry but it is more praiseworthy to remain celibate in order to be a better servant of God. There is surplus value to be wrung out of this because works of supererogation by saints are kept in a kind of delivery-from-penance bank to be used by God to exempt (some) repentant sinners from acts of expiation that might otherwise be required. Supererogation was a particularly sore point with Martin Luther and his objection was widely brandished in the Protestant Reformation in which theologians attacked the notion of "super-meritorious" actions and the resulting corruption which flourished in commercialization of institutionalized indulgences for which supererogation served as a cover. The Anglican Church went so far as to say in its Thirty-Nine Articles (1571) that works of supererogation "cannot be taught without arrogancy and impiety." Moreover, the dissident theologians understood how easily "morality" can be milked in the form of big donations from the guileless, and were thus giving a prescient glimpse of what was to come with late-twentieth-century charitable foundations and philanthrocapitalism.

Peter Singer[67] quotes "Saints and Heroes," a 1958 paper by J. O. Urmson, who suggests that imperatives of duty function to prohibit behavior that is intolerable if people are to live in society, and this is different from doing something that's good but it's not wrong not to do it. Singer suggests that, "this may explain the origin and continued existence of the present division between acts of duty and acts of charity," a distinction which he opposes since he says he is trying to ground moral behavior in the social (as opposed to the religious, for example) terrain. Moral attitudes, then, "are shaped by the needs of society," which "needs people who will observe the rules that make social existence tolerable." But his "social" perspective begs the questions of whose needs, what rules, who makes them and to what end, as if society was some kind of homogenous mass without this thing called political economy.

Morality, in this framework, seems to float above almost all social reality: in moral terms, preventing the starvation of people in other countries is as important as upholding property laws within a society. But what if the "property" norms embrace land grabs, upheld by national and international law that dispossess millions of people? Yet we are only obliged to observe the rules that make our social existence tolerable and our moral needs can be assuaged, if we wish, by giving to some or other charity (which, often dodgy anyway, channels the money back home again). Singer says, "[…] we ought, morally, to be working full time to relieve great suffering of the sort that occurs as a result of famine or other disasters." But how? He concludes that "[…] the best means of preventing famine, in the long run, is population control," thus niftily shifting moral responsibility onto disaster victims. So, as part of our supererogatory goodness, we in the rich countries should make sure that the people we have dispossessed in the plunder of empire and in the forms of capitalism that followed should tone down their breeding, and we can help them to do so by supporting organizations working for population control.

But do these population control organizations help anyone other than excessively fertile outlanders? Self-declared conservative Steven W. Mosher says yes. Taking as an example PSI

(Population Services International), an NGO (or "arm of government" as Colin Powell once recognized) bountifully funded by USAID, Mosher points out that this is an arm with a lot of state muscle. PSI, he says, is "[…] in effect, a mask worn by Western governments to avoid the unpleasantness that would ensue if U.S. officials themselves were to tell Africans or Latinos that they were having too many children." Oh, and by the way, the founder of PSI, one Phil Harvey (described by *Mother Jones* as a "hard-core philanthropist") founded "Adam & Eve," one of the leading US porn companies so there is a "[…] natural fit between Phil Harvey's porn business and USAID's anti-population bomb agenda: Lots of sex and no babies."[68]

Singer's early paper provided the foundations of the growing movement called "Effective Altruism" whose supporters cogitate on where supererogatory beneficence is best spent and encourage the affluent to give accordingly (where the bucks bang best). The argument goes that we should stop spending money on things we don't really need and give it to aid groups working in disaster or poverty-stricken areas. Singer extrapolates from an example of saving a child drowning in a pond. We are duty-bound to save the child. Or our mirror neurons—deemed by some neuroscientists to be the bedrock of empathy and by others to be overhyped—kick in and make us save the child. Or not. Saving the drowning doesn't apply to everyone. In January 2017 a 22-year-old Gambian refugee, Pateh Sabally, didn't qualify as a recipient for dutiful empathy and there were no mirror neurons kicking in, only cell-phones filming as bystanders watched him drown in Venice's Grand Canal. One person yelled, "Go on, go back home."[69] Undeterred by differences like those that might arise between a hypothetical drowning child and a really drowning black refugee, Singer soldiers on: "[…] if it is in our power to prevent something bad from happening, without thereby sacrificing anything of comparable moral importance, we ought, morally, to do it." The principles, he says, take no account of proximity or distance so we must extend our altruism to people who are far away, in this case, people who are dying in East Bengal as a result of poverty, a cyclone and a civil war.

Peter Singer, of course, didn't invent the example of saving a drowning person, a framework also used by the Confucian philosopher Mengzi (Mencius, 372–289 BCE) with somewhat more sophistication when talking about compassion. In fact, the situation of saving an individual who is about to drown was a commonplace in a good part of the moral debate and discourse of his day. Mengzi says that if a man sees a child fall into a well, anyone in such situation would have in his heart a feeling of anxiety and compassion. This is not premeditated or pre-learnt, and saving the child is not the result of trying to make a good impression on the child's progenitors, or wanting to gain a good reputation among neighbors and friends, or disliking the sound of the child's cries. From this he concludes that if this man is without the feeling of compassion in his heart, he is not human.[70] [...]. However, this isn't a moral action because the point is that the act of saving the child is spontaneous, it doesn't take the element of time into account, and it is not influenced by reflection on the consequences feelings might have, and neither does the lifesaving action depend on the reproach or praise which others might express.

Another philosopher Chunyu Kun, presents a false dilemma in which he tries to force the stickler-for-rules Mengzi to choose between scrupulous respect for ceremonial regulations which define the moral order of the Confucian school and saving a life.

> Chunyu Kun asked: "Does ritual require that men and women do not touch when handing each other something?" And Mengzi replied: "That is ritual." Chunyu Kun then asked again: "If your sister-in-law were drowning, would you rescue her with your hand?" Mengzi answered: "Only jackals and wolves would not rescue their sister-in-law if she were drowning. It is required by ritual that men and women should not touch each other when handing each other

> something, but if your sister-in-law is drowning, to rescue her with your hand is a matter of emergency."

Mengzi's answer, countering Chunyu Kun's tricky approach to the dilemma, is to make use of the term *quan* 權, which designates part of a set of scales and which has, among other meanings in the ancient literature, "ponder," "assess" (in the sense of calibrate) and "gauge" a given situation but, in the context of this specific passage, he seems to use it to signal urgent circumstances, an emergency that requires instant evaluation and overrides ritual, so it can't be a moral action.

Another ancient text, the *Lüshi chunquiu*, seems to use an anecdote about a disciple of Confucius named Zilu to stress the exemplarizing value of the spontaneous (non-moral) action of saving a person from drowning:

> Zilu rescued someone who was drowning and the man rewarded him with a cow, which he accepted. And Confucius said, "The people of Lu will invariably come to the rescue of a person who is drowning." Confucius foresaw the end result of the events in their earliest beginnings since his ability to perceive future developments was far-reaching.[71]

Zilu accepts a reward for his action of saving the life of a drowning man. In Confucius' view, the apparent self-interest of Zilu in accepting a reward from the man he has saved is as exemplary and would encourage others to imitate his good deed.

Singer ignores the finer points of whether a spontaneous act can be moral, or whether a non-moral good deed can still be exemplarizing and, worse, seems uninterested in the *real* moral question of root causes. A child falling into a pond is (usually) an accident. But the dire situation he raises, that of at least nine million destitute refugees in East Bengal, has socioeconomic causes which he seems unwilling to address. Hence critics like Paul Gomberg note that this "presenting liberal politics as an ethical duty [...] short-circuits political discussions of large-scale causes of poverty."[72] In fact, among the causes of the 1974 Bangladesh famine (two years after Singer published his seminal paper) in which approximately 1.5 million people died, mainly poor laborers and non-landowners, were two key facts. First, the state rationing system and market led to speculative hoarding and hence rising prices, and, second, the US ambassador had made it clear that, since Bangladesh exported jute to Cuba, the US was not going to give food aid. Bangladesh yielded and stopped the exports but the food came too late. Worse than simply ignoring the political economy of disaster, Singer's version of altruism, as Paul Gomberg points out, "[...] promotes political quietism" by "[shifting] our focus from political, social, and economic issues to abstract philosophical arguments."[73]

Some altruists like Peter Unger[74] take giving to philanthropic organizations as a moral standard. He gives an example: if on receiving a request for a donation from UNICEF, asking for $100 to help thirty innocent children in a faraway land, you would be wrong to throw the envelope in the trash, even if writing the check means you have to give up an evening at the ballet. Never mind that philanthropic organizations are riddled with corruption and power abuse or that this kind of charity is essentially undemocratic (making decisions for the wretched of the earth, and disrupting their ways of life by imposing neoliberal systems for example, as Naomi Klein so eloquently describes in *The Shock Doctrine: The Rise of Disaster Capitalism*), as well as pushing private interests that undercut public services. Saving little children who accidentally fall into ponds is a lot easier than thinking about what social mechanisms are needed to respect and guarantee human rights, the universal human rights which that Singer seems to want to reduce to mere rescue in apparently unchallengeable social systems.

Altruistic tinkering isn't going to change things. This global system grabs land and water, drives poor farmers into debt, thrives on selling organs, sex slaves or children, pushes debtors to suicide, creates mass extinction, and extracts vast amounts of resources and capital from poor countries through debt service, "trade" policies, tax evasion and other financial shenanigans… all of this to enrich the already rich. This system creates "drowning" people every second and nobody's there to rescue them because, basically, altruism doesn't give a tinker's cuss about, or shrinks from changing the system. Altruism thrives in the system. Singer's "emotional empathy" philosophy actually shores up the system in many ways, including an if-you-can't-beat-it-join-it response from his young followers who are keen to make big bucks and make them bang loudly by, for example, working for a "hedge fund on steroids."[75] The global capitalist class wants to rescue the "drowning?" Or maybe, to use a New Testament metaphor provided by Mark (10:20–31), the rich man is still trying to squeeze through the eye of the needle. Then again, speaking of banging bucks, it has been widely suggested that the poor give more to charity than the rich and, according to one estimate, the wealthiest Americans donate 1.3% of their income and the poorest 3.2% while, in 2012, "not one of the top 50 individual charitable gifts went to a social-service organization or to a charity that principally serves the poor and the dispossessed."[76]

The upshot of Singer's utilitarian position is that he ends up gushing about the effectiveness of the richest people in the world (back to Thatcher's Rich Samaritan). For a specialist in the field, he seems unconcerned about studies showing that affluence is often antithetical to altruism, partly because it comes with a sense of entitlement. And generosity also declines as societies become less equal. This fairly easily observed truism is by no means insignificant. Two Berkeley psychologists, Paul Piff and Dacher Keltner, have studied whether social class (measured by wealth, occupational prestige, and education) influences how much we care about the feelings of others. And as an article about their work in *Scientific American*[77] suggests, "Given the growing income inequality in the United States, the relationship between wealth and compassion has important implications. Those who hold most of the power in this country, political and otherwise, tend to come from privileged backgrounds. If social class influences how much we care about others, then the most powerful among us may be the least likely to make decisions that help the needy and the poor." They may also be the most likely to engage in unethical behavior. Keltner and Piff [suggest that…] "their research helps explain why Goldman Sachs and other high-powered financial corporations are breeding grounds for greedy behavior. Although greed is a universal human emotion, it may have the strongest pull over those of who already have the most."

A poor person, especially if she's a woman, doesn't have the wherewithal to enjoy the warm glow of benevolence, or a website where she can boast that she's "working to reduce inequality," or to engage in "PHILANTHROPY BUILT ON PEOPLE AND PARTNERSHIPS" because she has no bucks to bang. But Bill & Melinda Gates are quite another story, as the self-assurance, not to say hubris, of the quote on their website suggests. In a 2013 TED talk[78] Singer draws attention to another slogan on the Bill & Melinda Gates Foundation website—"All lives have equal value"—and not because it may seem cynical. No, not at all. He concludes, "That's the understanding, the rational understanding in the world that has led to these people being the most effective altruists in history, Bill and Melinda Gates, and Warren Buffett (Applause)." No wonder a *Huffington Post* article titled "The New Social Movement of Our Generation: Effective Altruism"[79] breathlessly promotes Peter Singer as ranking among the A-listers. "[…] the audience frenetically rushed down to mob the speaker for autographs and selfies. The slight, grey-haired philosophy professor had celebrity status." Well, celebrity can rub off. You only need to check out the rise of the Kardashian groupies.

This costs-benefits approach to remedying human misery ends up in sterile, navel-gazing: altruism trying to work out what altruism is. Now we have the so-called "empathy wars," and it takes a Yale psychologist to tell us that empathy is biased.[80] In a recent book, *The Most Good You Can Do: How Effective Altruism Is Changing Ideas about Living Ethically* (2016), Peter Singer would seem to agree about the bias in his field when he describes as an "absurd" outcome the fact that people gave more to a cause featuring a photo of a single child whose life would be saved by a treatment costing $300,000 than to one showing eight children all of whose lives would be saved for the same amount. But this is not "absurd" at all because we're all afflicted by marketing manipulation in which images are designed to sell. One sick child can look a lot cuter than eight. And, prioritizing one child would seem totally logical in a system where individualism (and not sharing) rules.

The image wizard, Barack Obama, is an empathy fan, in favor of a new breed of "empathy economy" and preaching that, "Learning to stand in somebody else's shoes, to see through their eyes, that's how peace begins. And it's up to you to make that happen. Empathy is a quality of character that can change the world."[81] Change the world? Really? When in office, however, the same man did a great deal to change the world in the direction of making it more wretched for others with his aggressive control of information, negligence in not seeking accountability from those who broke the law in conducting and aiding torture, intensifying the use of drone warfare, deporting 2.5 million people, expanding the private prison system, his faintheartedness with regard to killings of unarmed Afro-Americans, racial profiling, a worsening climate disaster with more drilling and more pipelines, and betraying most of his campaign promises.

Sometimes, in fact, empathy can actually produce rejection because recognizing the vulnerability of others raises too many uncomfortable questions about our own complacency. Publicly paraded empathy tends to remain at the level of lip service and, when it tries to seem what it isn't, the result can sometimes be bizarre. For instance, in April 2016, Norway's conservative immigration minister, Sivi Listhaug, donned a flotation suit and jumped into the water off the coast of the island of Lesvos where she bobbed around for a few minutes because she wanted to "understand" the experience of refugees. Her little taste of being a refugee was duly excoriated and, as one critic put it, "Tonight I'll sleep with the window open to see what it's like being homeless."

Empathy experiments are quite fashionable. One which recently went viral is Amnesty International's video "Look Beyond Borders," which is based on the theory that four minutes of continuous eye contact encourages intimacy between strangers. Yes, it takes a heart of stone not to cry when watching it. Another experiment in empathy is called "Walk a Mile in My Shoes." You go to the new London Museum of Empathy, get fitted with shoes of someone completely different from yourself, and then set out to walk a mile of that person's life in an immersive audio video. However, as the Australian journalist Ann Deslandes writes, "[...] acts of empathy that rely on recognition are tenuous because of profoundly unequal dynamics, such as those between refugee and citizen, or white person and person of colour. As long as empathy can be taken away at any time by the dominant partner, these acts can't escape their founding inequality. Indeed, as solidarity theorist Sara Koopman points out, why should we need to know what it feels like to be another person before we can recognise their claim for justice? Before we can stop killing and torturing them, because of who they are? Do we really not know what happens to someone in solitary confinement or indefinite detention? [...]"[82]

"Cognitive" empathy is a variation on the same theme. Roman Krznarik challenged Peter Singer in Oxford, "Doesn't the slavery case [...] show that 'reason'—in the form of laws and rights—actually works hand in hand with cognitive empathy to produce the kind of ethical world we both care about?" Singer conceded that slavery is a good example and, "Cognitive empathy can make a difference."[83] The operative words in Krznarik's question are "laws" and "rights" but they require a revolution in thinking if the aim is a society in which laws protect rights instead of laying waste to them, which raises further questions of what kind of laws are needed to produce an ethical world, how to achieve them and how protect them. Altruism, throughout history, across the world, and from religious doctrine to philosophical and neurobiological cogitations, is almost always discussed, praised or presented as some kind of solution without any mention of the political, social and economic causes of distress, justice or human rights.

In this regard, Pope Francis isn't very helpful. *The New York Times*[84] reports that he has given a "prescription" for "dealing" with panhandlers. Yes, once again, it's all about the giver. What you have to do is just give the money and don't worry even if you know the lucky recipient of your largesse is going to spend it on rotgut. But you must give nicely, "look the person in the eyes, and touch his or her hands." Now comes the stunning hypocrisy. According to the writers, "The reason is to preserve dignity, to see another person not as a pathology or a social condition, but as a human, with a life whose value is equal to your own." And this is "scripturally sound, yet possibly confounding, even subversive." Yes, "don't worry" is certainly "scripturally sound," as discussion of charity in all religions demonstrates. No, the advice is not confounding but par for the course. As for "subversive," that's twaddle. It's upholding the system which, increasingly based on extreme concentration of wealth and power and its by-product of human redundancy, forces some people—"whose value is equal to your own"—to panhandle. So, right, we look the beggar in the eyes, "preserve dignity" and go on our merry way.

At the end of the day, our notions of altruism are embedded in a wider field of humanities where imperial, patriarchal, bourgeois and Eurocentric perspectives still hold sway so that, in this general framework, the bearers of altruism and charity are not all that different from missionaries brandishing the Bible as one of the gifts of salvation. Poverty and the suffering of others are taken for granted as collateral damage and, at best, an ill to be temporarily ameliorated but not abolished. The present unspeakable tragedy of rejected, dying refugees, fleeing from terrible situations mostly caused by the West, suggests that today's choice is to abolish not unjust social systems but their victims. You only have to read the 2016 World Economic Forum report[85] and note its emphasis on resilience in "islands of order in a sea of disorder" to understand that *this* is the state of affairs today. Only the wealthy can afford islands of order (real islands, gated communities, bunkers, panic rooms and so on): "In this scenario, by 2030 the world resembles medieval times, when the citizens of thriving cities built walls around them to protect themselves from the lawless chaos outside" (p. 31). These are walls that altruism will never penetrate because, in that world, the locked-out needy will no longer exist. There is only room for the "resilient" rich.

CHAPTER 5
CELEBRITIES

Viewed from the perspective of celebrity, charity takes on a still more complex and, at times, truly weird slant. The altruism debate apparently wonders why "people" (in general, without seriously considering the fact that rich people are showily altruistic while ordinary people might be generous or kind but few people would know) care about others at their own expense. But there are other questions. The very rich give away a tiny proportion of their wealth, so why do they feel entitled to own so much more than they need? Why does society tolerate and even adore them? Why does it showcase materialistic, greedy, narcissistic people and make their brattish behavior seem acceptable, or even something to aspire to? One answer is that this is hardcore neoliberalism, which is about consumerism. And consumerism needs advertising (celeb excess) plus a little leavening (celeb beneficence). Celebrities, superspreaders of the doctrine, oblige with smidgens of philanthropy but this isn't about loving humankind, as the word is supposed to suggest. It's more about self-promotion. Worse, the wealth that allows it often comes from pure maleficence. The magnanimity/maleficence nexus might be symbolized, for example, in Villa la Leopolda ($750 million, built on an estate once owned by the "humanitarian" King Leopold II, the one who brutalized and killed ten million or more Congolese), now owned by the "philanthropist" Lily Safra who, from her latter-day fiefdom, gives to homeless Hurricane Katrina victims. What might a Kinshasa slum dweller make of this generosity squeezed from genocide?

Celebrities who show how much they care about the homeless can't have modest homes. Otherwise they wouldn't be celebrities. So they splurge on themselves: around $32 million (Jerry Seinfeld), about $147.5 million (Bill Gates), or $150 million (Aaron Spelling). They have superhuman needs. Take Bill Gates. His "pleasure-dome," Xanadu 2.0, with lots of security ("walls and towers... girdled round"), covers 600,000 square meters. Half a million board-feet of lumber (500-year-old Douglas fir trees) went into this monstrosity (bye-bye "forests ancient as the hills") with twenty-four bathrooms, six kitchens, twenty-three-car garage, and lakeshore frontage with sand annually imported from St. Lucia. Then there's the 228-acre ranch, the horse farm, the nature "reserve" (i.e. reserved for Bill), Grand Bogue Caye, the Republic of Belize's largest island, which he's rumored to own. And the Codex Leicester, a collection of writings by Leonardo da Vinci which cost $30.8 million. And whatever else he owns. Yet the man is taken seriously when he says, "I've been very lucky, and therefore I owe it to try and reduce the inequity in the world."

Why do celebrities need so much? Not only that, how can they, knowing and making a point of knowing (at some statistical level) with their charity that half the world is hungry? Bill Gates is showered with honors. One of the 100 people who most influenced the twentieth century (*Time*). Humanitarian person of the year (*Time*). Presidential Medal of Freedom (from Barack Obama—who also likes private islands and lost no time flying off to Sir Richard Branson's bit of paradise Necker Island[86] when his second mandate finished). An honorary knighthood from an antediluvian queen. Silver Buffalo award, the highest Boy Scout honor in the U.S (shared by other luminaries like Nazi sympathizer Charles Lindbergh and Colin Powell). Britain's (sic) second most powerful person after Tony Blair (*Sunday Times* Power List, 1999), just above the Governor of the Bank of England and way above the royal family.

When you're that rich your driblets of eleemosynary snake oil are liberally sprinkled as pearls of wisdom in TED talks. Here are a few Gatesisms.

- If you are born poor it's not your mistake, but if you die poor it's your mistake.
- Life is not fair, get used to it.
- If you can't make it good, at least make it look good.
- Money has no utility to me beyond a certain point.
- The most amazing philanthropists are people who are actually making a significant sacrifice.

So what "significant sacrifice" is Bill Gates, altruist icon of Peter Singer, "actually" making? It's calculated that he earns $250 every second or about $20 million a day. He's the "most generous person" in the world with donations exceeding $27 billion (to his own foundation). He earns money much faster than he gives it away. He is revered across the political spectrum for sorting out a feckless aid sector with his business models. Politicians hang on his every smarmy word. He lectures nations about allocating more taxpayers' money to foreign aid when Microsoft's tax avoidance represents 3.5% of the world's aid budget.[87] It's so dumb-ass blatant it might be hilarious if Gates didn't represent such a putrid system (and if we weren't making him even richer because we're writing this book using Microsoft).

It's not just Bill Gates. There are plenty of celebs playing holy charity. It has the cute name of "actorvism." And they're all more or less hypocritical idiots and/or power-hungry narcissists. Global spokesman, Richard Gere, took to *The Electronic Intifada* website and urged people to vote in the 2005 Palestinian presidential elections: "I'm Richard Gere and I'm speaking for the entire world..."; peacemaker extraordinaire Jude Law went to Afghanistan in 2008 to negotiate a ceasefire with the Taliban;[88] super-greenie Leonardo DiCaprio zooms around in his private jet lecturing on climate change; diva-diplomat Sharon Stone says the Middle East process is like going to the gym, and lays her libido on the line announcing she'd kiss just about anyone to achieve peace in the region; bounty-bountiful Bruce Willis put a million dollars on the head of Bin Laden; and yummy mummy Gwyneth Paltrow thinks that celebs owe it to "humanity" to adopt babies from poor countries (but never got round to it).

A closer look at DiCaprio, known for his over-the-top, star-studded fundraising events (€45 million from one gala in Saint-Tropez in July 2016, for example), suggests that he is rather dodgier than a mere arrogant chem-trailer. The source of the donations he gets for the Leonardo DiCaprio Foundation is being questioned, in particular when it was found by a US federal probe into money laundering to be linked with a $3 billion scandal involving a Malaysian sovereign wealth fund, 1MDB, which used misappropriated funds to back his 2013 film—oh irony!—*The Wolf of Wall Street* and to donate to his charity. And 1MDB happens to be a major driver of deforestation in Malaysia where politicians are given rainforest logging contracts worth billions in exchange for their support for the beleaguered government. US prosecutors have said that 1MDB had non-official help in its money-laundering operation from Jho Low, a playboy friend of DiCaprio's. But Jho Low is also a philanthropist and supported the Leonardo DiCaprio Foundation (devoted to the "long-term health and wealth of all [sic] Earth's inhabitants") by buying three million dollars' worth of marked-up champagne at DiCaprio's 2013 birthday party and donating very pricey works of art, including a Lichtenstein sculpture, to be auctioned to the actor's celebrity supporters.

Needless to say, not all celebrity charity is bad, although "celebrity" and "charity" are concepts that need much closer scrutiny than they usually get if a more decent and just society is the aim of the exercise. Exceptions range from, say, former San Francisco 49ers quarterback Colin Kaepernick and his response to Donald Trump's federal budget aiming to de-fund charity initiatives (donations to the Meals on Wheels America initiative, and the Love Army for Somalia), through to Wystan Auden whose many discreet acts of charitable—or solidary, more like it—kindness only came to light long after he died.

What kind of society breeds the self-serving sanctimoniousness and downright greed of people who tell you that if you die poor it's your mistake? Anyone trying to analyze the celeb phenomenon has to stomach the hogwash of the media with which they engage in a mutually profitable love-fest: in other words, negligible fact-checking, sensationalism and out-and-out fabrication. Stunt-wise, almost anything goes (filmed getting an ice bucket tipped over themselves through to Angelina Jolie nabbing former British Foreign Secretary William Hague for a four-day, £5.2 million "global summit" on sexual violence in war zones). Even if all those famous wet napes actually raised money for amyotrophic lateral sclerosis research and treatment, better public health systems would be a far more effective way of dealing with this and other diseases. As for the pricey global summit, it produced a "Statement of Action" of just over two hundred words with a logo resembling a clapperboard (yes, really). That's £26,000 a word.

But, surely celebrity philanthropy has a copycat effect? The industry thinks so. It's called "encouragement by example." That's why *Forbes* has a list of the most charitable celebs. People wanting to be like Gisele Bundchen will copy her and give. But, no, it doesn't work like that. In the United States, charitable giving per household has stayed at around 2.2% of income (if giving) for forty years. A long time ago, Christopher Lasch observed that, "In his emptiness and insignificance, the man of ordinary abilities tries to warm himself in the stars' reflected glow."[89] But the glow is without warmth and doesn't encourage kindness. Celeb charity can't be done discreetly. It needs the pomp and circumstance once supplied by religion. So high on the agenda of charitable activity are gala events. The diamond-studded display makes the innocent[90] gasp in wonder. How beautiful charity is! Symbolically, some beauty's exhibition of a mammaplasticized bosom gets associated with charity, just as the virgin's lactescent convexities did centuries ago. All this wealth hanging off flawless frames suggests some kind of deiform quality, above good and evil.

Charity celebs and fashion ooze together. A quick Google News (sic) "Amal Clooney" search yields "human rights lawyer" but, much more, digital oohs like "stuns in floral look," "outshines husband George," "major maternity style," "tousled locks effortlessly pushed away from her face," "ambrosial Amal Alamuddin" (who immediately became "Hollywood royalty" after floating around Venice where she had dropped in to "plight her troth to George Clooney"), or "baby bump in feathered Versace gown."

With the juxtaposition of "human rights lawyer" (who charges $750 per hour) and "gorgeous in ladylike florals," we're supposed to believe that flaunting, say, $20,000 in frippery every time you go out—never wearing the same thing twice—is compatible with "human rights." Amal in her florals and stilettos is laying waste to human rights. Yet *Vanity Fair*, in its "Celebrities" section (March 29, 2017), cites other human rights lawyers who bask in her reflected glory. One United Nations human-rights lawyer says that, thanks to Amal Clooney, interest in her own work has spiked "100 percent." With an eye for the main chance big charity-businesses therefore employ full-time "high-profile personality" liaison officers, and almost all the celebs support some or other charity. Charity and showbiz are so closely entwined that "Make Poverty History," starring *inter alia* Paul McCartney, Bono, and George Clooney, prompted *Time* (December 19) to declare 2005 as the year of "charitainment." Nevertheless, whatever the hooey, a survey by professors Dan Brockington and Spencer Henson, of Manchester and Sussex universities, finds that celebrities don't make people more aware of their pet charities but they do gain themselves by becoming more popular with the public.[91]

Star power is wonderful for consumption. Film and TV stars, athletes, pop stars, reality stars, royal families, chefs and tycoons are all paragons of taste, examples to follow in buying behavior, the kind of squandering that actually harms invisible vulnerable populations. In the United States one in four advertisements features them. In South Korea and Japan, the figure is 70%.[92] After Nicole Kidman was signed up by Chanel No. 5 in 2003, global sales rose by 30%. Celebrities are trusted because they are, well, celebrated, squeaky clean, surrounded by lovely things, and are so touted that we "know" them. Even non-fan consumers are more prone to remember celebrity-pushed products because they subliminally associate success or beauty with them. For fans, "it is as if they are receiving advice from a valued friend."[93]

This friendly advice also rises to rarified circles. At the 2005 World Economic Forum Sharon Stone heard the president of Tanzania describing how people were dying from malaria because they lack basic amenities. She stood up and pledged $10,000. Then she challenged business leaders to match her and, in no time at all, a million dollars were offered. But the pledges weren't honored and the United Nations had to make up the shortfall. So, whatever her original charitable impulse, Stone influenced UN spending on a cause she knew little about. Celebrities, understanding the power of advertising, need their pet campaigns to work and tend to trumpet their success so Bob Geldof gave Tony Blair's government credit for setting poverty on the way to becoming "history."[94]

Luxury and charity are in cahoots. You can stay in Barcelona's beachfront hotel, La Vela and fork out upwards of €255 per night but feel good about it because your money is working philanthropically since it allegedly supports UNICEF and Nutrition Without Borders. And charity couldn't exist without fashion. It's so vogue to hug a charity, especially when Gucci, Prada, Armani and Jean Paul Gaultier (who will kindly use you as their clotheshorse at galas if you're famous enough) have got there before you through the entwined joys of philanthropy and freebie advertising courtesy of, say, UNICEF, the United Nations Children's Fund, and its star-studded list of goodwill ambassadors.[95]

Charity pizzazz is a fun way of papering over nasty stuff for Gucci, which has been sullied for more than a decade by accusations of sweatshop labor.[96] It's not as if UNICEF is unaware of this since, as early as 2003, it was in possession of a damning report showing that Indian suppliers were paying workers less than one euro per day. But it's a lovely loop. Fashion house gets celebrity to sport its gala finery ↔ tabloids sell by trumpeting designer/celebrity names ↔ UNICEF, celebrity and designer get their press as immaculate do-gooders ↔ all sales rise more.

Some UNICEF staffers aren't convinced. The UN brand is tainted enough (with moral relativism, the Population Fund's involvement in coerced sterilization in Peru, unchecked powers of the Security Council, Oil for Food scandal, child sexual abuse by peacekeepers in Congo, Haiti, Cambodia, Côte d'Ivoire and elsewhere, the peacekeeper-caused Haiti cholera outbreak, Rwanda, Srebrenica, for example) without celebrities swirling in, causing chaos, and making local staff look like props. After they and the entourage have swept out, having turned the disaster into a spectacle and/or framed it as a profit-making opportunity (as Condoleezza Rice did when she said that the 2005 tsunami that took some 300,000 lives paid "great dividends" for the United States), people remember not suffering and the toiling of some relief workers but that a star came to that country called "Africa," without knowing whether the actual place was Dakar or Darfur.

Malawi and Cambodia are eternally linked with the Madonna and the Angel(ina) who swoop in and leave with a saved little baby or two. Their faux philanthropy, complete with heavenly names, magicks away harsh realities. The objects of their charity don't get a look-in except in photo-ops. Neither do charity icons always have much idea of what they are looking for on stunts called "fact-finding tours." In 2011, Save the Children took X-Factor runner-up Stacey Solomon to Malawi because it needed backing by "the power of famous [sic] voices." Solomon had a ball investigating maternal mortality (675 maternal deaths/100,000 live-births during the period 2004–2010): "It was one of the nicest experiences I have ever had."[97] And, for *People*, if Christina Aguilera (spokeswoman for Yum! Brands and its Kentucky Fried Chicken) goes to Rwanda with the UN World Food Program, the country must be "war-torn," even if the fighting ended two decades earlier.

UNICEF is so impressed by banging bucks that in 2002 it teamed up with the McJob company to invent a McDonald's World Children's Day, by which means it raised about $20 million in twenty-four hours. UNICEF's UK spokeswoman prated, "Unicef is protective of its brand and chooses partnerships carefully. We do not enter into partnership or allow use of the Unicef brand without a minimum six-figure contribution."[98] UNICEF is a "brand," a business, so McDonald's low wages and poor working conditions are part of the deal. McDonalds is accused of dodging, from 2009 to 2013, corporate tax worth about €1 billion by means of a Luxembourg-based structure through which it paid a mere €16 million in tax on revenue of €3.7 billion. You'd think McDonalds could have given UNICEF a little more for its whitewashing job.

The other corporate partners of the UNICEF "brand" include the H&M Foundation (accused of exploiting child labor in Myanmar), ING (illegal movement of billions of dollars through the US financial system for Burmese, Libyan, Iranian… clients), and Unilever (mercury poisoning in India, child labor, general exploitation, environmental crimes, deforestation …). But to return to the charity look and UNICEF's partner Gucci, the "human rights" lawyer Amal Clooney who so expeditiously learned the art of being "Hollywood royalty" after marrying George and shutting down Venice in the process, attended a UN Women in the World reception in September 2016 with the

Yazidi human rights activist Nadia Murad, a former ISIS captive. Amal wore Gucci. There's a website[99] that tells us these things:

> AMAL CLOONEY WORE A
> GUCCI DRESS
> WOOL SILK WEB DRESS
> € 1,500

It doesn't say what sad-faced Nadia Murad wore.

This crassness is no recent phenomenon. In the eighteenth century Adam Smith not only pointed out the moral dereliction of celebrity idolatry but got neatly to the point of political economy: celebrities play a necessary part in creating and maintaining social stratification.

> "[The] disposition to admire, and almost to worship, the rich and the powerful, and to despise, or, at least, to neglect persons of poor and mean condition, though necessary both to establish and to maintain the distinction of ranks and the order of society, is, at the same time, the great and most universal cause of the corruption of our moral sentiments. [...] It is from our disposition to admire, and consequently to imitate, the rich and the great, that they are enabled to set, or to lead what is called the fashion. [...]. Even their vices and follies are fashionable; and the greater part of men are proud to imitate and resemble them in the very qualities which dishonour and degrade them."[100]

In general, celebrities are shoring up a system of brutal inequality, which erodes democracy and public trust, destroys civic values, and undermines public health. Research shows that "[...] you are better off living in a community with a lower standard of living, but greater equality" because it has more social cohesion and networks of mutual aid and caring than those with high levels of inequality.[101] Despising "persons of poor and mean condition" to "maintain the distinction of ranks and the order of society" is today cruelly distilled into the World Economic Forum's gospel of "resilience." The non-resilient are taking the form of "surplus populations" which, unable to consume, are dysfunctional for the market. They are hotbeds of chaos which require the policing and penal powers of the state to detect and contain the risk they represent by means of surveillance, discipline and exclusion. This is the cesspit lying just beneath the red carpet.

If the inequality gap is so insane that, according to OXFAM, eight men own the same wealth as half the world, i.e. 3.6 billion people,[102] then it would be reasonable to assume that celebrity charity is more necessary than ever to do the makeup job for an unsustainable system. The demigods of celebrity culture are a symptom of a general moral and ethical malaise in which, as capitalism is foundering in its own morass, mythmaking is essential for keeping the show going. They help to keep people out of politics for, as Lewis Lapham wrote in *The Wish for Kings*, belief in princes, princesses and fairytales is easier than political engagement. Politically disengaged or disenfranchised people may feel a bit better when Demi Moore and Robbie Williams tootle off to succor Haiti but they'll never know about the role of the United States in causing its catastrophes.

Even when some celebrities make sincere, well-informed attempts to raise awareness of a calamity or atrocity, the gesture may fall into a vacuous pit of empathy, of weeping and lamenting over, for example, an image of a father wailing over his dead child, a sinking boat crammed with refugees, a line of small coffins, or taking the verbal form of encouraging comforting all-embracing, manifestly untrue slogans like "We are all refugees." The appropriate feeling is rage, rage against politicians who are more interested in arms sales than human lives, who cause wars, and build real and virtual walls to keep their fellow-human victims of their actions—refugees—out of our line of vision, rage against the system that is destroying the planet, many members of our own and other species, and our very humanity with it. Rage, which demands serious thinking about what action to take.

Jerome Phelps raises some hard questions about the guilt-assuaging role of celebrities and addiction to images in his article "Why Is So Much Art about the 'Refugee Crisis' So Bad?"[103] using the example of Ai Weiwei's performance when he lay on a Lesvos beach imitating the pose of the dead three-year-old Syrian child Alan (initially reported as Aylan) Kurdi who was found on a Turkish beach. His comment is harsh but it should at least cause some discomfort about the generally uncritical view of celebrities and the role society has allocated to them. "Once again, a celebrity sees a humanitarian crisis and realises that what the world needs is an image of himself."

Ai Weiwei is a political artist and wants to draw attention to "humanity's struggles" when he is really representing a particular atrocity, the result of antihuman political decisions made by so-called democratic authorities. His empathy, especially since he is a celebrity, distracts attention away from the real person, Alan Kurdi, and what he really represents. This is where Peter Singer is misguided about empathy and altruism because when politics is glossed over with fame (including his own) ordinary humans are lulled into a false sense of security. Important people really care about humanity. We can leave the solutions to them. They have the wherewithal. Then, only very few people ask why the emphasis of the "crisis" is on Europe's problems rather than on the dire situation of real human beings in other places, or why Europe has so dismally failed to respond to the true crisis. Worse than failing, the Italian Coast Guard let 268 refugees including sixty children die in the Mediterranean on October 10, 2013 when an officer told the Maltese navy that they would not move their nearby ship to rescue the refuges because it needed to spot "new targets," and Italy didn't want to transfer them to the nearest coast. This is the true nature of the refugee crisis but it challenges the humanity of the privileged, the people who go to art galleries wrapped up in refugee blankets to express their solidarity. It is too hard to think through all the implications. Fuzzy empathy may be well meaning but, in these times, it is shirking responsibilities and declining to engage in even the simple action of confronting political leaders with hard political questions about their awful, literally murderous policies.

The academic industry named Celebrity Studies has grabbed its niche in a context of crisis in the humanities, reflecting and also reinforcing the general "Crisis" usually referred to as "economic." If the crisis is understood as one of values in which ideas of "humanity" itself are at stake, then the humanities epitomize it and Celebrity Studies throw revealing light on a dehumanized and dehumanizing culture. Celebrities are part of a system that sees famous people as brands and thus consumer products (so the Beckhams have trademarked their children's names). Without consumer culture there could be no celebrity culture. Culture is a major asset of postindustrial capitalism, offering new goods for consumption and, to some extent, setting up new altars to worship at. It is a means of shaping subjectivity and obedience (preferably as self-policing) to the state and political structure which, in turn, adapts to the new needs of the Fourth Industrial Revolution (or postcapitalism). One of the "cultural" goals of this digital age is to develop brainpower beyond the bounds of human consciousness and create a new kind of extra-human "intelligence" inscribed in matter (the Internet of Things, genetic design, big data, and so on) with certain skills and intelligence as offshoots of the biological, physical and digital domains, mobilizing all forms of knowledge to turn the new "intelligence" (information, algorithms) into a productive force above and beyond the human being.[104]

Thinking about what it means to be human is reduced to software metaphors. Human lives become data and data is turned to profit. This process is managed by a very tiny technical elite, so massive concentration of wealth would be just a harbinger of a still more baneful appropriation of knowledge because, with this radical fusion of human with technology, individual personhood stands to be obliterated by data. For example, a venture capital company called OS Fund "invests in entrepreneurs working towards quantum leap discoveries that promise to rewrite the operating systems of life."[105] Another well-known "education" philanthropist, the billionaire Elon Musk, says that people will soon need to become cyborgs: a "merger of biological intelligence and machine intelligence" will be necessary if humans are to remain economically valuable.[106] The implications for intelligence as an autonomous reflective power, the basic need of humanity to use ideas freely, are scary. And human rights will have no place in this freedomless world.

Freely used ideas are not much loved by the very wealthy so "education" (where are you Pink Floyd and "We don't need no thought control?") is a field of experiment and enterprise much favored by philanthropists. No Child Left Behind (NCLB) sounds like a presents-for-every-kid initiative which consumerism-promoting philanthropists would love. But, no, it's an Act, part of United States federal law passed in 2002 and, in the belief that, by establishing measurable goals, the NCLB can improve individual results, statewide standardized tests were introduced and students had to meet set values of Adequate Yearly Progress. NCLB incentive schemes took funds from low-performing schools, thus compounding school failure and encouraging cheating. The schools themselves cheated too, fiddling the figures or covering up wide-scale cheating when improved test scores meant funding rewards and low scores meant no funding. Humanities subjects like art, history, geography, and language are not tested by NLCB and were therefore dropped by schools.

Bill Gates is a spreader of mosquito nets,[107] which makes him seem like a practical-minded philanthropist, identifying the problem of malaria and applying the "obvious" solution of "especially" treated (i.e. Africans can't design their own nets, and there is zero contact between researchers and the actual problem) insecticide-impregnated nets which are costly for poor folk and need regular re-dipping in Gates-approved insecticide. Further inquiry makes one wonder if this is a benign cover for his nefarious ideas about "education." He actually pontificates on "Mosquitos, Malaria and Education" in a TED talk.[108] But our "optimist" seems blithely unaware that malaria and poverty aggravate each other, and that good public health, clean drinking water, sanitation, and hygiene education would be much more democratic and effective.

It's not just a problem of naivety. It's worse than mere ignorance. To give one example, the WHO reported that—by means of old-fashioned public health methods like clean drinking water, hygiene, sanitation, community medical clinics and eradicating mosquito breeding sites—Eritrea reduced malaria mortality by nearly 80% between 2000 and 2015. This didn't make headlines but, Gates, on shoulder-rubbing terms with the organization and so concerned about malaria, should have known about it. Yet he announced that he was giving $1 billion for his quick-fix solution of vaccine to prevent malaria. As Thomas C. Mountain points out, "A 'donation' of $1 billion or so to develop a malaria 'vaccine' could turn into 'a gift that keeps on giving' in the form of tens of billions of dollars in new, patented 'vaccine' sales in Africa alone, and Bill Gates, through his investment portfolio of drug company stocks, will quietly pocket a continuous flow of African blood money. What Bill Gates' 'donation' amounts to [is] a malaria drug addiction program for Africa's people."[109] Not to mention the long reach of his interference around the world.

Bill Gates is so high-profile he can nudge state and global funding towards the areas he wants to prioritize. Global health scholar Laurie Garrett writes that at the WHO, hardly any major policy decisions are taken without being "casually, unofficially vetted by Gates Foundation staff."[110] The Gates Foundation was (after the US government) the WHO's second-biggest donor in 2014 and its donations are "earmarked," which is another way of saying how much it influences WHO policy. Indeed, the WHO

Director-General, Margaret Chan, admitted that her "budget [is] highly earmarked, so it is driven by what I call donor interests."[111] It's not difficult to work out which donor.

In February 2008, Dr. Arata Kochi, the former head of WHO's malaria program, complained in an internal memorandum that, with its homogeneity of thinking, the Gates Foundation had created a "cartel" with closely linked research leaders, was dominating research in the area of malaria treatment, obstructing the possibility of independent review, and undermining scientific creativity in a way that "could have implicitly dangerous consequences on the policymaking process in world health."[112] It isn't surprising to learn that Gates is vehemently against public health systems and considers them a "complete waste of money" and claims that there is no evidence that they work.[113] The policy line between public and private is hard to see, especially as there is no governing framework, oversight or stipulation that these influential charitable foundations must detail how they operate and what their results are, and there are no mechanisms to ensure that the money donated is used for an international agency's goals rather than others shaped to meet donor interests. There is a widespread perception that states are leaving their social responsibilities to private foundations but many are, in fact, opting for market-based solutions to health and development and, in the process, doing themselves out of taxes.

What Bill really likes is "bricks in the wall," educational "thought control." He loved the NCLB "gold standard" (overhauled when President Obama signed the Every Student Succeeds Act in 2015—a law with a demonstrable lie in its title) and is a leading donor to primary and secondary education in the United States. Gates is still standardizing, with help from the gutter press magnate Rupert Murdoch, a big investor in online education who, in 2010, calculating that this could end up being a $500 billion business, bought Wireless Generation, an educational technology firm, saying that he hoped News Corps' content would go straight to the students' terminals: tabloid press meets education meets celebrities. In 2013, the Gates Foundation teamed up with the Murdoch empire by funding an electronic database of personal information—names, addresses, test scores, interests, aptitude, problems, and outside activities—of millions of children in primary and secondary schools. The project folded in 2014 following a hue and cry when it was discovered that inBloom Inc., which ran the database, was feeding information to for-profit groups supplying schools. That was a charitable $100 million down the drain.

The privatized business models applied in education today depend on measurement, a lucrative business in which private sector metrics standardize and streamline shareholder value. It might be difficult at first sight to see where celebrities fit in here, but they are a typology, setting a standard of wealth and success and, more important, providing an apparently pretty face for a world in which the perpetrators of great wretchedness lurk in mysterious hideaways measuring and plotting humanity. Their in-group control of "intelligence" means that extra-human qualities are confined to those at the top of the stack in a world in which an all-knowing, omnipresent new faith called Dataism, worshipping the power of the algorithm, supposedly makes sense of human existence. Human beings used to be seen as the source of meaning but intelligence has been uncoupled from consciousness, as Yuval Noah Harari puts it.[114] Sophisticated networks extract our ideas of meaning and use them to determine our fate, and this is where reorienting the educational system comes in. This grisly project really needs pretty faces.

Culture is no longer a space for free creation but a competitive market of talents, skills and patents and, accordingly, depoliticized cultural and educational policies are designed by promoters, consultants, enterprises, richly endowed foundations, and think tanks. Knowledge has ceased to be a condition for emancipation, for freely transforming our lives. You are either a competitive consumer or redundant. The old problem of white, privileged, European, male conceptions of what is human is worse than ever. The fate of humanity is concentrated in the hands of people like the 2,500 attendees (83% male; average age about 50; one-third American; using 1,700 private jets; paying $71,000 subscription fees; and largely unconcerned about climate change) of Davos, a social engineers' clique funded by 1,000 of the world's biggest companies. They plan what to do about "risks" they see in demographic phenomena like growth, aging and migration of populations, and concoct a new kind of leadership to deal with them. If the besuited Davos denizens are working to bureaucratize sovereign power over death, with their wars, refugee regulations, and selective business-style humanitarianism, celebs might be something like their dazzlingly robed high priests.

Celebrity "culture" as a field of academic study is quite wacko, as its subject might suggest. The fare is picked over and reconstructed in PhD theses and conferences replete with titles like "Fake or Flawless? A Discursive Analysis of Beyonce's Feminist Identity"; "I'm Not a Kardashian: Framing Celebrity Reluctance Towards Social Media"; and "'A fashion designer, a politician, and a Jesuit walk into a bar…': Authenticating the Iconography of Vivienne Westwood, Barack Obama, and Pope Francis in Celebrity Culture." What kind of society presents this rubbish as intellectual? It's all very well to discursively ponder Beyonce's feminism but these academics are talking about people who flaunt their privilege as if it were not shining bright against an appalling backdrop of suffering.

The journal *Celebrity Studies* declares[115] that its work "ranges across such topics as the relationship between celebrity and the construction of self and identity under consumer capitalism," or "celebrity confessional" and weightier issues like "interconnections between celebrity, politics and citizenship" or "human rights and popular culture." Its "celebrity manifesto" states that the journal will "explore the political economy of fame" but it hasn't progressed far along these lines, if one judges by its latest articles (2017): "Flesh-Images, Body Shame and Affective Ambiguities in Celebrity Gossip Magazines"; "His Own Kind of Honour: Reluctant Celebrity Chef Michael Van de Elzen"; and "'Ah, love! It's not for me!' Off-Screen Romance and Pola Negri's Star Persona," for instance.

Meanwhile Staffordshire University (United Kingdom) has offered "David Beckham Studies." "[He] doesn't actually [...] take a political stand or engage with any kind of social issues of the day. But maybe that's just we want in the early 21st century, a person who doesn't actually do much, but onto which we can displace all our fantasies."[116] Spot on! Tailor-made for neoliberalism. Confine your studies of social issues to Murdoch-covered charitable galas ("disease parties," they're jestingly called) and never ask why Mr. Beckham, needs palatial homes in London, France, Madrid, Beverley Hills, and Dubai, or to own twenty-two cars, and how this squares with the charitable image he wants to project, preferably crowned with a "fucking knighthood."

In academia women celebs become postmodern feminist icons. In 1992 Harvard offered the course "Madonna [no, not the lactating one] Studies in Women and Popular Culture" which examines how the song "Like a Virgin" offers a "deconstruction of fixed female identities."[117] For Camille Paglia, professor of Humanities at the University of the Arts Philadelphia, "Madonna has cured all the ills of feminism." One Princeton lecturer in Postmodernism and Contemporary Culture rejoices in students' willingness to "write papers about Madonna at the drop of a hat."[118] Then there's Oprah. The University of Illinois offers "History 298: Oprah Winfrey, the Tycoon": "[...] how Winfrey came to be a cultural icon and to build a formidable media empire [...]." Is anyone teaching that Oprah Winfrey is a stalwart of neoliberalism and meritocracy or how her "positive thinking" denies the structural processes that entrench race and gender inequality? How role models like Oprah are privatizing liberty and reinventing it as market conduct? One white student took the course because he wanted to know more about African-American history.[119] He'd do better to study why African-American kids are getting shot in the street by trigger-happy whites.

Oprah might even run for president. If fellow celebrity Trump can do it, so can she. "I thought, 'Oh gee, I don't have the experience, I don't know enough.' And now I'm thinking, 'Oh.'"[120] She might have competition from other celebs because it's also rumored that Mark Zuckerberg and Kanye West could run for the nation's highest office. And *Time* reported in October 2014 that, "The Odds of George Clooney Running for President Just Doubled." Why? Because he "married prominent human rights lawyer Amal Alamuddin." And he's "not just one of the most recognizable faces in the USA, but in the world." If Sharon Stone thinks she'd like to achieve what Camp David couldn't by osculating her way to Middle East peace, anything's possible.

In this money-spinning milieu of academic journals, magazines, websites, television channels and shows, and mainstream newspapers celebrities play several roles. One is to provide a public, easily recognizable face for philanthropy. But this "love of humanity" is only for the very rich who are also busy destroying humanity and its environment. Poor people can't do philanthropy. Small private acts of charity—or kindness—belong to the commons, common people and their struggles for social justice. Celebrities, religiously arrayed in secular finery, draw attention to social distress but immediately cover it up by giving the impression that something is being done about it. Their aura suggests they are the chosen beings who might inhabit the brave new world of the likes of Elon Musk. And this rarified world has been announced, for example in the "wealth porn aesthetic," as Zoe Williams[121] calls it when speaking of the show *Big Little Lies*: "[...] the more expensive the spaces, the more empty and sterile. [...] The sheer, uncluttered cleanliness of wealth [...] conveys at once the desire to sever ties with the complicated world, the quest for elite purity and the urge to forget the excesses of your accumulation."

Not only do the ultra-rich try to purge their wantonness, they are aided by a high degree of impunity in a brain-numbed society so their charitable work, even when inappropriate, inept and corrupt, is taken at face value (charity is always good) with little examination of subtexts. "Mother" Teresa of Calcutta was a perfect charity idol for a rich world with a poor conscience.[122] The good nun wasn't fussed about praising the atrocious Duvalier family of Haiti as they funded her projects, or accepting millions from devout Charles Keating, one of the US's most notorious fraudsters, or from big-time pension-funds embezzler Robert Maxwell, but neither was she going to be flustered by having to explain how it was spent. Her celebrated center in Kolkata didn't noticeably benefit (so "Mother" preferred to seek medical treatment in California) and her order declined to publish audits. But never mind: bowing before the tawdry altar "of showbiz, superstition and populism," the Church broke its own rules about devil's advocacy and a five-year wait after the death of a candidate for beatification, and Pope John Paul II rushed in to nominate her a year after her death. Who cared about mismanagement of funds when the Church had a superstar saint in the making?

Another celebrity with the moral crown of the Nobel Peace Prize, Aung San Suu Kyi, tucks flowers behind her ear and prohibits any talk of the genocide she superintends against the Rohingya in Myanmar[123] where, naturally, she heads a charity, the Daw Khin Kyi Foundation, which aims to "lay the foundations for peace, security and freedom in our country." (Rohingya need not apply.) Another genocidaire, Henry Kissinger, is trustee (together with other warmongering benefactors, Madeleine Albright, Condoleezza Rice, and Colin Powell) of the International Rescue Committee. Kissinger cares about blankets for refugees and clean water for kids? So does the woodheap,[124] as some of us used to say long ago in hicksville Australia.

Or there is the impunity long enjoyed by charitable pederasts and sex offenders like Jimmy Savile and Rolf Harris. Or sought by Paris Hilton who, after being convicted for drunk-driving, managed to get hundreds of people to sign a petition addressed to California governor Arnold Schwarzenegger saying she should be freed because, "She provides beauty and excitement to (most of) our otherwise mundane lives." Or gracing the "environmentalist" Harrison Ford, vice-chairman of Conservation International (accused of green-washing for BP, Cargill, Chevron, Monsanto and Shell) who almost crashed into a Boeing 737 when he landed one of his eleven planes on a taxiway, but won't face any penalties.

Celebs live in fortified houses, often with "panic rooms" and have bodyguards in round-the-clock attendance. Yet they are often depicted as normal, like the rest of us, walking kids or dogs, darting out for an ice cream or enjoying a carefully staged and photographed country stroll. They are even prone to negative press with divorce, financial and legal struggles, weight problems, drug issues, cheating partners, problem children, and professional flops, issues that, rather than tarnishing their Olympian status, make sure that the public can identify with them because we are all human and nobody's life is perfect after all.

Lurking behind celebrity hijinks is the dangerous entropy that can be ignited at any time by the excluded masses. The rich are taking it seriously, are preparing for this dystopia, especially in Silicon Valley and New York. Survivalists stock up on Bitcoin, buy real estate havens in far-flung places, get second passports, and have fuelled-up helicopters and lavishly fitted-out underground bunkers on the ready. They preach "radical self-reliance" and construct sniper posts to protect them from the "chaos outside."[125] This catastrophic scenario is, in many senses, a much realer aspect of what celebrities stand for on their side of the social gulf and is probably, at least partly, why the media keeps presenting them and fuelling the aspirations of a voracious voyeuristic public with a pernicious subtext of possible equal privilege. In the end, if one cares to look into it, charity is a merciless mirror that reflects much about social fears and desires of a declining western civilization.

In all the celebrity tabloid coverage and studies programs, there is little interest in the fact that a society based on inequality and fast-appearing "surplus" or "bare-life" populations needs charity and celebrities to gild over its harshness. But not any old charity. It must be visible. It must convey the false promise that if celebs can make it, others can too. Celebrity is also a political spectacle, as Trump understands. Guy Debord wrote in 1967 that, "The spectacle originates in the loss of the unity of the world, and the gigantic expansion of the modern spectacle expresses the totality of this loss. [...]. In the spectacle, one part of the world represents itself to the world and is superior to it. The spectacle is nothing more than the common language of this separation. [...] The world at once present and absent which the spectacle makes visible is the world of the commodity dominating all that is lived."[126] As spectacle, celebrity seeks, in its widely purveyed media narrative, to unify fractured social life, to become a "family" for isolated, alienated individuals, and replace the community. Rampant postmodernity.

Perhaps the most sinister aspect of celebrity charity is the idea that it's a wonderful thing that, in this "world of the commodity," some white-toothed rich people drop a few crumbs off their table into the gaping mouths of the starving, that there's something acceptable about this "loss of unity" in society, this division between "the best" and "the rest" who are condemned to *zoe* existence by the same system that spawned the beautiful ones. Of course the system needs celebs (either cynical accomplices or stupid enough to think that they really are doing good) to help deny and hide atrocious reality. And when this is the case real, empathetic concern for others becomes revolutionary.

CHAPTER 6
A MUNIFICENCE OF MALFEASANCE

It's fairly indicative that many charity "scandals" are understood in the sense of "activity that is morally or legally wrong" but few seem to be discussed in the sense of "causing outrage." Most people are reluctant to speak ill of charity, or can't associate it with scandalous wrongdoing because it is so widely believed to be good *per se.* Scandals are rarely seen as intrinsic to the system of charity itself and the larger system within which charity plays its part, even though they are profuse and multifarious, including tax avoidance or evasion, the "development Disneyland," the wheeling and dealing of a philanthropic grandee like Jeffrey Sachs, predatory humanitarianism, Big Charity's G8 power-wielding, the love-triangle consisting of celebs, big corporations and upper echelons of international political power, megalomaniac delirium, fake foundations, and illegal or legal-but-dishonest cooking of the books. These are not isolated instances of dishonest practice but combine to characterize the everyday functioning of philanthropic endeavor in the unjust system of which it is nearly always an all-too-willing part. Change is not on the agenda and do-gooding institutions are often less concerned about feeding the multitudes than making sure they get a hefty slice of the cake.

One day after the Haiti earthquake on January 12, 2010 the FBI issued a lame "Haitian Earthquake Relief Fraud Alert"—immediately echoed by *Forbes*—warning would-be donors not to respond to unsolicited emails or click on links or files they may contain, and to be wary of individuals claiming to be survivors or officials, urging them to check the veracity of nonprofit organizations,[127] not to give personal or financial information to people soliciting contributions, and to donate only to tried-

and-true organizations like the Red Cross. This kind of advice might be more suited, perhaps, to Internet scams like Nigerian emails, frisky Russian girlfriends, or mugged-on-vacation pleas, or might alert out-of-touch users who have been meditating on a remote mountaintop for twenty years but, basically, it only suggests that charity scams exist and, moreover, is naïve or slapdash. The reality is that a good many well-known nonprofits are disgracefully inept at best and criminal at worst.

The institution of charity is open to massive fraud but the problem isn't the online vulnerability of people who might like to contribute $50 for a good cause. The real iniquity is that offenses are committed in the name of charity, aided by a system that turns a blind eye or actually encourages them, and these crimes affect traumatized people, the supposed beneficiaries of philanthropy. Perfunctory email security warnings distract attention from the elephant in the room, the neoliberal society which creates and perpetuates inequality, and uses an ancient benevolent institution to gloss over its wrongdoings, making it an accomplice in doing so.

A charity, by its own lights, should aim to abolish itself as soon as possible. Its "consumers" are people hard hit by natural disasters, war, poverty, systematic oppression and dispossession, and they need help to recover as well and as quickly as possible. But charities tend to be a strange, self-perpetuating business in which people make careers and retire with pensions, so poor or zero results are more amenable to career-enhancing "long-term missions." The money supporting them doesn't, of course, come from "clients," the beneficiaries of its work, but from third parties, sometimes anonymously or, if they aren't anonymous, they might be using the charity to showcase their magnanimity, as would be the intention of many celebrities who then need "their" charities to appear to be effective and to generate good publicity. Keeping up appearances is a strong incentive for swindling, which isn't too difficult as nonprofits are largely exempt from the usual market pressures and oversight. Several charities might deliver similar goods or compete for "clients," a further inducement to dishonest practice. At the end of the day, all this means that missions are poorly executed and "customers" underserved and often undeserving (like the charity itself or a building contractor in its home country).

In Haiti, after the collapse of a $30 million partnership with USAID, the American Red Cross (ARC) was left scrabbling for projects to spend the money on: "Any ideas on how to spend the rest of this?? (Besides the wonderful helicopter idea?)," the ARC chief Gail McGovern wrote to the chief international officer David Meltzer in a November 2013 email obtained by *ProPublica* and National Public Radio (NPR).[128] The ARC had been in Haiti for years before the 2010 earthquake but still didn't know how to spend its large donations garnered with the help of Michelle Obama, the NFL and *tutti quanti* in a long list of celebrities. Since it was out of touch with local actors and needs, the ARC brought in clueless outsiders with all kinds of "hardship" perks, when qualified local people could have done the job much better.

If they are to keep existing, charities must keep pulling in funds and leverage the system to attract donors and produce gratifying results for them. Modest, untelegenic agricultural projects ensuring food security in out-of-the way places won't appeal as much as, say, Brad Pitt's "Make It Right" designer houses (with no neighborhood facilities and presently rotting in post-Katrina New Orleans). But if charities are assumed to be evaluated in accordance with the work they are meant to be doing—meeting the real and desperate needs of those on the receiving end—most are failing.

One of the more disreputable cases of this perversity at the heart of charity was revealed in the United States in 2015 by the National Public Radio and *ProPublica* investigations into the disappearance of some $488 million donated to the American Red Cross (ARC) for earthquake relief in Haiti, almost 14% of the country's GDP of $6.62 billion at the time. One Red Cross official described the earthquake as a "spectacular fund-raising opportunity." And, yes, the funds were spectacular, at least for the Red Cross. A report by Senator Charles Grassley details how the ARC spent about 25% of Haiti relief money on "administrative" costs and "fundraising" (when it already had the funds) and also earmarked $2 million for a $4.3 million contract it awarded to a partner organization, the International Federation of the Red Cross. Unsurprisingly, it downsized its ethics office from sixty-five employees to three.[129] The ARC built only six of the 130,000 homes it claimed to have constructed and would seem to be guilty of massive fraud in Haiti, but it has only been perfunctorily chided and never charged.

When a cholera epidemic (introduced by UN peacekeepers of the MINUSTAH mission, but never properly acknowledged or compensated) raged through Haiti nine months after the earthquake, the ARC's response was crippled by "internal issues that go unaddressed." These "internal issues" had a devastating effect on the people of Haiti. "None of these people had to die," says Paul Christian Namphy, a Haitian water and sanitation official.[130] Constructing a clean water system would cost about $800 million, the same as the MINUSTAH annual budget (and why on earth did Haiti need a *peacekeeping* force after an earthquake?) and just 8% of the more than $9 billion which had been pledged in public and private donations. In addition, official bilateral and multilateral donors pledged $13 billion and the UN Office of the Special Envoy for Haiti noted that only $6 billion of that had been disbursed. On what? It wasn't used to provide safe water infrastructure or to prevent the spread of cholera. By 2016, about 770,000 people were affected and some 9,200 had died. And this appalling situation came about with the FBI's endorsement of the ARC *after* the organization had been criticized when its state chapters had kept money donated to 9/11 victims, and for its wretched performance after Hurricane Katrina in 2005. The

ARC's priorities left little room for doubt when, on one occasion after Hurricane Sandy in 2012, nearly half its rescue vehicles were diverted from their work to be used as props for news conferences.

Vijaya Ramachandran and Julie Walz unpacked the numbers[131] and found that approximately 94% of humanitarian funding for Haiti aided intermediaries like the donors' own entities, UN agencies, international NGOs and private contractors. Not local NGOs. There is no information about how the money was spent, either from foreign NGOs or private contractors. USAID contractors are supposed to provide bi-weekly and quarterly reports on how they are using the aid but, then again, the Agency is not "responsible for directly monitoring subrecipients unless otherwise required by law"[132] and is therefore unable to determine where the money paid to contractors is going. A breakdown of donor figures shows that high percentages (for example, nearly 70% of Canada's aid to Haiti) of funding are "not specified." EU figures reveal that 67% of humanitarian aid and 43% of recovery funding went to international NGOs. Ramachandran and Walz found that only 45 organizations or projects—out of thousands—had submitted reports on their work by the end of 2011. Just four specify how the money was spent. The Haitian government, required by donor conditions to be transparent, is given little information about aid and its uses. The result of this malpractice is that some 55,100 IDPs are still living in tents today, in the squalor and danger (especially for women) of thirty-one resettlement camps. Haiti still lacks good roads, a reliable electricity supply and potable water. And cholera is far from being eradicated.

Philanthropic performance after the Asian tsunami of December 26, 2004 was also bad enough to suggest grave cause for doubt over what charities actually do. By 2006, the Red Cross, which had been pledged $2.2bn globally, still had more than a third of that stashed away in banks. It promised to build 50,000 houses in Indonesia, Sri Lanka and the Maldives but just 8,000 were completed while only about 166,000 of the 500,000 people rendered homeless had been rehoused. Many aid agencies were too small to manage the necessary tasks but this didn't deter them from pocketing funds to prolong their existence so they could enter the fray when the next disaster struck. Incompetence is a "steep learning curve." At the victims' expense, but this is never mentioned. The expression says a lot about priorities.

How is this misconduct possible in the midst of such great suffering? One answer is that it is almost impossible to monitor how nonprofits operate. When a major disaster strikes, as happened with the 2004 tsunami and the Haiti earthquake, international charities promptly get huge cash inflows from millions of small donors. The charity often creams off as much as possible and parks the loot in some tax haven. Sums declared as inflows can be accredited by obliging contacts through false invoices if records are required. International donations exist in a "black hole" of accountability[133] and crony trustees are far from independent. Governments don't hold nonprofits accountable for deliberate or inadvertent mismanagement and the "clients," the victims, can't. Instead of trying to demonstrate good-practice credentials by transparency and rigorous accountability—the need for which would seem clear given the sensitive, painful nature of their work—and striving to stand out as shining examples of good works in times of grief and strife, charities are usually less than forthcoming about their activities. The money you give to the Red Cross might buy good feelings of doing something to help but it probably won't save lives or build homes or hospitals for victims of a disaster. The undeclared role of charity is to paper over and maintain the system that produces the disasters.

"Mother" Teresa of Kolkata was not known for financial transparency, as we have noted. If *Stern* magazine calculated that her order, Missionaries of Charity, received about $100 million in annual revenue supposedly for "wholehearted free service" to the poorest of the poor, nobody seems to know where the money went. Certainly not in pain relief because, as the now-canonized "Mother" asserted, "There is something beautiful in seeing the poor accept their lot, to suffer it like Christ's Passion. The world gains much from their suffering." She was also a zealot of religious imperialism, as Vijay Prashad writes (in what could also be a succinct definition of the Jeffrey-Sachs-style humanitarian intervention):[134]

> [...] the quintessential image of the white woman in the colonies, working to save the dark bodies from their own temptations and failures. [...] The Euro-American-dominated international media continue to harbor the colonial notion that white peoples are somehow especially endowed with the capacity to create social change. When nonwhite people labor in this direction, the media typically search for white benefactors or teachers, or else, for white people who stand in the wings to direct the nonwhite actors. Dark bodies cannot act of their own volition to stretch their own capacity, for they must wait, the media seem to imply, for some colonial administrator, some technocrat from IBM or the IMF to tell them how to do things. When it comes to saving the poor, the dark bodies are again invisible, for the media seem to celebrate only the worn out platitudes of such as Mother Teresa and ignore the struggles of those bodies for their own liberation.

Back in the metropolitan heartland, one of the playgrounds of charitable wrongdoing is tax avoidance or evasion, although it's called tax "incentives." Despite all the evidence to the contrary, people usually understand charity as a kind of redistribution, but the rearrangement of bank balances tends to be limited to fairly tight circles. If governments are giving tax incentives to charities so that they can do a lot of the work which, arguably, governments themselves should be doing in terms of health, housing, clean water and so on, then at least they have the obligation to ensure that subsidized philanthropic grants are used to alleviate some of the harm caused by increasing inequality because, although some charitable endowments can create public value, all charity tax breaks represent a huge public investment.

In the US alone, there are more than 200,000 charitable organizations and Americans were set to give $400 billion to charities at the end of 2016, an average of $2 million per charity. According to the *Giving USA* annual report on philanthropy, charitable giving rose 3.5 percent in 2012 to $316.23 billion, an all-time record that surpassed the record of $311 billion in 2007 before the financial crisis. In 2010, public charities in the United States reported $1.51 trillion in revenue, $1.45 trillion in expenses, and $2.71 trillion in assets. (How are expenses and assets related?) Yet poverty rates keep climbing: 20% of American children are from families that struggle to put food on the table, and the number of homeless minors has grown by 60% in the last six years (the same figure as for the country's wealth). Charity is supposed to remedy social ills. The facts don't square. If the institution of charity has slotted itself into an unscrupulous system, it is because it allows altruistic instincts to be exploited by corporations, not only bamboozling the public into thinking that a few dollars donated to a children's home make a difference to the children concerned, but also making a few people very rich. Charities acting like for-profit corporations are not into ending poverty, homelessness or hunger. They manipulate the system that aggravates them.

In a hardline neoliberal context, Australia provides a view of charities in which the perspective is lack of official oversight in a sector that is prone to corrupt practice. The nonprofits business is booming with an income exceeding $100 billion each year and more than a million people on the payroll. There are approximately 54,000 active charities, or about one for every 445 people (a ratio about four times higher than in the United States). Until 2012, and the establishment of Australian Charities and Not-for-profits Commission (ACNC), there was no national regulatory body. The Tax Office registry was never updated, so there was no serious monitoring of the sector, although 38% of its income comes from government and very little (less than 4%), from donations. The rest is "self-earned," from services they provide, which means nonprofits function like businesses. There is no official code of ethics addressing commercial agreements between charities and fundraisers, which account for 90% of regular donations. Although the ACNC required charities to report on their activities, many declined to do so and only thirteen were delisted after investigation.

Australia's recent neoliberal governments are chary of NGOs because they are more likely to advocate their causes in public or to decry, for example, the country's shockingly high proportion of indigenous incarceration or its refugee policy—subject of a 108-page submission alerting the International Criminal Court to crimes against humanity—while a for-profit organization tends to lobby the government quietly and directly. These governments, not outstanding for intellectual agility, see charities as damaging to private entrepreneurship. Perhaps they're not well-informed about charity scams which offer plenty of scope for untrammeled entrepreneurship, as demonstrated by the Sydney-based Appco Group which obtains donations on behalf of some of Australia's biggest charities. For example, it raised $12.2 million for the nonprofit organization Special Olympics Australia, which only got 4% while Appco took a fee of 57% and, in a program it ran for World Wildlife Fund, it took 85% of the first year's funding as fees. An agreement between a fundraising company and a nonprofit is deemed to be a commercial arrangement that does not require transparency. Indeed, former Prime Minister Tony Abbott believes that, "the people serving our community don't deserve a new level of scrutiny."[135]

In the United States, the Internal Revenue Service (IRS) stipulates that charities only have to spend about 5% of their investment assets annually. This money doesn't necessarily go to good causes but can be written off as salaries or "expenses." A billionaire can set up, tax-free, a charitable trust to give his kids a lifelong job and salary, and no estate tax is due on the "donation." The trust is protected from creditors because, by law, the heir does not own it but only "controls" it.

In Great Britain, charities are exempt from tax on income including donations, rent and investments. However, since the profits they make on operations are taxable, many charities conduct their business operations through a separate company which would theoretically pay tax on its profits if it didn't donate them all to the charity through the "Gift Aid" scheme, a facility offered by HM Revenue so that charities can reclaim the basic rate on taxation. Although these companies are simply a tax-dodging device, this activity is not illegal and is resorted to by charities that are reputedly impeccably honest like OXFAM. Another OXFAM dodge is its "Tag Your Bag" scheme which represents some £80 million per year in tax relief. Gift Aid allows a charity to claim 25% of a donation as tax relief, even though the charity hasn't paid any tax. And higher-rate tax payers can also claim extra tax relief but this doesn't work for goods donated to a charity shop. Accordingly, the donor lets OXFAM sell the goods on his or her behalf and then gives the charity the proceeds. These are classed as a cash donation and eligible for the 25% Gift Aid tax relief.

There is a difference between tax evasion, which is illegal, and tax avoidance which is defined as legal utilization of the tax regime to one's own advantage in order to reduce the amount of tax payable. What this means—how easy it is for the wealthy to use charities for tax avoidance—supposedly upset even George Osborne, Britain's Tory Chancellor of the Exchequer from 2010 to 2016 (himself not adverse to the odd sizable tax dodge involving his residences): "I was shocked to see that some of the very wealthiest people in the country have organised their tax affairs, and to be fair it's within the tax laws, so that they were regularly paying virtually no income tax."[136] In operational terms, the distinction between evasion and avoidance is blurry, while slippery organizational definitions and lack of transparency open up loopholes leading into full-blown evasion and profiteering by large corporations with their teams of savvy lawyers, wily tax advisors, and other useful resources like shell companies.

Tax evasion and fraud through abuse of charities, which is becoming more organized, diverse and sophisticated, is a serious problem in several countries where it costs treasuries hundreds of millions of dollars, as the OECD Sub-Group (of Working Party No. 8) on Tax Crimes and Money Laundering reports in a 2008 study based on nineteen countries. Nevertheless, large-scale charity abuse would seem not to afflict all countries. The OECD report says that five of the countries surveyed—Austria, Chile, Denmark, France and Germany—were apparently unaffected. In the United States, the most common means of tax evasion is said to be overstatement of charitable donations given, but the CNN reported[137] another kind of scandal, namely that the "50 worst" charities received a total of more than $1.3 billion in a decade and paid nearly $1 billion of that back to their fundraising companies. Thirty-nine were disciplined by state regulators, some up to seven times, so they were not exactly deterred. Eight were banned in at least one state. One reopened with a new name after being shut down. One third of their founders and executives had relatives on the board of directors or payroll. This suggests not only that there is something wrong with the way many charities are run but, worse, that they enjoy a high degree of impunity.

Many charities are a godsend for ill-intentioned taxpayers, donors, tax-return preparers and, yes, for charities themselves. Deemed unquestionably good, they are virtually above public suspicion, which shows how little the public understands the history of charity and its relationship with political economy, or how sophisticated charity PR has become. Nonprofits turn over large amounts of money and, since they often shift funds across borders, they attract big-time felons, including terrorists, and yet they are not subject to the stringent accounting vigilance applied to for-profit businesses. They can fund decidedly uncharitable political campaigns abroad, as the David Horowitz Freedom Center (operating as a 501(c)3 nonprofit) did with its substantial support in recent years for Geert Wilders and his xenophobic People's Party for Freedom (PVV) in the Dutch elections, although IRS tax rules prohibit tax-exempt charities from funding explicit political party activity. It then broke the rules by failing to disclose its donations to PVV in its annual tax return. But it is still up and running.

Nothing is sacred. The worst tragedies can offer the best opportunities for racketeering. At the end of 2016, the chief operating officer and the CEO of the Irish-based nonprofit GOAL, employing 3,000 people around the world and recipient of $37 million in funding from the EC, the US, Ireland, and Germany in 2016, both resigned as the result of investigations into graft related with aid crossing from Turkey into Syria. Between 2011 and 2015 GOAL's income rocketed from €60 million to €201 million, mainly due to USAID grants. Despite revelations in the Irish media that one of GOAL's major shareholders was the twin of a trustee of GOAL's UK charity, and that it was doing business with a commercial logistics firm set up by its own employees (including the chief operating officer), international funding is still being disbursed on the basis of existing agreements.

Criminals can falsify donations to generate Gift Aid tax relief, or set up a charity for purposes of fraud, hijack the identity of a charity, or obtain a position of influence in existing charities. The OECD report gives an example of the smaller-scale skullduggery that can occur. A tax preparer produced 1,190 income tax returns for clients allegedly wishing to make a charitable donation. Then, falsifying receipts using the names of legitimate charities, she claimed unwarranted deductions for her clients who were charged a fee for her services. The total in tax returns to the clients was some €2.4 million for which she collected €525,885 over a period of three months. The tax authorities lost €675,804 and also had to pay the cost of reassessing the 1,190 tax returns. This time, the relatively small-fry fraudster ended up in prison.

A more convoluted case is Britain's Cup Trust, set up in 2009 by Matthew Jenner—head of NT (No Tax) Advisors and well known in Her Majesty's Revenue and Customs (HMRC)—and his NT partner Anthony Mehigan, with a single trustee, Mountstar PVC, based in the Virgin Islands. The company, registered with the "watchdog" Charity Commission, borrowed money and used it to purchase bonds, which it then sold at a price well below market value. These buyers sold the bonds at market value and donated the proceeds to the Cup Trust, after which they claimed Gift Aid relief. Under Gift Aid rules, the Cup Trust would then be entitled to claim the basic rate tax paid by the donors on those gifts. In terms of income (£97 million in 2017) it is huge but in 2011 the "charity" allegedly spent an astonishing 99.98% of this on fundraising costs, as the table shows:[138]

THE CUP TRUST

STATEMENT OF FINANCIAL ACTIVITIES
(Incorporating Income and Expenditure Account)
FOR THE YEAR ENDED 31 MARCH 2011

	Note	Unrestricted funds 2011 £	*Total funds 2010 £*
INCOMING RESOURCES			
Incoming resources from generated funds:			
Voluntary income	2	78,934,026	*97,580,707*
Activities for generating funds	3	7,542	*9,457*
Other incoming resources	4	30	-
TOTAL INCOMING RESOURCES		78,941,598	*97,590,164*
RESOURCES EXPENDED			
Costs of generating funds:			
Costs of generating voluntary income	5	78,918,422	*97,451,195*
Charitable activities		55,000	-
TOTAL RESOURCES EXPENDED	7	78,973,422	*97,451,195*
MOVEMENT IN TOTAL FUNDS FOR THE YEAR - NET INCOME/(EXPENDITURE) FOR THE YEAR		(31,824)	*138,969*
Total funds at 1 April 2010		*138,969*	-
TOTAL FUNDS AT 31 MARCH 2011		107,145	*138,969*

The upshot was that donor tax benefits were around £55 million while the Cup Trust, which paid out 3p out every £100 of donations to good causes, claimed £46 million in Gift Aid.

Cup Trust was investigated by the Charity Commission but was found not to have broken the law because its activities came under the heading of tax avoidance and not evasion, despite the dubious offshore connections and Gift Aid fraud. "Contingency" fees of £7.7 million were not explained. The Commission, which "regulates" some 180,000 charities, claimed it has insufficient funding and resources to investigate thoroughly. In the ensuing enquiry by the House of Commons Public Accounts Committee it was found that the Charity Commission had failed to act with due diligence with regard to the corporate trustee—in the Virgin Islands, which should have rung alarm bells—before Cup Trust was entered on the Register of Charities. The bar for due diligence was set very low because it would only have taken a phone call to HMRC to discover what the true purpose of the enterprise was. But, the point is, the Charity Commission acted as if Cup Trust were above suspicion and criticism, precisely because it is a "charity."

Tax crimes and misdemeanors are countered by data gathering by domestic intelligence agencies, customs and immigration authorities, foreign tax agencies, law enforcement agencies like the FBI or Royal Canadian Mounted Police and, in Italy, the Finance Police, data matching, use of informants, and risk profiling and analysis, all of which can erode individual freedom and privacy, so in more than one sense everyone pays for tax fraud. And what the public is paying for can be pathetic, almost funny, if cancer-stricken adults and children weren't involved. A US federal investigation into the operations of cancer charities, including The Breast Cancer Society (BCS) and Children's Cancer Fund of America (CCFOA), found that organizers, who pilfered more than $187 million from donors, spent some of the loot on luxury cruises, dating site memberships, Victoria's Secret lingerie, cars, gyms, jetski outings, and tickets to sports events and concerts.

One much-favored tax dodge is the "donor-advised fund" (DAF). In the United States, this is a donating device administered by a public charity. An individual or entity opens an account in the fund, surrenders ownership of the cash, securities or other financial instruments thus deposited, but retains advisory status as to how they are invested and how the funds are distributed to charities. Anyone who stashes money in a DAF gets a tax deduction, and the deposit grows tax free. A hedge-fund manager can invest $12 million in highly appreciated stock at the National Philanthropic Trust (NPT). This grows to $15 million after a year and, since the NPT allows "custom investments," he can put his DAF into his own hedge fund because US charity law doesn't prohibit direct grants from a private philanthropist to for-profit companies, although it does detail provisions that must be met before a foundation receives tax relief for the donation. However, the proviso isn't very stringent, or the definition of charity includes charity towards oneself. The Gates Foundation, for example, even though it supposedly must demonstrate that a grant is used solely for charitable purposes, frequently funds for-profits.

DAFs, 8.4% of all charitable donations in 2015, receive the same tax benefits as other operating charities but there is no time limit for their distribution. The journalist Kelley Holland, cited by Linsey McGoey, describes them as "financial holding pens for the assets of people who want to grab a tax deduction but have no immediate plans for any actual charitable giving," and notes that "the effect on the rate of overall giving is negative."[139] This kind of "charity" has generated expressions like "tax-smart philanthropy," "flexibility," "tax-advantaged items," "custom investments," "give-'em-away gambit" (allowing contributors of appreciated assets to deduct their full market value), "savvy benefactors," "charity stash" or "tax write-off." A cozeners' lexical jamboree. The real emphasis of "tax-savvy" philanthropy becomes fairly clear in a recent *Forbes* article citing Neil Kawashima, a Chicago estate lawyer:[140] "The Trump presidency makes it tax-savvy for many donors to give to charity in the 2016 tax year [...]." The dodge has been around for a long time. Way back in the 1959 film *The Young Philadelphians*, Paul Newman, playing the ambitious tax lawyer Tony Lawrence, boosts his own career when he suggests that a client would benefit more by donating appreciated stock to the Society for Prevention of Cruelty to Animals than by selling the shares and giving cash.

Another succulent perk is double exemption, which can be carried out on an international scale. Between 2012 and 2013, a time of drastic public spending cuts, Vodafone distributed £4.8bn in cash dividends to shareholders but, for the second consecutive year, paid no corporation tax thanks to inordinate tax breaks. Its chief executive Vittorio Colao was paid £11 million that financial year. The Gates Foundation stepped in to support the good cause of Vodafone, reducing its overheads even more by offering its subsidiary Vodacom a non-repayable grant of $4.8 million to roll out M-Pesa, a system allowing villagers in Tanzania to pay bills by mobile phone text messages. The scheme had been a huge success in Kenya where it accounted for a good part of the $150 million annual turnover of Safaricom, East Africa's largest and most profitable company, which is partly owned by Vodafone. The Gates Foundation gets a tax break for its contribution to Vodacom, and Vodafone keeps avoiding taxes via its holding company VIL (Vodafone Investments Luxembourg). Basically, these "liminal profiteers," as Linsey McGoey calls them, shape government policy as they champion *laissez-faire* non-interference and "exploit tax loopholes that deplete government financial reserves even as they charitably lament the seeming inability of states to enforce measures to combat global hunger or poverty."[141]

"Corporate philanthropy" is usually understood to mean the charitable donation of corporate profits or resources to nonprofit endeavors. This is basically business as usual, whitewashed to garner public approval. However, in the 1990s, charitable donations by US companies as a percentage of profits fell by 50% or, measured by percentage of pretax profits, fell from 2.1% at its peak in 1986 to around 0.8% in 2012. This drop roughly coincided with spectacular rises in executive pay (400% for CEOs in the 1980s). For society as a whole, giving as a percentage of GDP remained essentially unchanged.[142] This recalls Milton Friedman's 1970 argument in *The New York Times* that business has only one social responsibility: to increase its profits. Charitable activity, he said, was hypocritical window-dressing, stealing the money of customers and shareholders. But Milton didn't foresee that private, tax-exempt donors would soon be charitizing for-profits, including Mastercard, Monsanto, media companies and pharmaceutical corporations.

The Gates Foundation says its $11 million donation to Mastercard is for "financial inclusion in Africa," East Africa to be precise, where Mastercard will, to use the Foundation's ineffable prose, "open up a world of inclusion and help people to build better, brighter futures."[143] These are not equity or endowment investments but donations to reduce corporate overheads for wealthy companies when they are expanding into new markets. The companies don't have to repay these grants no matter how profitable the ventures turn out to be. Naturally, there's mutual backscratching so it's not altogether surprising to read headlines like "MasterCard to Simplify E-Commerce for Microsoft Dynamics Countries around the Globe." These gainful corporate favors are financed with public money. According to US law, foundations must give their grants to 501(c)(3) nonprofit organizations, but almost any outfit can pass as nonprofit if it undertakes not to distribute profits (directly) to its owners. Moreover, they can donate to for-profits so long as they are "compatible" with their charitable goals. When charity is ruled by and embraces neoliberal ideology, almost anything goes. If profits go back to foundation owners by marginally roundabout mechanisms, nobody seems to notice.

Just as Warren Buffett, billionaire and one of the three trustees of the Bill & Melinda Gates Foundation, was honest about class warfare and who is winning, he was also candid about the perks of philanthropy and advantages of a billionaire-friendly Congress. "Some of us are investment managers who earn billions from our daily labors but are allowed to classify our income as 'carried interest,' thereby getting a bargain 15 percent tax rate. Others own stock index futures for 10 minutes and have 60 percent of their gain taxed at 15 percent, as if they'd been long-term investors. These and other blessings are showered upon us by legislators in Washington who feel compelled to protect us, much as if we were spotted owls or some other endangered species."[144] It's interesting that Buffett chose a perch-and-pounce predator for his allegorical protected species rather than, say, an innocuous little creature like an Amargosa vole.

Mark Zuckerberg's not inconspicuous pledge that he and his wife would give away 99% of their net worth in their lifetime, or $45 billion, actually gives him more control over what happens to the money he is promising to pungle up and still provides tax benefits. What he and his wife Priscilla Chan have actually set up is not a charitable trust but a limited-liability corporation (LLC), enabling Zuckerberg much more financial leeway than a charitable trust would do. LLCs can make for-profit investments and political donations but, unlike charitable trusts, are not obliged to report political donations. Giving money to existing charities or nonprofits entails loss of control but the LLC structure would give him much greater control over where and how the money is used. The "charity" angle is a mealy-mouthed assertion that money earned by the foundation will be used for charitable efforts. Zuckerberg isn't alone in this kind of gesture. Silicon Valley tech billionaires who "give away" large chunks of their net worth include Gordon Moore (about $3 billion of his assets), Pierre Omidyar and Jeff Skoll (about a billion each) and Paul Allen (about $1.5 billion), and they are no more interested in ending or mitigating inequality than Zuckerberg is or Andrew Carnegie was.

Zuckerberg offers insights into the vapidly hubristic workings of a billionaire do-gooder's mind in a 5,700-word Facebook meme titled "Building Global Community." Maybe it's actually a wewe since, as John Naughton[145] counts, he uses the word "we" 156 times to mean anything from "I" to "I and my 86 million followers" and "I and everyone in the world." "Community" (98 times) is similarly nebulous. As the critic Nicholas Carr[146] observes, the thing is that "[...] from his virtual pulpit [...], the young Facebook CEO hesitates not a bit to speak for everyone, in the first person plural. There is no opt-out to his "we." It's the default setting and, in Zuckerberg's totalizing utopian vision, the setting is hardwired, universal, and nonnegotiable." For Zuckerberg, society's ills can be fixed by technology, another Elon-Musk-style take on humanity. Global tensions would end and a peaceful, harmonious global "community" would be achieved, he implies, if everyone joined Facebook ("social infrastructure"). Appropriately po-faced, he says, "In recent campaigns around the world—from India and Indonesia across Europe to the United States—we've seen the candidate with the largest and most engaged following on Facebook usually wins." Some of us, "we," don't want to partake of the "community" in which Narendra Modi, Joko Widodo (and the murderous generals for whom he provides a front of democracy) and Donald Trump go about their work of trampling on communities everywhere. What if a Kolkata Dalit started talking about the world "we" all want?

In *The Ragged Trousered Philanthropists* (1914), Robert Tressell described as "philanthropists" a bunch of workers who bowed to the bosses' demands and gave their work away in back-breaking, ill-paid conditions. Philanthropy is undemocratic, one of the most unequal of human relations, and it entrenches the inequality even further when it interferes with state functions and masquerades as an alternative for welfare and labor protections. At this level, it safeguards and expands personal assets, and opens up markets for corporations which can partner with big foundations to benefit from the associated tax privileges. Whatever they claim, most big philanthropists don't give their wealth (power) away. They just shift it around. The Mexican magnate Carlos Slim, richest person in the world from 2010 to 2013, is fairly forthright. "Wealth is like an orchard. You have to share the fruit, not the trees." The steel baron Andrew Carnegie was also emphatic that philanthropy is both an essential way of distracting the militant working class and their demands for structural change and a distraction from the need for state regulation in the service of public interests. Governments seem unfazed about subsidizing billionaires and few questions are asked about what, in theory, society might be getting back or what is really being squeezed out of its coffers.

Zuckerberg and his megalomaniac notions about imposing what he wants in the name of what "we" want, has immense power and this raises questions of whether the state should be making him more powerful. And should massively funded "charities" like Harvard University be eligible for tax breaks as if they were modest neighborhood soup kitchens? In 1969 Richard Nixon brought in the Tax Reform Act but today philanthropic institutions actively work to undermine this attempt to distinguish between grant-giving organizations funded by a small number of rich individuals through private, powerful foundations and small charities directly engaged in charitable work. The Act sought to strengthen oversight on private foundations, for example by means of the IRS 5% payout rule to ensure they contribute to public good but this can be dispensed with by claiming administrative expenses which include the donor's salary, or by contribution to a donor-advised fund, which avoids the payout requirement.

Big givers and big beneficiaries are hand in glove. The former want something back from the latter and often it's not just tax breaks but power. For example, the Koch brothers fund some 350 programs at over 250 colleges and universities across America and this philanthropy is not about democratizing education. If the Charles Koch Foundation pledges $1.5 million to Florida State University's Economics Department, the rub is that a Koch-appointed committee will select professors and undertake annual evaluations. Higher education has become a top Koch priority in recent years. According to a Center for Public Integrity analysis of Internal Revenue Service tax filings, a couple of private charitable foundations headed and bankrolled by Charles Koch combined in 2013 to spread more than $19.3 million across 210 college campuses in 46 states and the District of Columbia. David Koch, a fossil-fuel pusher and donor of tens of millions of dollars to the American Museum of Natural History in New York and the Smithsonian National Museum of Natural History, is not disinterested either. He sits on their boards and sponsors exhibitions imposing his own anti-climate-science views. Koch educational charity aims at brainwashing students in free market economics, influencing what should or should not be investigated and revealed in science, and tightening the stranglehold of wealth and power over everything in order to benefit wealth and power.

The veterans' charity scam is a field of rich pickings and, in the warmongering United States, logically includes quite a lot of charities. Among dubious organizations claiming to support veterans are American Ex-Prisoners of War Service Foundation, American Veterans Relief Foundation, AMVETS National Service Foundation, Freedom Alliance, Help Hospitalized Veterans/Coalition to Salute America's Heroes, Military Order of the Purple Heart Service Foundation, National Veterans Service Fund, NCOA, National Defense Foundation, Paralyzed

Veterans of America, and Vietnow National Headquarters. The National Vietnam Veterans Foundation, without any independent board of directors, sets a pattern for this particular kind of war profiteering. From 2010 to 2014 it received $9 million, of which it spent less than 2% on actual veterans. Yet its expenses, listed for 2014 tax return purposes, included $133,000 for travel, $21,000 for unspecified "awards," $70,000 for "other" expenses and $8,000 for parking. The charity's CEO and founder, former veteran, J. Thomas Burch, is a federal employee, an attorney working at the Department of Veterans Affairs with a salary of $127,000 in 2014, when he also drew a wage of $65,000 from his "zero-star" charity. Veterans Affairs did not see the situation as a conflict of interest *per se*.

On a much bigger scale, another famous veterans' charity, the Wounded Warrior Project, which raked in $372 million in 2014–2015, mainly from elderly small donors, squandered millions every year on travel, dinners, hotels and conferences. It takes the notorious tax dodger Starbucks (which from 2009 to 2012 paid no tax on sales of £1.2 billion in the UK) as its business model. In 2014, about 40% of the organization's donations, about $124 million, went on overheads including a large amount to counter criticism of its spending and to fight legislative efforts to restrict the amount that nonprofits spend on overheads.

Charity Watch's "Hall of Fame"[147] provides a list of miscreants and their favored forms of cheating. More important, the offenders reveal some disturbing constants in charitable shenanigans which signal grave systemic issues in the ways in which philanthropy is understood and practiced. The wrongdoers tend to be devout Christians, respected people (some of them sex offenders) with lavish lifestyles and celebrity supporters. They build personal fiefdoms, falsify tax filings, use their organizations to support friendly politicians, are greedy, nepotistic, hubristic, and have no scruples about conflicts of interest. Their organizations are notable for lack of transparency and financial and governance controls, and show high "administrative" and "fundraising" costs. The real problem is, once again, the system in which they flourish and, to a scandalous extent, get away with their crimes which, at the end of the day, take advantage of and work against vulnerable people.

Some examples from the "Hall of Fame" illustrate how easily, in a system of entrenched inequality that is loath to change, the "unlimited love and kindness" of charity turns from benevolent to malevolent.

- The late Father Bruce Ritter, with Mother Teresa among his fans, used Covenant House, allegedly a safe shelter for homeless teenagers, for sexual contacts with the teenagers and staff members.
- William Aramony, highly respected CEO of United Way of America, umbrella group for thousands of organizations funding social projects nationwide, was convicted in 1995 on twenty-five felony counts of defrauding the UWA, in many cases for purposes of sexual advances to and harassment of young women.
- Foundation for New Era Philanthropy headed by John Bennett, Jr. a prominent Christian with VIP contacts, which he used to reel in the naïve and unwary, was a Ponzi scheme which defrauded victims of $135 million.
- Lorraine Hale of Hale House, a charity for needy children (referred to by her husband as "cash cows"), used a good part of its donations to fund a profligate lifestyle.
- Roger Chapin, "non-profit" entrepreneur, raised $168 million for veterans and kept most of it for himself though he did pay $100,000 to General Tommy Franks in exchange for his endorsement.
- Larry Jones, president of Feed the Children (FC), awarded a $40 million annual, no-bid, television buying agreement to

Affiliated Media Group, which employed his son. He also took kickbacks and kept a stash of pornography in his private area at this Christian charity.

- John Donald Cody, using the stolen identity of Bobby Thompson and claiming to be an ex-military man, set up a sham charity, The United States Navy Veterans Association, and bilked donors out of nearly $100 million.
- Greg Mortenson, founder of Central Asia Institute, author of *New York Times* best-selling books, used the charity for his business interests, book promotion ($1.7 million) and speaking events, to the tune of some $7.2 million.
- The pastor Joe Wingo and his family of the charity Angel Food Ministries were subjects of a 49-count federal indictment for multi-million-dollar theft, fraud, kickbacks, and cover-ups as well as using charity funds for political campaigns.
- Somaly Mam, famous for her work in two nonprofits, Agir Pour Les Femmes en Situation Précaire and the Somaly Mam Foundation, for women and girls ("my girls") abused by sex traffickers, falsely included herself among the victims. One of *Time*'s 100 most influential people, she jetted around courting celebrities—including Angelina Jolie, Susan Sarandon, Sheryl Sandberg, and Nicholas Kristof—with harrowing, fabricated tales.
- James Reynolds Sr. (plus 24 family members) used the so-called Cancer Fund of America, and four additional "cancer" charities, to embezzle more than $187 million to benefit professional fundraisers and Reynolds' extended family.
- Zvi Shor (aka "Steve Shor" and "Demetrie Bennett") founded the National Children's Leukemia Foundation (NCLF) in 1991 and, even though he was convicted of bank fraud in 1999, kept going for more than twenty years, raising millions of dollars

for fictitious treatment programs and "cures" discovered by a fictitious NCLF "research team."

Nobody knows better how money rules than the members of a plutocracy so they are careful about husbanding it and dictating how their charity (they call it "self-taxing") is spent. The Giving Pledge, brainchild of Warren Buffett and Bill and Melinda Gates, and signed by more than 120 of the world's richest people, has little to show except self-congratulatory antics and tighter dynastic control over wealth by pledging more money to family-controlled foundations. In some cases, however, the political results can also be substantial.

As the Saudi-led coalition continued its bombing of densely populated areas of Yemen—using internationally outlawed cluster munitions manufactured in the US and UK, as well as white phosphorus, and targeting markets, schools and, notably, hospitals and facilities run by humanitarian organizations (including double-tap attacks), in what UN Secretary-General Ban Ki-moon denounced as war crimes in January 2016—the "colorful" Prince Alwaleed bin Talal, a man of influence in the Saudi foreign ministry, announced that his foundation was donating $29 million to the British nonprofit Save the Children, one of the main NGOs working in Yemen.

Alwaleed, described by *Time* as the "Arabian Warren Buffett," is a member of the Saudi royal family, a big game hunter, keeper of a troupe of court-jester dwarves (who he uses for "midget-tossing" fun and games), a big stakeholder *inter alia* in General Motors, Twitter, Time Warner, Citibanks's top shareholder, the largest individual foreign investor in the United States (he says), and member of the Gates-Buffett Giving Pledge, has announced that he is donating his entire $32 billion fortune to charity or, more accurately, to his own foundation Alwaleed Philanthropy, which he wants to model on the Gates Foundation. The prince is a loudly self-proclaimed champion of women's rights—which looks good in the West—and even employs a female pilot, Hanadi

Zakariya Hindi, in a country where women aren't even allowed to drive. Well, no, she doesn't actually fly his planes and he told his aviation staff she never will. His philanthropy, of course, includes the small jesters. "Little people [...] are often among disadvantaged individuals who come to ask for HRH Prince Alwaleed's assistance as a philanthropist." He's giving them a job and a "work ethic."[148] Why is this man, of supposed political acumen, who enjoys humiliating the dwarves who receive his "charity" and killing big game, now "giving away" his fortune? One former employee provided a partial answer, "I was there over five years. I went to every African country. Cash was given out in millions of dollars. They would go for a meeting and we would give a bag man millions of dollars of cash. And then we'd return two or three years later and guess what, we're going to build a hotel there. Anything [Alwaleed] does worldwide is for a reason."[149]

Alwaleed is chummy with Bill Gates, not only in the Giving Pledge but also as co-owner of Four Seasons Hotel and Resorts and habitué of Gates' annual Microsoft CEO Summit. He hangs out with all kinds of celebrities, among them Prince Albert of Monaco who has set up the "Prince's Roundtable on Philanthropy," a closed-door international camarilla of lovers of humanity held every year in Monaco immediately after the World Economic Forum in Davos—striking while the iron is hot. In 2016 Prince Albert presented the Arabian Warren Buffett with a Special Prize for his decision to allocate his personal fortune to support charities worldwide, combating poverty, empowering women and developing communities, and understanding through education, or so the Prince of Monaco said.

The donation to Save the Children, to be used for setting up a Humanitarian Leadership Academy (roping in Mark Goldring, the CEO of OXFAM to sit on its board), has led to some debate. Some see it as dirty money, saying that taking it would undermine respect for international humanitarian law. Others declare that, since humanitarian aid is usually tainted anyway, Saudi Arabia shouldn't be singled out for criticism. That would be racist. The big shots in Save the Children, acting as if they are unaware of the man's character and favorite pastimes, are "delighted" to partner with him. After all, his dynasty is producing plenty of mangled, starving children, so Save the Children will have work in Yemen for years to come. The new training centers are to produce "professional humanitarian responders" who will save lives in the toughest places in the world. The House of Saud is obligingly creating tough places. In Yemen, as even the "delighted" Save the Children complains, it is blocking aid while 460,000 severely malnourished under-fives risk dying of pneumonia, diarrhea and other preventable diseases.

Hence, Save the Children is "saving lives" by teaming up with a man with "tremendous influence" in the foreign affairs of his country which is deliberately killing children and aid workers. How would they reconcile the new partnership with the fact that, in a 2015 tweet, which he soon deleted, their benefactor offered a hundred Bentleys to Saudi Arabian pilots who were attacking civilian targets in Yemen? It seems that the official line of Save the Children is no-comment except to praise the generosity of the Bentley giver because the fundraising principle is "anything goes" (though Save the Children calls it a "robust" donation acceptance policy). This time, the bucks are banging with bombs. One senior UN official commented that any aid agency, UN or NGO, taking UK or US money but queasy about grants from Saudi Arabia is applying a double standard because the Yemen war couldn't continue without the support of the Americans and the British. Which casts a very grim light on most official aid policy.

This situation is probably related with another humanitarian morass. Saudi Arabia recently blackmailed the UN, threatening to withdraw hundreds of millions of dollars in funds if the Saudi-led coalition was not removed from the Secretary-General's "list of shame" for its murder and maiming of hundreds of children in Yemen. It was removed. At the end of 2016 Saudi Arabia was reelected without opposition to the UN Human Rights Council. Blackmail may work but it can't be repeated too often. The House of Saud, loath to invest in charity at home where it doesn't need to because it's in control, needs a celebrity hugging philanthropist to brush up its international image. It doesn't matter if he's a zebra killer and dwarf tormentor. International soft power, which is really hard power when wielded in the billionaires' league, is another big factor lurking behind this apparently surprising benevolence from Riyadh. It would be reasonable to assume that, if this prince is not suffering from dissociative identity disorder, soft-power drives his charity all the way to hard power. And crimes against humanity in Yemen go almost unmentioned in a vacuous media which respectfully reports the prince's presence at gala events and praises him for his generosity.

This rich people's "philanthropy" cheapens human life. In this regard, the words of William Pickens, educator and son of liberated slaves, are a stern warning. "To cheapen the lives of any group of men cheapens the lives of all men, even our own. This is a law of human psychology, of human nature. And it will not be repealed by our wishes, nor will it be merciful to our blindness." If charity fits snugly into a system where love of humankind is a cover for war crimes and a grotesque form of power whereby billionaires can impose their whims on "democratic" governments, perhaps the cameo of a munificent prince entertained by the sorry spectacle of dwarves being tossed around might serve as an awful metaphor. Zuckerberg's "we" really refers to approximately 2,000 billionaires. Are "we," the rest of us, also dwarves who will be tossed around in the dreadful societies and calamities they are bringing about?

CHAPTER 7
BLEEDING NEED: A BRIEF HISTORY OF HUMANITARIANISM

THE NON-PROFIT SECTOR IS NOW THE WORLD'S EIGHTH LARGEST economy, with nineteen million salaried employees.[150] Many are engaged in humanitarian work at a time when crises are lasting longer and needs growing faster as climate change, failing economies and conflict lethally combine in many parts of the world. There is much to criticize in the way large and small nonprofits operate in the humanitarian space, but our concern here is not to scrutinize their actions or those of individual humanitarians whose motives are often laudable. Rather, we focus on humanitarianism as a form of charity operating within unjust systems and producing a vassalage of largesse.[151] Given that this sector is so enormous, why are the people it is supposed to be serving not more present in the media? They include 18.8 million people (69% of the population) in Yemen; 13.5 million people in Syria plus another five million refugees; at least five million in South Sudan; and a total of some 65.3 million people forced from their homes. This absence raises the question of what the humanitarian project is all about.

On March 8, 2012, the Nigerian-American writer Teju Cole responded to the *Kony 2012* video with a quick-fire seven tweets[152] offering a crisp summary of today's humanitarianism:

1) From Sachs to Kristof to Invisible Children to TED, the fastest growth industry in the US is the White Savior Industrial Complex.

2) The white savior supports brutal policies in the morning, founds charities in the afternoon, and receives awards in the evening.
3) The banality of evil transmutes into the banality of sentimentality. The world is nothing but a problem to be solved by enthusiasm.
4) This world exists simply to satisfy the needs—including, importantly, the sentimental needs—of white people and Oprah.
5) The White Savior Industrial Complex is not about justice. It is about having a big emotional experience that validates privilege.
6) Feverish worry over that awful African warlord. But close to 1.5 million Iraqis died from an American war of choice. Worry about that.
7) I deeply respect American sentimentality, the way one respects a wounded hippo. You must keep an eye on it, for you know it is deadly.

Cole ruffled a few philanthropic feathers but it seems that his challenge to think about the origins and results of the white man's do-gooding was not taken up in the humanitarian trade. Nicholas Kristof was politely wounded, when identified as a white savior, "uncomfortable to think that we as white Americans should not intervene in a humanitarian disaster because the victims are of a different skin color." The really uncomfortable issue, however, is not the color of Kristof's skin and whether it disqualifies him from what he decorously calls the "humanitarian disaster." Doing the usual white-man's-burden thing of not knowing exactly where in Africa, Kristof has "middle-class" Cole coming from Uganda (instead of Nigeria), and seems unaware or not to care that his inexplicit, non-committal "humanitarian disaster" might actually be something that "middle-class" Cole sees all too clearly, namely the "militarization of poorer countries, short-sighted agricultural policies, resource extraction, the propping up of corrupt governments, and the astonishing complexity of long-running violent conflicts over a wide and varied terrain [...] serious problems of governance, of infrastructure, of democracy, and of law and order." Stating the obvious, Cole is rocking the benevolent boat and his description of Kristof's mental blinkers encapsulates one of the basic problems of humanitarianism: "All he sees is need, and he sees no need to reason out the need for the need."

Charity, philanthropy and humanitarianism are conceptually entangled. If charity is Christian love, man reenacting towards man God's love for man, the online *Oxford Dictionary* definitions suggest that philanthropy is the work of a rich person who "seeks to promote the welfare of others, especially by the generous donation of money to good causes," and humanitarianism seeks to "promote human welfare." Most writers on the subject seem to take the meaning of "humanitarianism" as clear and unproblematic, containing just two references "humans" or "humanity," and "ism" as the relational element. In its interventionist form, humanitarianism might be the charity of nations. One privileged person or group of people decides what is good for another less privileged person or group. Thanks to their privilege, the former usually don't have a clue about what the latter actually need and why.

Except in cases of grassroots fundraising for social justice, part of a struggle for social change, human rights don't appear as part of the framework. Yet, if it is accepted that everyone has the right to subsistence, the right to exist, three duties are inescapably entailed: 1) not to deprive a person of his or her means of subsistence; 2) to protect people against deprivation by other people of their means of subsistence; and 3) to provide subsistence to those unable to provide their own.[153] Humanitarianism only attends *post hoc* and partially to the third requirement, as part of a fairly general pattern in which aid-giving countries cause disasters and then make a show of patching up while engaging in further plundering, as Naomi Klein trenchantly describes in her book *The Shock Doctrine: The Rise of Disaster Capitalism* (2007).

Meeting the first two duties, more concerned with rights than charity, would demand another social, economic, and political system. If humanitarianism recognized the three essential human rights principles of freedom, justice and dignity, which both empower the individual and demand a social spirit, it would have to challenge the entitlement of benefactors, the system and conditions that create the need for them. Since all human rights depend on the right of material existence, they are not "soft power" but belong in the domain of political economy. Freedom (surely what any endeavor in the name of love for humanity should aspire to for all humanity), means independence from the arbitrary will of another, including the most charismatically well-intentioned political authority, and this independence always necessitates possession of sufficient material resources to assure one's social existence. Anything else is one or other degree of servitude or slavery. People who have survived a catastrophe or crisis only to become recipients of humanitarian assistance are in this situation of "anything else." They don't enjoy the *right* to exist because their lives depend on others. The life they are "given" is what Giorgio Agamben calls "bare life." Affecting hundreds of millions of people, this bare, biological (*zoe*) existence—or Aristotle's "mere" life as contrasted with a "good" life, the primary aim of the polis—is an enormous injustice which is supposed to be made somehow palatable by "humanitarian assistance."

Anecdotes of the humanitarian worker's experience can be shocking, surprising or offered with the aim of entertaining. NGO pros dine out on their experiences and write books with titillating titles like *Emergency Sex and Other Desperate Measures; A True Story from Hell on Earth.* An email from East Timor in 1999—just after the population had overwhelmingly voted for independence in a referendum after twenty-four years of brutal occupation by Indonesia, only to see many more people killed and their country reduced to rubble and ashes by well-orchestrated militia groups—describes a fairly usual situation. "Dozens of brand-new four-by-fours were parked along the waterfront, half a kilometer of them, from the cold beer in the Hotel Dili to the floating hotel, complete with Jacuzzis and bars, exclusively for aid workers, dwarfing tents made with plastic bags lined up along the beach and housing homeless Timorese. The NGO that hosted us claimed it was Timorese but it worked with the World Bank and big international NGOs. The director was drooling as he spoke of the millions pouring into his coffers. The house where we stayed was one of the few in Dili with all its walls and a generator. It had been the residence of a senior Indonesian army officer and its fence was made of missile shells."

A certain kind of humanitarian mindset is expressed in another email to one of the authors from a man giving news of his son who was unhappy with his posting. "He yearns for an African disaster, and the omens seem good for that outcome." Some humanitarian workers pray for disasters in their favorite parts of the world, or see their jobs as a business where the recipients of their aid can be "warehoused" before being abandoned to their fate when a more lucrative crisis somewhere else beckons. Others are self-sacrificing and brave and there are many hues of humanitarian humanity in between. The anecdotes point to serious underlying issues.

The Paris surrealist group which published the tract "Murderous Humanitarianism" in 1932[154] didn't mean their title as an oxymoron. They were enraged. The pamphlet, drafted mainly by Réne Creval and signed, *inter alia*, by André Breton, Paul Eluard, Benjamin Peret, Yves Tanguy, Pierre Yoyotte and J. M. Monnero, the latter two from Martinique, laid into colonialism, capitalism, the clergy, the black bourgeoisie and "counterfeit liberalism." A few fragments of the tract give an idea of its fury. "Now these slavers, knowing their days to be numbered and reading the doom of the system in the world crisis, fall back on a gospel of mercy, whereas in reality they rely more than ever on their traditional methods of slaughter to enforce their tyranny. [...] The clergy and professional philanthropists have always collaborated with the army in this bloody exploitation. [...] The white man preaches, doses, vaccinates, assassinates and (from himself) receives absolution. With his psalms, his speeches, his guarantees of liberty, equality and fraternity, he seeks to drown the noise of machine guns."

The pamphlet drew attention to the fact that the real "intervention" almost always precedes the crisis. The adjective "humanitarian" turns out to be anti-humanitarian (in the sense of love for humanity), just as "non"-governmental organizations are increasingly governmental organizations, or exist within governments (US Agency for International Development (USAID), the UK Department for International Development (DFID), the Humanitarian Aid Department of the European Commission (ECHO)), or are closely linked with governments and the UN (OXFAM, CARE International, Médicins Sans Frontières). And the ICRC is mandated by an international treaty to uphold the Geneva Conventions. The NGO is really a GO, the green light for interventions which often have little to do with succor. One Davos habitué, Naser Haghamed, CEO of Islamic Relief, says that NGOs must accept that private companies play a major role in terms of infrastructure and data services and in delivering cash-based aid, as well as being, in some cases, contractors for big funders like DIFD and USAID.[155] He neglects to add that the US and European governments openly define their development assistance in terms of trade facilitation, geopolitics and business interests.

Language, its inversion and perversion is a big problem when thinking about what humanitarianism really is, and it is perhaps unsurprising that the surrealists, who did try to grapple with it, have come to be associated with bizarre, incomprehensible extravagance rather than with powerful, rupturist ideas for dark times. Quibbling over language is one way of thrusting aside the unthinkable that must be thought about. Meanwhile, the way things are, if neoliberalism didn't have humanitarianism and philanthropy, it would have to invent them to distract us from the terrible reality it has forged. "Murderous Humanitarianism" uses strong words. No language is strong enough to condemn the enormous damage charity, humanitarianism and philanthropy cover up and cause in the catastrophe of a global system run by a few billionaires. The humanitarian crisis is not an isolated event but a systemic phenomenon and humanitarianism is the opposite of a philosophy of social change.

In a society dominated by cupidity and half-witted irresponsibility, careless or cynical use of language is the order of the day. For a Pentagon policy maker, "humanitarianism" has nothing to do with the needs of a traumatized woman in a Darfur refugee camp, yet he invokes her humanity when his policy is made public. In general, "humanitarianism" depoliticizes military (and non-military) interventionism for geopolitical or economic purposes by stripping the humanitarian object of any sociopolitical identity. Of humanity itself. Without basic identifying features—age, gender, ethnicity, religion, citizenship and so on—"it" cannot demand or exercise human rights.

In the United States foreign affairs tradition, also shared by European international law and the United Nations system, humanitarianism is summarized as having five main theoretical commitments: 1) to engage with the world by government and citizenry; 2) a commitment to multilateralism and intergovernmental institutions; 3) repudiation of power politics, militarism and the aspiration to empire; 4) moral idealism in the service of offering better conditions in projects of "moral uplift, religious conversion, economic development, and democracy"; and 5) a commitment to cosmopolitanism and respect for other nations' cultures.[156] In policy-making terms, these goals have mutated into institutional projects with all the problems of global power relations. Humanitarians hobnob with people who plan wars, sharing the language of rules of engagement, collective security, self-defense, intervention, collateral damage in a mission of governance, although most would deny that this project of determining the hows, wheres, whens and whys of life-saving distribution among selected people is political.

The evident, unavoidable results are all too visible. International humanitarian law has no role in places like South Sudan or Rakhine State in Myanmar where political strategies take the forms of slaughter, torture, and "surrender or starve." Signatories to the 1951 Refugee Convention wash their hands of legal responsibilities in favor of deterrence measures aimed at blocking people seeking refuge from the terror of war zones or tyrannical regimes. Europe makes aid to the Sahel and Afghanistan conditional on pushbacks or migrant suppression. Some of the world's poorest countries host 86% of the global refugee population. Accordingly, xenophobia is on the rise in many places, hand-in-hand with dwindling support for international norms.[157]

The Sphere Project: Humanitarian Charter and Minimum Standards in Humanitarian Response and the Ombudsman Project (coordinated by the British Red Cross) take a technocratic approach when stipulating standards of performance and transparency for humanitarian workers. Sphere attempts to establish benchmarks for measuring the quality of the "humanitarian space," closing it off from the real world in which, for example, relations between combatants and civilians in refugee camps are life-and-death factors in areas where aid agencies work. After the genocidal conflict in Rwanda in 1994 the humanitarian response to the refugee crisis in Goma, eastern Zaire, ignored the question of accountability for the slaughter in Rwanda. This reinforced the killers' belief that their murder of some 500,000 people was warranted so, in the absence of any attempt at justice, Hutus, still committed to their genocide, kept killing Tutsis from a nearby camp. The Zairean official from the Catholic relief agency Caritas which was running the Tutsi camp shrugged off the violence. "This is normal because they have been in conflict in their country for so long."[158] Twenty-three years later, few commentators are willing to match the fact that about a million Rohingya Muslims have fled Myanmar since the 1970s with the other fact that they were rendered stateless in 1983, an early step in what is now a fully-fledged but mainly unheeded genocide, presently overseen, *inter alia*, by Nobel Peace laureate Aung San Suu Kyi.[159]

Donor governments might insist on efficiency criteria as a condition of funding but these are defined in terms of donor interests. The British government is clear enough: "development aid" should be in the "national interest" and used to bolster foreign policy and trade objectives. Aid agencies like the International Rescue Committee often refer to the recipients of aid as "clients," as if they were free consumers, only subject to the laws of the market. These are "clients" with little chance of autonomous action as their human rights are at their lowest ebb and still being violated, whether by omission or commission, when aid agencies in disaster-hit places bring in food, shelter and medicines but then move on after a certain time because humanitarianism is not unconditional but always time-bound and space-bound.

These limitations clash with the philosophical claims of human rights, especially the essential universal dimension which is of a moral order preceding contingent historical, social, spatial and temporal conditions to apply to humans everywhere. The moral universalism underlying human rights posits the existence of trans-cultural and trans-historical moral truths, according to which each individual has an innate and equal worth as the bearer of human rights in a community of which all humans are members. A thumbnail sketch of the social microcosm of one of the world's many refugee camps shows the enormous gulf between human rights principles and humanitarianism in action.

The Kakuma camp, accommodating 185,000 permanently displaced people, was opened in 1992 by the UNHCR in Kenya's Turkana Desert. Kakuma, lying between two dry river-beds in a poor region of Kenya, is subject to dust storms and flooding, infested with malaria, cholera, poisonous spiders, snakes, and scorpions. Rape and sexual assault are rife. The autochthonous community consists mainly of nomadic pastoralists who resent the presence of the refugees—for them, an externally imposed disruption to their way of life—and this sometimes leads to violence. The camp is managed by the Kenyan government and the Department of Refugee Affairs in conjunction with the UNHCR. Aid agencies in the camp include the World Food Program, International Rescue Committee (IRC), the Lutheran World Federation, the National Council of Churches of Kenya, the Jesuit Refugees Services, Don Bosco, an Italian NGO, and Rädda (Swedish Save the Children). Although almost all the refugees in the camp—mostly from South Sudan; Sudan, Somalia, DR Congo, Burundi, Ethiopia, Rwanda, Eritrea. Uganda, Tanzania, and Congo-Brazzaville—depend for their lives on food aid, supplies are erratic and below the minimum dietary requirement of 2,100 calories per day. The refugees are constantly hungry and never sure that they will receive the next rations or if they will be enough.

On arrival, refugees are given a four-by-five-meter piece of reinforced plastic with which to construct their shelter and are expected to scavenge in this inhospitable landscape for other building materials like wood, grass, and mud. The 5 p. m. curfew means refugees can't be helped at night. By this hour, aid workers are installed in three large compounds outside the camp, complete with electricity, water, air conditioning, a swimming pool, bars, shops, recreational centers, and gyms. Donor support is precarious and conditioned by conflicts elsewhere in the world, thus fostering a constant atmosphere of uncertainty and fear, especially as the Kenyan government keeps threatening to close down the camp in the name of "national security interest." At present (August 2017), the camp is unable to cope with the huge influx of refugees from South Sudan. Most refugees, especially young people, despair of ever escaping. They know they are being warehoused. One refugee leader summed up humanitarianism from the receiving-end perspective. "We're vulnerable, we're voiceless, [and] we're neglected by the UN, the media, [and] the international community, as well by our host government."[160] Even the UNHCR calls it "life in limbo."

In 2015, the UNHCR estimated that there were 65.3 million displaced people in the world, 21.3 million of them refugees, more than 10 million of whom are under the age of eighteen. Just seven countries—Turkey, Pakistan, Iran, Lebanon, Jordan, Ethiopia, and Kenya—"host" over half of the world's refugees, often in conditions like Kakuma since they prohibit the installation of facilities that would give a camp a more permanent feel. But refugees are trapped for seventeen years on average. The longer a camp exists, the lower the international funding and the worse the human rights situation. Statistics on refugees aren't hard to find but the real conditions of their bare existence are rarely mentioned.

The extreme vulnerability of refugees and displaced people doesn't necessarily end when they reach the "safety" of camps and zones that are supposedly protected by UN peacekeepers who, according to the UN website, must stand out for their "utmost sensitivity towards the local population and upholding the highest standards of professionalism and good conduct." In 2003 the UN declared that its policy on SAE (its sanitizing acronym for sexual abuse and exploitation) was "zero tolerance" but, since then, an Associated Press investigation has found nearly two thousand allegations (more than three hundred involving children) of sexual abuse and exploitation by peacekeepers and other

UN personnel around the world. Only a fraction of the alleged perpetrators have served jail time. UN secrecy surrounding these crimes and its deterrence of whistleblowers suggest that the figures are probably even higher. Many UN member states asked by the Associated Press investigators for information declined to respond.

However, it is known from one internal UN report that, in Haiti, at least 134 Sri Lankan peacekeepers exploited nine children in a sex ring from 2004 to 2007. Although 114 of the offenders were sent home, none was ever imprisoned. One teenage boy told the Associated Press investigators that he was gang-raped in 2011 by Uruguayan peacekeepers who filmed the assault on a cellphone, and dozens of women reported they were raped while many more said they had to engage in "survival" sex with peacekeepers when they had no other way to stay alive or feed their children. In June 2017, the UN removed from the Central African Republic a contingent of 630 peacekeepers from the Republic of the Congo after it was revealed that they had been engaging in sexual exploitation and abuses that indicated systemic problems in command and control. Ugandan peacekeepers were also accused of raping young girls.

The UN now has a new SAE plan which, claiming to be transparent, based on accountability and ensuring justice, calls for tighter vetting of job applicants and proposes the appointment of a high-level official at UN headquarters as a victims' advocate, and similar in situ appointments to the four missions with the worst SAE records, namely Central African Republic, Democratic Republic of Congo, Haiti and South Sudan (which—and this is no coincidence when you think about whether such crimes could occur in Switzerland, for example—are among the world's most shattered countries with the most vulnerable populations). A "high-level" meeting on SAE is planned for the UN General Assembly in New York in September 2017 but it is expected that countries (usually poor countries funded by rich countries) providing peacekeepers will refuse to punish individuals or groups among their military and police contingents. With the threat of withdrawal of both troops and funding if action is taken against offenders the UN, just as it did in the case of the cholera epidemic its troops caused in Haiti, suppresses information and undermines investigations. In fact, UN administration and staff do their utmost to control, influence and stymie the work of the Investigations Division of the Office of Internal Oversight Services. The new plan is basically a rehash of earlier schemes and pronouncements. The UN, claiming to be neutral, polices itself and is its own court, defense, prosecution, jury and judge in cases of abuse committed by its employees. Unsurprisingly, the bottom line is that the United Nations fails to protect human rights.[161]

Human rights tend to be pigeonholed in the norm-creating process whereby values become norms through decision-making or laws if the legal institutions are involved. Theories on human agency meet biological constructs through the back door, positing in a social evolutionary framework that agreement on rules is a matter of utilitarian principles and public reasoning. This is a culturally specific process and the evolving human rights standards may end up being stipulated in constitutions or, paradoxically, in international "universal" human rights instruments. But, the "public reasoning" that produces the human rights codes is a privilege of the powerful. Historic bills that grew out of revolutions have been coopted and are given lip service in official documents. Government is a pragmatic business.

One big problem of guaranteeing and protecting human rights is the systematic confusion between moral and legal rights. Moral rights can't be enforced without being recognized as legal rights, enshrined in codes and protected by laws. Doubt as to the existence of a legal right is not resolved by discussion of its universal or ethical validity but by checking the relevant legislation, the limits of which are set by the jurisdiction of the body that passes the law in question. Justice is then defined in relation with the state and not as a general moral principle. But charity, especially in its forms of humanitarianism and philanthropy, steps in to give an appearance of justice. The nature of law-bound humanitarianism was laid bare at the 2002 World Food Summit in Rome when, standing alone among 182 nations, the United States opposed the inclusion of the right to food in the final declaration, insisting (basically as it had done in 1996) that the right to food cannot give rise to any binding duty to feed the hungry adequately, or to guaranteed entitlement, either at the domestic or the international level. Food is a *commodity* and access to it is exclusively limited to purchasing power or charitable schemes. In 2017 the FAO estimates that 100 million people worldwide are facing acute malnutrition and risk starving to death.

A hundred million. We are referring to human beings, not just a number, shockingly large though it might be. These human beings, with names and people they love and who love them, who feel pain, despair and perhaps know what joy is, must be turned into a single abstract thing like a cause-less catastrophe or, in the case of refugees, an "avalanche" or "flood" in which the individual components can't be taken into account, precisely because they are humans, supposedly with the same human rights as Bill Gates.

From the western standpoint, they exist in a non-social, apolitical and anti-historical bubble. But they are a product of the developed world and the historical conditions for its development, as the poverty specialist Thomas Pogge recalls:[162] "[…] the existing radical inequality is deeply tainted by how it accumulated through one historical process that was deeply pervaded by enslavement, colonialism, even genocide. The rich are quick to point out that we cannot inherit our ancestor's sins. Indeed. But how can they then be entitled to the fruits of those sins: to their huge inherited advantage in power and wealth over the rest of the world?" The plunder Pogge speaks of was not peanuts. The £7.5

trillion that Britain extracted from African countries in the slave trade alone was the basis for the industries and banking systems that transformed its economy. The eighteenth-century slaving enthusiast Malachy Postlethwayt saw the vile trade as the "Great Pillar and Support" of British commerce with America, and the British empire as a "magnificent superstructure of American commerce and [British] naval power on an African foundation."[163] Part of the "magnificent superstructure" was the seed of the humanitarian endeavor which expanded with the growth of Western economic and cultural power, becoming a means of transmitting Western liberal values and acting as a Trojan horse for capital.

A recent report, *Honest Accounts 2017*, shows that African countries receive about $19 billion in aid grants but lose more than three times that much ($68 billion) in capital flight when multinationals misreport the value of their imports and exports to reduce tax. According to the report, 101 companies listed on the London Stock Exchange, 59 of them incorporated in the UK and 25 in tax havens like the British Virgin Islands, Guernsey and Jersey, control $1.05 trillion worth of resources in Africa in five commodities: oil, gold, diamonds, coal and platinum. By 2011, the African Development Bank estimated that 82% of Africans, over 800 million people, lived on less than $4 a day.

However well-intentioned humanitarian workers might be, they are working within the institutional frameworks of global powers and their benevolence is used as a tool to shape foreign affairs in favor of the "givers." In David Kennedy's words, "[…] humanitarians have a hard time acknowledging our own participation in rulership,"[164] and are helpless before the harsh realities of power politics. If calling for a human right means in Henry Shue's terms,[165] calling for social protection against "standard threats," international protection amounts to the wretched "bare life." Humanitarian organizations are not concerned to ensure that everyone present in the humanitarian space enjoys the same rights. And "standard threats" faced by the "other" are a condition of their work. They need the status quo, which is preserved by little more than damage control. Some aid workers have attempted, with greater or lesser success, depending on the specific crisis and the agency in question, to protect human rights. But the project founders on the fact that rights must be socially guaranteed if the powerless are to enjoy them, and social guarantees need to be protected by international law, which would have to act against human rights abusers. But this international law would be the law of the perpetrators. Basically, any shift to rights-based humanitarianism can go no further than window-dressing, a competition between agencies to invade some kind of moral high ground.

The humanitarian project nestles in a contradiction between "hard" and "soft" law. The former is the "black letter" text of an act of parliament while the latter mostly languishes in international agreements which are not incorporated into national laws. To the extent that conventions become hard law, they usually deal with negative rights so, for example, the "right to life" is less the right to have one's life guaranteed than the right not be deprived of life, which is what humanitarian workers try to protect. They don't have the wherewithal to guarantee the right of the means of existence.

The core structuring principle of human society is political. Every attempt to reduce any part of that to a non-political status is a political act. Humanitarianism, with its limited conceptualization of human rights and avowed neutrality is supposedly apolitical. Yet, in the humanitarian space every choice is political, if somewhat random, in a practice that benefits do-gooders, misfits, adventurers, opportunists, warlords, ethnic cleansers, banks, big business and governments more than recipients of aid. Since the 1990s a "new humanitarianism" has appeared to challenge the founding notion of neutrality and demand the chance to engage in development projects, conflict resolution, advocacy and even policy-making. This has given rise to much casuistic wriggling and little clarity. For a long time, neutrality was the defining feature of humanitarian action, going back to its origins with Henri Dunant's nineteenth-century Red Cross Movement. Victims of war and disasters would be given succor on the condition of turning a blind eye to the causes and effects of the emergency, theoretically because this allowed humanitarian action without discrimination.

The Swiss jurist Jean Pictet, who was instrumental in drafting the 1949 Geneva Conventions, drew a distinction between "legal justice" and charity, noting that the former is given according to a person's rights, while charity is given according to a person's suffering. Since the two principles clashed in conflict zones the International Committee of the Red Cross (ICRC) had to opt for charity because any pronouncements about violations of international law would mean no access. Contemporary humanitarian law followed suit, disregarding questions of justice in international conflicts and delimiting a narrow set of protections aimed at minimizing "unnecessary suffering." International humanitarian law did not challenge Westphalian sovereignty or militarism and imperialism. In the ICRC founding principles, national sovereignty is inviolable: the succored existed within borders and not beyond them. These "neutral" principles implied a pragmatic relationship with military professionals and, taking over some obligations of a regime towards its citizens, the ICRC bestowed legitimacy on the government in question.

Modern international humanitarian law at the heart of the First Geneva Convention for the Amelioration of the Condition of the Wounded in Armies in the Field (1864), which was signed by twelve European nations (but not the United States), has its origins in the rescue and relief work carried out by Dunant in June 1859 in the Battle of Solferino. The International Red Cross Movement, founded in 1863 with a call for "compassion in the midst of battle" also constituted an attempt to codify the laws of war. Neutrality, symbolized by the white flag held up in order to gain access to the wounded, was a founding principle, together with "humanity" (prevent and alleviate human suffering, protect life and health, and ensure respect for the human being), "impartiality" (aid must be given according to need without discrimination of any kind or on any grounds), and "independence" (operating without interference, in accordance with humanitarian considerations free of political, military and economic interests).

Protecting life and health and ensuring respect for human beings cannot be based on neutrality. Giving impartial assistance to all sides in a conflict actually means aiding at least one party that is attacking the rights of another or others, usually on the grounds of race, nationality, religious beliefs, social class or political, military or economic interests. Respect for the human being requires confronting and abolishing the causes of disrespect. And if humanitarianism involves one outcast group being saved by another privileged group, which is usually closer to the perpetrators than the victims, then white-flag neutrality is, at most, a means of gaining access to populations at risk. Nowadays, the blue helmet, the red cross, and the white flag are often seen as something to shoot at, perhaps in part because it is so clear that they are not impartial.

Given that such unequal relations obviously define a humanitarian space, it seems incredible that it can still be presented as a sanitized anti-political zone. "Need" never comes alone. It comes conditioned by economic status, race, religion, nationality, ethnic group, gender, age, geographic location and other factors. Outside cloud-cuckoo-land, it can never be "irrespective" of those factors. Indeed, if it believes that its principles are violated the ICRC will withdraw from a humanitarian crisis, no matter how great the need. Neutrality also means that other basic principles are compromised, freedom of speech, for example. When Peter Maurer, president of the ICRC joined the World Economic Forum's board in 2014, he was asked if this was proper when the WEF embraces arms manufacturers among its members. He gave the "neutral" answer that it is essential to talk to all "stakeholders" of conflicts. Obviously the victims aren't "stakeholders." The argument is presented in a means-ends framework while also ostensibly creating—*per impossibile*—some kind of moral equivalence between oppressors and their victims. ICRC workers aren't allowed to testify about abuses they have witnessed, on the grounds that this might endanger other aid workers in the zone and damage ICRC's reputation for "confidentiality," the condition for future access, as if avoidance of the issues were a proper moral stance. Moreover, what is neutral when donors choose not to aid cases where the need is greatest?

In the political order after World War Two, relief agencies operated within clearly defined limits. Charities and "non"-governmental organizations faced expulsion from the countries where they worked if they were seen to take any kind of political stance. Hence, where possible, disasters were dubbed "natural." If the citizens of a country were starving as a result of corruption, incompetence or counterinsurgency operations, the weather was blamed. The terrible 1983–1985 famine in Ethiopia was a "drought." Most humanitarian workers believed it and those who didn't kept mum so they could keep working. After the end of the Cold War, "weather" became less guilty with a new confluence of multilateral security and humanitarianism which, now in the sphere of foreign policy, has expanded its activities to include development and peace-building initiatives. Since much funding for aid agencies comes from state coffers the end, interventionism, justifies the means, supposedly by protecting human rights. This has required a little tweak in humanitarian identity, updating it as "new" humanitarianism, where "new" means what it did with Tony Blair's "new" Labor and Bill Clinton's "new" Democrats.

With George W. Bush's "with-us-or-against-us" doctrine, neutrality was laid to uneasy rest with the insistence that humanitarian agencies and the powers-that-be must share the same values. This idea marked planning for the military intervention in Iraq, when agencies were invited to join the coalition as an embedded sector of "operation Iraqi Freedom," in accordance with one of the eight "war objectives" (sic) of the Pentagon: "… immediately providing humanitarian aid, food and medicines to displaced persons and the many Iraqis in need." The Pentagon then magicked up an Office of Reconstruction and Humanitarian Assistance. This cooption of humanitarian agencies to the coalition's political project didn't fool Iraqis, so the lives of aid workers were endangered.

The propaganda possibilities held out by the humanitarian project were too good to miss. In April 2003 the military-run Humanitarian Affairs Coordination Center in Jordan stressed the need to get NGOs into the strategically-important city of Basra in southern Iraq to show people how great life was going to be after Saddam Hussein was ousted. A similar attempt to demonstrate the "genuine goodness" of the United States was made in Somalia in 2003 with the "Gift of the People of the United States of America" in the form of 50-kilogram sacks of grain bearing the American flag, when the grain was actually supplied by the UN World Food Programme. In one fell swoop the United Nations was reduced to the United States and food was used for political propaganda. In fact, the virtue-posturing "gift" was part of a bigger story. At the end of the 1970s, Somalia, now notorious for its pirates and as a "failed," famine-stricken state, was self-sufficient in food but the debt repayment policies imposed by the International Monetary Fund and the World Bank in the eighties included liberalization of the country's markets and hence a massive influx of non-traditional foodstuffs produced by subsidized western multinationals, which deprived local producers of their livelihood. So famine ensued.

Another propaganda concern is gagging critics, or what Arundhati Roy calls NGOization. Her coinage signals the fact that heavily-funded NGOs are "part of the same loose, political formation that oversees the neoliberal project and demands the slash in government spending in the first place."[166] In this scheme, aid recipients become "pathological victims," the usual fare of another "malnourished Indian, another starving Ethiopian, another Afghan refugee camp, another maimed Sudanese," racist typecasts fattening the White Savior Industrial Complex, which is fervently represented by the man who is saving "people that have nothing and are not successful enough even to stay alive right now," Jeffrey Sachs.[167] Resistance is defanged, both among recipients of aid doled out as charity from a superior civilization, and also among NGO workers, most of whom want to help even while they are gagged in their role of kind-hearted envoys of empire.

A number of academic centers, calling for better NGO accountability and governance, have begun to act as think-tanks in a kind of nexus between government and nonprofits. These include the Yale School of Management, the Hauser Center for Non-Profit Organizations at Harvard, the Centre for the Study of Global Governance at the London School of Economics, and the Centre for Study of Globalisation and Regionalisation at the University of Warwick. These institutions recognize the non-neutrality of nonprofits, as a Hauser Center Working Paper[168] makes clear when arguing that local and international NGOs are "important policy makers." Moreover, when thousands of NGOs are accredited to the UN—more than 4,000 to the Economic and Social Council (ECOSOC), for example—they often end up working in international alliances like NATO.

The end of the Cold War saw many changes in multilateral security organizations which previously operated in accordance with a statist concept of security viewed in military terms. Without changing their formal structures, they have now introduced a humanitarian dimension into their strategic goals and activities and, where necessary, with an artful sleight of hand, they transform "humanitarianism" into "human rights," which are then used to justify military intervention. Meanwhile, relief agencies have expanded their mandates into the realm of peacemaking, also with vague references to "human rights." With the philanthropic disengagement of western governments in Africa, nonprofits are used as a policy instrument to such an extent that inexpert relief workers can end up working as government advisers.

Relief agencies must negotiate the humanitarian space in a process called "fieldcraft" (also a kind of US Army survival training), entailing *inter alia* deals with government authorities about silence on human rights abuses for the "greater good" of the relief program. One harrowing account of this kind of moral morass is Deborah Scroggins' book *Emma's War* about a young British aid worker in South Sudan. She married the western-educated Nuer warlord, Riek Machar, and then tried to turn a blind eye to his atrocities even when she knew he was manipulating the flow of food aid by means that included massacres and keeping children half-starved in order to extract more aid from foreigners. For many NGOs, silence is an "operational" strategy.

Another "fieldcraft" option is to panic and call for international intervention, as happened in Somalia with CARE-US being the loudest voice. The Pentagon joined the humanitarian club and the result was the disastrous "Operation Restore Hope" (1992–1993). Yet humanitarian intervention was fatally denied in Rwanda, partly because of the military debacle in Somalia. Aid mostly goes to "middle-income countries that are also poorly governed."[169] The "too-difficult" situations are ignored. There are many "surplus," "redundant," dehumanized or "basket-case" (Henry Kissinger) populations in great need which, for dark reasons of state, are not humanitarian priorities. These include West Papuans, the Rohingya, victims of genocide; South Sudanese, victims of ethnocide; the dispossessed San in Botswana; and refugees on boats sent back to sea, left to drown or held in terrible prisons like those of Australia on Manus and Nauru islands.

Zimbabwe reveals some of the catch-22s of humanitarian "neutrality." After the country was hit by floods and drought in 1992–1993, international appeals raised generous amounts of support. The government's relations with the international non-profits were relatively good and aid was channeled through its ministries of Health, Social Welfare, and Agriculture. Now, with the collapse of key economic sectors like mining and agriculture, and hyperinflation, levels of foreign investment and aid are falling, cash is running out and the "death spiral" (as *Bloomberg* puts it) looms. The Mugabe government's image abroad is one of human rights abuse, political repression and controversial land reforms. If the government gained political legitimacy in its distribution of aid in 1992–1993, it now asks for aid from governments that criticize its policies.

The government views international aid agencies as a form of external intervention. Which they are, and Mugabe turns this to his own advantage. In September 2002, the activities of Save the Children (UK) were temporarily suspended after twenty-two years of work in the country on the grounds that its operations were not neutral. Indeed, it was impossible to save children without taking the family context into account, and this entailed extended families, clans and tribes and, ultimately, affected the balance of power. Local chiefs are responsible for assisting their people in times of need. If they can dip into the pork barrel to discharge that responsibility, their power base is greatly enhanced. If NGOs select beneficiaries according to need in a consultation supervised by an external agent, they undermine traditional authority, shift the balance of power and even bring about the collapse of community institutions. The question of whether neutrality means respecting the status quo of local customs (as well as that of the donor sphere) is never properly addressed.

Food humanitarianism in Africa is nothing less than aggressive. The US government, USAID, and industry, plus the Bill & Melinda Gates Foundation, are using the current situation to force the introduction of Genetically Modified (GM) crops on countries desperately needing food aid. When these countries are obliged to buy designated products from US agribusiness, American wheat, maize and soya-bean farmers receive large subsidies and a guaranteed market. Zimbabwe and other African countries have made it clear that they don't want to be guinea pigs or dumping grounds for GM products. But USAID, as a vehicle for the GM industry and taking advantage of famine, coerces developing countries into accepting GM technology and strong-arms them to pass favorable intellectual property and biosafety legislation (with a shift from precaution to promotion with minimal public oversight) allowing GM corporations, including Monsanto and Cargill (sponsors of the UN World Food Programme), to swamp the market. Once the GM food enters the scene as aid, African governments find it difficult to resist the corporate take-over of the agricultural economy.

The third principle of the Charter of Médicins Sans Frontières (Doctors without Borders – MSF) states that it "observes neutrality and impartiality in the name of universal medical ethics and the right to humanitarian assistance." Yet, its co-founder Bernard Kouchner attempts to dodge the thorny neutrality issue simply by declaring that MSF is "impartial." Apart from the problems raised by succoring Interahamwe killers in refugee camps in the Democratic Republic of the Congo, impartiality is not what results when the international and local power relations behind a humanitarian crisis are disregarded but Kouchner is breezily indifferent to the *context* of taking "care of the victims on both sides of the conflict." He describes "three main eras of the medical community's involvement in international humanitarian crises" and his words are quite shocking because, in in his waggish way, he is saying that it has gone from respect for governments and neutrality, to rebellion against uncooperative governments, to humanitarian doctors laying down the law to governments and wielding the might-is-right power of the so-called international community, or let's just say the Pentagon. Yet he still insists that this behavior is neutral and impartial.[170]

> In the first era we asked the government: "Are we authorized? Can we receive the clearance to go and take care of your people, Mr. Government, Mr. Dictator?" If they refused, there was no way to cross the border. It could only be through ICRC involvement and neutrality.
>
> The next era was that of the French Doctors. We were asking the government the same question: "Mr. Dictator, will you allow us to care for your patients?" If they said "Yes, okay," we'd come. If they refused, we'd say, "Sorry, but we're coming anyway"—and would cross the border. It was physically difficult, and some of our people died. Others have been imprisoned for years.
>
> In the third and present era, we put it like this: "Mr. Dictator, in the name of the international community, in the name of the UN system, we advise you not to massacre your minorities."
>
> "Why not?"
>
> "Because we will use measures: embargos, travel restrictions, freezing your bank accounts, and eventually military pressure."

In Kouchner's stage three, doctors intervene in issues that properly belong in the legal sphere of *jus ad bellum*, the set of criteria consulted before engaging in war to determine whether it is justifiable. Yet he claims that the humanitarian task lies strictly in the "impartial" domain of *jus in bello*, the laws that apply once the war is underway. Participating in the decision as to whether a war should be waged is hardly impartial and, anyway, humanitarian impartiality requires that only consequences are dealt with. Concealing or disguising causes are exactly what policy makers want, and humanitarian agencies are their witting or unwitting instruments. Hence, Point 52 of the UN Document "An Agenda for Peace: Preventive Diplomacy, Peacemaking and Peace-Keeping"[171] begins, "Increasingly, peace-keeping requires that civilian political officers, human rights monitors, electoral officials, refugee and humanitarian aid specialists and police play as central a role as the military."

NGOs in Europe, with higher levels of private funding, tend to be more autonomous than those in the United States and can choose among different sources of government support. The main differences between European and US humanitarian organizations are autonomy in sources of funding, the role of advocacy, security issues, NGO-military relations, transparency and rules of internal functioning, and logistics of aid provision in situations of conflict. In the US, CARE and Save the Children receive large amounts of funding from the government and, making a geographical statement about their priorities, moved their headquarters from New York (closer to the UN) to Washington (closer to the Pentagon) in the 1990s. This palling-up with power allows aid agencies to fall back on the excuse of "only following orders" when things go awry, even when they depict humanitarian power as an abstract, neutral thing that simply doles out money, food, and medicines.

Points 9 and 10 of the "Code of Conduct for the International Red Cross and Red Crescent Movement and Non-Governmental Organizations in Disaster Relief"[172] are more wishful thinking than operational principles:

> 9. We hold ourselves accountable to both those we seek to assist and those from whom we accept resources.
>
> 10. In our information, publicity and advertising activities, we shall recognise disaster victims as dignified humans, not hopeless objects.

Being "accountable" and recognizing that victims are "dignified humans" require equality of circumstances, and this simply doesn't exist in the humanitarian space. NGOs are first and foremost accountable to their funders and, even then, "accountability" is rather absent because the main concern is notching up brownie points. As for Point 10, no recipient of charity can be "dignified" when depending on others for the right to material existence in one of the most unequal relationships that exists.

Helping to maintain the status quo, humanitarianism appeals to charity and acts of benevolence by the rich and powerful whose power, hardly undermined by magnanimity, may even be enhanced because of the systematic confusion between humanitarian and humanist. Humanism, seeks general solutions to human issues through rational argument rather than relying on governments, deities or sacred texts. The nature of humanism—which is not confined to western philosophy (in which it came into prominence in Europe from the fourteenth to sixteenth centuries as an expression of the rights of the common man against feudalism) but dates back to the Buddha, Socrates and Confucius for example—is not particularly clear but, roughly speaking, it is a branch of moral philosophy. It is born in the West as a rather lame concept since, as Bertrand Russell acidly observes, "The humanists of the time [...] were too busy acquiring knowledge of antiquity to be able to produce anything original in philosophy."[173] Nonetheless, humanism is quite close to human rights in positing that all human beings should have the right and responsibility to shape their own lives.

Humanitarianism, however, is an activist reaction, circumscribed by limits of time and space, to specific calamities and governed by the "can-do" approach without reflection on the fact that those who "can do" are those with the means to do. Humanitarianism, as a form of charity, is practically the antithesis of humanism. It is basically a withered relativist offshoot of moral universalism (which is deemed to be applicable to all humanity and derivable from moral codes existing in all cultures). Humanitarian relativism goes back a long way, as is illustrated by the 1772 common-law case of the runaway slave James Somerset. He had been brought to England, had escaped and been recaptured, and was about to be shipped back to Jamaica. At issue was the question of whether Somerset was subject to the medieval law of villeinage, in which case he was a serf whose master could pack him off to the plantation again. But this had explosive legal consequences as it would call into question the status of British agricultural workers. If a black man could be enslaved under the law of villeinage, they could too. Resort to this law could mean the demise of common law. In his ruling, William Murray, First Earl of Mansfield, pronounced that villeinage did not apply and that, on the basis of local, customary, organic law, slavery was prohibited. But he did not rule that this "odious" institution should be abolished throughout British territory. So slavery continued in the British West Indies for another sixty years and in India for ninety.

To keep backtracking, one of the basic assumptions of humanism is the dictum of the pre-Socratic philosopher Protagoras (c. 481 BCE–420 BCE) that "man is the measure of all things, of those that are that they are, and of those that are not that they are not."[174] The universalism of this pronouncement might be challenged by interpreting it to mean that each human being is the measure of all things, so there is no objective way of gauging who is right when individuals differ, in which case it is a skeptical doctrine that underscores the untrustworthiness of the senses. As an objective view of the human condition, Protagoras's statement has been seen as a refutation of absolutism in western philosophy while also being claimed by both relativist and universalist camps. The former sees ethics as derived from the individual and the latter takes the view that what is ethically good for one must be ethically good for all.

Humanitarianism, decked out in universalist garb, postulates a scientific or metaphysical foundation for global politics but also hints at Kant's political question, "Who are we?" which suggests a self-conscious moral community. However, humanitarianism creates a certain sort of "moral" community that perforce excludes others in a world where enormous inequality, racism, xenophobia, religious intolerance, sexism and many other human failings are the order of the day. In Gini Coefficient terms, if the humanitarian "community" were a country, it would be the most unequal one on the planet. Four percent of the total number of emergency aid agencies received about 85% percent of total funding in 2013. The relativist/universalist tension lies at the heart of humanitarianism, a wispy notion cocooned in pretentious prattle frequently invoking hackneyed expressions like "international community."

Darwin sowed the seeds of suspicion in western philosophy about Greek and Enlightenment ideas of human nature but, politically speaking, nebulous humanitarianism bolstered by humanist claims is a resilient concept. Pragmatist thinkers as unlike as Nietzsche and William James see metaphysical questions as disguised political questions concerning the group or groups with which one hopes to be affiliated or to create. The notion of "We, the people…" of the world, the "international community" may sound all very fine in the "multi-stakeholder world" of humanitarian discourse but it rings terribly hollow in the humanitarian space which underlines, like no other context, the absence of freedom, justice, dignity and fraternity supposedly characterizing the imaginary universal community.

Charity has constructed a massive ideological edifice of humanitarianism. But it's shaky because the real-world conditions which belie its basic claims are ever-more evident. The latest version is what some observers call "post-humanitarianism," the quick fix for the specific challenge, rather than seeing the humanitarian system as a whole, as if it ever were a "whole." Europe's donations to UN agencies have plummeted since the onset of the economic crisis, in the days when most refugee and IDP crises were far away from its borders. Meanwhile the US remains the single biggest donor of humanitarian aid. If the present geopolitical priorities of USAID are anything to go by, some people might look back on old-fashioned humanitarianism as a golden age of human kindness. But the surrealists were right. The White Savior Industrial Complex was never kind.

CHAPTER 8
HOW CAPITALISM LOVES HUMANITY

If the word "philanthrocapitalism" appears to be comprised of two unhappily cohabiting contradictory terms trying to suggest there is such a thing as humanity-loving capitalism, that's what it's really all about. Squaring the circle. People who fancy they've achieved this feat say it's the new philanthropy, modeled on the way profit-making business is done. Capitalist products must be "new" so this one is too even if, as with many another product, "new" is not exactly the case. As Linsey McGoey points out, there's nothing new about the "new" philanthropy: "[...] a business-like, impact-oriented approach to charity has been dominant within large-scale philanthropy for at least 120 years, ever since industrialists such as Carnegie and Rockefeller vowed to apply business techniques to the realm of philanthropy"[175] as they sought ways to shield some of their income from taxation and to boost their power and prestige in the national and world arenas. Yet, in some ways, this self-serving philanthropy goes back even further, to pre-capitalist charity which was, in its own way, "business-like" and "impact-oriented" as it did its bit to prop up an unequal social order in which rich and poor had to be kept in their places.

"Philanthropy" has undergone several mutations through history. In the second century BCE, Plutarch used the term *philanthrôpía*, taking the original Greek idea which was philosophical, metaphysical and ethical, to refer to superior human beings in the sense of full self-development of mind, body and spirit, a state of being well-educated and productive for the benefit of humans. It was also associated with freedom and democracy and, accordingly, both Socrates and the laws of Athens were described as "philanthropic and democratic." Then, in the Middle Ages charity, selfless love promising salvation, took over in a harsh feudal system, consigning earlier humanism to the scrapheap until the Renaissance humanist philosopher Pico della Mirandola in his *Oration on the Dignity of Man* (1486) revived the philanthropic account of human creation, now with a Promethean Christian God. In the seventeenth century, Plutarch's concept was somewhat revived by Francis Bacon who viewed it as a political philosopher. In his essay *On Goodness*, harking back to Aristotle's concept of virtue, he spoke of "the affecting of the weale of men... what the Grecians call philanthropia" or deliberately instilled habits of good behavior while also highlighting the political nature of *philanthrôpía*. Since his philosophical instinct extended not to man *per se* but to man as a political subject, his philanthropic formula postulated that "reliefe of Man's estate" was the "last or furthest end of knowledge."

However, with Samuel Johnson's influence in the eighteenth century etymology took over and philanthropy became "love of mankind; good nature," which was twisted into something else by the end of the nineteenth century when immensely wealthy US industrialists like John Pierpont Morgan, Andrew Carnegie, John D. Rockefeller, and others, understood that private philanthropy was the "blonde child of capitalism" and began to set up philanthropic trusts and foundations. For John D. Rockefeller (senior), the power of making money was a gift from God and he therefore had a duty to enter the "business of benevolence." And this version of do-gooding meant ensuring the cultural reproduction of these gentlemen's version of American values, in particular individualism, meritocracy, discipline and obedience. They saw themselves as embodiments of a kind of theologically prescribed stewardship, whereby they held their possessions as trustees for a higher authority, or as epigones of divine providence. This was missionary activity at home, fostering good causes like education, immigrant assimilation and poverty mitigation, public health and science, medical research and the arts. And making sure that possible recipients of their generous endeavor were well behaved. The *Hand-Book for Friendly Visitors among the Poor* stressed the need to detect unworthy beneficiaries: "where too much is paid for rent, or tobacco, or liquor, or dress, or in any unwise expense, and *economy needs to be taught*."[176]

Their particular brand of social engineering was geared to the country's capitalist-imperialist pursuits, patriarchal society, tight social control, white supremacy and settler colonialism. As early as 1914, the National Education Association passed a resolution in which it expressed alarm about "[...] the activity of the Carnegie and Rockefeller Foundations—agencies not in any way responsible to the people—in their efforts to control the policies of our State educational institutions, to fashion after their conception and to standardize our courses of study, and to surround the institutions with conditions which menace true academic freedom and defeat the primary purpose of democracy as heretofore preserved inviolate in our common schools, normal schools, and universities."[177] Capitalism was now well and truly cobbled onto philanthropy and vice versa. Despite the incompatibility of the two terms, one apparently giving and one clearly exploitative, they are kept together because capitalism, increasingly greed-driven and ruthless yet hampered by modern social values, needs a gloss of benignity. Luckily for the richest people on earth, the politics of manipulated popular memory can be a powerful instrument. Nostalgia is long-lived and present-day perceptions are easily polished with sentimentality drawn from alleged past glories. Hence, old religious ideas of the benevolence of charity are frequently invoked by some of the worst exploiters.

By 2013 there were more than 100,000 private foundations in the United States with assets of over $800 billion. Their emphasis is pragmatic and donor-centered, as the oft-cited definition of the John Hopkins professor Lester Salamond suggests: philanthropy is "[...] the private giving of time or valuables (money, security, property) for public purposes; and/or one form of income of private non-profit organizations." But what kind of "giving" is this when a joint JP Morgan and Rockefeller Foundation report titled, "Impact Investments: An Emerging Asset Class" (2010) says, "Increasingly, entrants to the impact investment market believe they need not sacrifice financial return in exchange for social impact?" Or, as Chris Williams, a Gates Foundation press officer, puts it, "fulfilling a charitable objective does not preclude revenue generating activity." Impact investment is also called "doing good while doing well."

The former UN Secretary-General Ban Ki-Moon also believes in impact. In a 2015 visit to Silicon Valley, trying to drum up support from techie kings for the UN's Sustainable Development Goals, he expressed, and not for the first time, his faith in the transformative power of capital. "You are the most brilliant innovators. What matters is that some creative and innovative people who have the entrepreneurial capacity help these visions be carried out."[178] Willful blindness as to what a lot of corporations actually do, or commit, permeates the highest echelons of power. Or perhaps a kind of Omertà rules. Melanne Verveer, President Obama's first ambassador for global women's issues, admires Nike (of sweatshop fame) and Walmart for their "game-changing" philanthropy. Walmart even launched a Global Women's Economic Empowerment Initiative. One woman, apparently not noticed by Verveer or economically empowered by Walmart, was Betty Dukes, the lead plaintiff (of a million) in a 2001 landmark class-action lawsuit against her employer, alleging that Walmart discriminated against women employees and retaliated against women who reported it.[179]

Unsurprisingly, modules on "social entrepreneurship" are booming at elite business schools which send students off for "life-changing" experiences in Africa and teach them how to achieve maximum "impact." One example of the business-benevolence plutocracy they aspire to join is furnished by a list of some members of the Rockefeller-Foundation-inspired Global

Impact Investment Network (GIIN), which was founded in the United States in 2009 as a tax-exempt non-profit organization: the Bill & Melinda Gates Foundation, United States Agency for International Development (USAID), Goldman Sachs, J. P. Morgan Chase, Morgan Stanley, Zurich Insurance Group, Ford Foundation, Deutsche Bank, International Finance Corporation, and the Inter-American Development Bank Group. Find one big philanthropist and it's not difficult to find the rest. They have formed a cartel. It protects their impunity and, more benignly, is proof of the old adage that birds of a feather flock together.

How does the Bill & Melinda Gates Foundation aid billions of people? Well, it invests in equities and securities in financial markets, in countries like Saudi Arabia and Egypt, in companies like Verizon, Walmart and Dow Chemical, in mortgage and student loan financing firms, and in Morgan Stanley, Barclays, Bank of America, CitiGroup, Lehman Brothers, Wells Fargo, Bear Stearns and Deutsche Bank. "Improving health," it invests in Coca-Cola, Pepsi Cola, Kraft products and, until quite recently, McDonald's, Burger King, Taco Bell, Pizza Hut and KFC (which it has been busy spreading in Africa). It "combats climate change" by investing in oil companies like Conoco, Chevron/Texaco, BP, Anadarko Petroleum, the oil, natural gas and mining company-cum-environmental polluter and human (especially Navajo) rights violator Kerr-McGee, and depredator mining giants like Rio Tinto and the Brazilian company Vale, considered by many environmentalists to be the world's worst corporation in terms of contempt for the environment and human rights. For the Gates Foundation, clean energy means nuclear power, so Bill Gates is chairman of the board of the nuclear reactor company TerraPower and, undeterred by Fukushima, he rabbits on about the important role of "reliable power in eradicating global poverty."

The Bottom of Pyramid model of wealth is another staple of Gates-style philanthropy because, though the poorest billions at the bottom may not know it, that's where the money is. Here Gates applies the last turn of the screw: "impact investing is a powerful model with the potential to build markets and drive change for the people who need it most," meaning what The Financial Times Lexicon calls new business opportunities in designing and distributing goods and services for poor communities, or hitherto untapped "profit generators."

Matthew Bishop and Michael Green, authors of one of the "new" bibles of philanthrocapitalism—whose title, *Philanthrocapitalism: How the Rich Can Save the World*,[180] makes its position clear—claim that philanthrocapitalist "hyper-agents" like Bill Gates, Ted Turner, Bill Clinton, George Soros, Pierre Omidyar, Michael Bloomberg, Sir Richard Branson, and David Rockefeller, moved by something they cringefully dub "richesse oblige," use the skills and "intellectual vigor" which made them rich to apply their wealth and "convening power" (covening power at places like Davos) to philanthropy. Unlike state agencies, they are unaccountable yet the state still lurks behind billionaire generosity, thanks to the fact that, given the large tax breaks for philanthropic endeavors, and depending on the laws of different countries, up to two thirds of what they "give away" is, in fact, taxpayers' money. But there is no active involvement of either governments or citizenry. One commentator distils this kind of entrepreneurship into what he calls his "favorite quote," from George Soros: "I indulge in political philanthropy. I try to use my money to influence how governments spend money."181 As if there were nothing ideological or antidemocractic about billionaire largesse.182

Most foundations have high "administration" costs, offer little information about what they do, and are especially reticent about their failures. Robert Monks, a long-time campaigner for better corporate governance describes the variety that springs from private billionaire endeavor: "Perpetual existence, no need to conform to competitive standards, it is all too much for human nature. Hence the palatial offices, fancy conferences and increasingly lavish pay for the professional philanthrocrats."[183] It's a closed network, a club whose members, bankers, politicians, businessmen, Silicon Valley techies, film stars and reality show divas, are more than willing to pronounce on what's good for the poor, adept at spinning through revolving doors, and great at scratching backs.

The philanthropy they do is shrouded in mystery. It's known, for example, that in 2013 donor groups gave just over $41 million to ninety-two think tanks and groups promoting climate change denial and opposing regulation of carbon emissions. But, in general, these groups can easily fail to disclose who their funders are since a legal loophole protects the "right to privacy," as established in the Supreme Court's 1958 *NAACP v Alabama* ruling according to which association members can "pursue their lawful private interests privately." This means that governments can't force even controversial groups to identify their members unless there is a compelling state interest in disclosure. This is understood as a very good thing by corporations like BP or Exxon (which make a great show of sensitivity to environmental issues) because the Supreme Court ruling allows them to fund conservative think tanks opposing the scientific consensus on climate change. According to Adam Meyerson, president of the Philanthropy Roundtable, "So-called "dark money" illuminates our free society."[184] There was more joy for dark money in May 2016 when the US House of Representatives passed the Roskam Bill (GOP) which eliminates the stipulation that nonprofit groups must disclose their donors to the IRS. They said this was to protect privacy and free speech.

One main difference between today's philanthropy and earlier modern versions is scale thanks to the abyss of inequality caused by extreme concentration of wealth and power. However, as Bishop and Green nonchalantly concede in their panegyric on world-saving philanthropy, the rich are aware that if they "do not take on this responsibility [of philanthropy] they risk provoking the public into a political backlash against the economic system that allowed them to become so wealthy" (p. 12). Risk management is what they call the basis for a "new social contract," Carnegie-style. The deal is that the rest of us accept increasing inequality in exchange for "the rich regarding their surplus wealth as the property of the many, and themselves as trustees whose duty it is to administer it for the common good." This book would seem to have a lot of followers as private foundations are mushrooming by the thousands every year.

George Soros, globe-trotting do-gooder, and less known nowadays as the hedge fund man who broke the Bank of England in 1992 by short selling sterling and reportedly making a billion pounds on a single trade, wrote in his book *The Crisis of Global Capitalism* that he sometimes feels like a "gigantic digestive tract, taking in money at one end and pushing it out at the other." His beneficiaries get his shit ("money is feces, because the anal eroticism continues in the unconscious"—oh, Norman O. Brown, where are you?). Another caca from Mr. Soros is his insistence that "[...] in making the rules, people ought to be concerned [...] not to bend the rules to their benefit or their advantage. [...]." Worth about $5 billion at time he expelled this ordure, he was operating in some dodgy parts of the world where short-selling attacks in unchecked currency markets is within the rules, tax rules, for example, the loophole which allowed him to defer taxes on fees paid by clients and reinvest them in his fund, where they kept growing tax-free. According to Irish regulatory filings, by the end of 2013, Soros—through Soros Fund Management and the use of deferrals—had amassed for himself $13.3 billion. Soros certainly does "indulge."

In this world where the rich can "indulge" in what some call "venture philanthropy" there is a "Market," the one that gobbles up millions of small markets around the world. But markets are not institutions of a pre-social nature. They are political and seek to defend certain interests, whether they are private or of the majority of the population. This was seen by early political economists, some of them, including Adam Smith, influenced by Bernard Mandeville's long poem, *Fable of the Bees* (1724). One of the famous lines in this work is, "Private Vices by the dexterous Management of a skilful Politician may be turned into Publick Benefits." The Dutch-born physician and man of letters, Mandeville (1670–1733), is prominent in the scholarship about the rise of consumption. It was he who comforted uneasy consciences by reconciling individual avarice and national prosperity, pointing out that greed could be good, at least for the economy. "Thus every Part was full of Vice / Yet the whole Mass a Paradice," he wrote, offering as proof that, "Luxury Employ'd a Million of the Poor / And odious Pride a Million more." However, if the early political economists believed that under *laissez-faire* conditions private enterprise would bring collective benefits they also set provisos. In Mandeville's opinion, "So Vice is beneficial found / When it's by Justice lopt and bound." Modern philanthropists tend to dispense with lopping and binding to parrot the idea, "Private Vices may be turned into Publick Benefits."

Mandeville's book was much admired by Friedrich Hayek who, with *Prices and Production*, produced "one of the most frightful muddles" Keynes had ever read, but Keynes was talking economics not politics. If Hayek believed that, "[...] the adoption of a system of central planning necessarily produces a totalitarian system,"[185] he must have turned a blind eye to Mandeville's warning that "Private Vice" had to be lopped and bound in the public sphere. Paul Krugman put his finger on the crux of the matter here, namely the appeal for philanthrocapitalists of the idea of applying their own "dexterous Management" of their personal indulgence to produce public good: "[...] the Hayek thing is almost entirely about politics rather than economics. Without *The Road to Serfdom*—and the way that book was used by vested interests to oppose the welfare state—nobody would be talking about his business cycle ideas."[186]

Mandeville is interesting because he was perfectly aware of the sociopolitical function of charity, which he detailed in his "An Essay on Charity and Charity Schools" (1723), causing a scandal because overtly religious charity schools for the poor were the most admired and popular form of benevolence in eighteenth-century England. He attacks respectable do-gooders whose renown, he says, comes from their hypocritical hiding of their private vice behind public benefit. Charity schools were a fad, like hooped petticoats and there was no reason for them because people were born into their life stations and should be content therein. Britain's growing prosperity depended on exploiting the poor. This being the case, individuals who indulged in works for the public benefit were merely acting out of self-love. "Pride and Vanity have built more Hospitals than all the Virtues together."

Adam Smith is also picked and picked over—starting with nineteenth-century utilitarians who turned him into a proto-libertarian of the Hobbesian ilk—by philanthropists. Pierre Omidyar, founder of eBay and one of the most active philanthropists in the United States, funding nonprofit and for-profit ventures alike, quotes Adam Smith as his philanthropic model, purportedly because he was "a very eloquent proponent of the notion that individuals pursuing their self-interest in the right environment will make society a better place." Accordingly, "in the right environment profits are a sign that society is better off."[187] However, as the Catalan philosopher Antoni Domènech points out, the market envisaged by the now much-maligned (often from the left) Adam Smith was not remotely like eBay. It "did not mean a market left to its supposed self-organising spontaneity, but one that was politically and institutionally constituted and supervised in such a way that rural rentiers, financial magnates, oligarchs, monopolists and all the other *gentiluomini* would be reined in by the republic."[188] Moreover, in *The Wealth of Nations*[189] Smith uses the Great Fire of London as a metaphor in terms that are of deep ethical and political significance when he observes that natural liberty must not be left to run rampant. It needs fire-breaks: "[...] those exertions of the natural liberty of a few individuals, which might endanger the security of the whole society, are, and ought to be, restrained by the laws of all governments, of the most free as well as of the most despotical. The obligation of building party walls, in order to prevent the communication of fire, is a violation of natural liberty exactly of the same kind with the regulations of the banking trade which are here proposed."

As described above, in this special kind of political economy called charity, there are few fire-breaks but nobody seems to notice or care. Today's equivalent of the "hooped-petticoat" club members, celebrity philanthropists, "celanthropists," are more admired for lending their brand and advertising skills to "good" causes than criticized for blatant self-promotion and dumbing down policy debates. Very few observers wonder where "celanthropists" fit into present-day political economy.

Philanthropy in the United States might be traced back to what Alexis de Tocqueville called "voluntary associations" constructing colonial society and established for the public good, which he saw as a form of democratic philanthropy going back to the Mayflower Compact of 1620. Written by the Pilgrim Fathers and signed by forty-one male passengers, this was the first governing contract of the Plymouth Colony and also a social contact which the settlers agreed to follow "[...] for our better ordering, and preservation [...] and by virtue hereof to enact, constitute, and frame, such just and equal laws, ordinances, acts, constitutions, and offices, from time to time, as shall be thought most meet and convenient for the general good of the colony." The first corporation, Harvard College (1636), was a philanthropic voluntary association created to train young men for the clergy. Early philanthropic associations in the new colony aimed at promoting the "common wealth" along the lines of Christian ideas as expressed by the preacher Cotton Mather who, with his famous essay "Bonifacius, or an Essay to Do Good" (1710), echoed the founders' original idealism and advocated philanthropic magnanimity as a way of life. In 1775, the Continental Army of volunteers, financed by private donations, was created for concerted action of the Thirteen Colonies against Great Britain. Its *pro bono* general, George Washington, unpaid for three years, signed his letters, "Philanthropically yours."

Since the "Founders at Independence Hall" was a Philadelphia-based philanthropic association, the Declaration of Independence (1776) was preceded by a mission statement, as was common with documents published by such organizations. Hence, the famous sentence from the Preamble: "We hold these truths to be self-evident, that all men are created equal, that they are endowed by their Creator with certain unalienable Rights, that among these are Life, Liberty and the pursuit of Happiness." Although some thinkers believed that America had been created by and for philanthropy, the thoughts of Founding Father Alexander Hamilton (now revived in the Broadway hip-hop show) were of a different kind. In the very beginning of the first of *The Federalist Papers* (1788), he made an early declaration of imperialist benevolence, declaring that Americans were acting on behalf of and for the benefit of all mankind, which "adds the inducements of philanthropy to those of patriotism." But this needs to be seen in the context of subsequent Papers. His was an elitist view. In *Paper* 35 he argued that the "weight and superior requirements of the merchants render them more equal" to govern than the other classes. Basically he agreed with Founding Father John Jay that the people who own the country should govern it. At the Constitutional Convention of 1787 he was reported to have declared that, "All communities divide themselves into the few and the many. The first are the rich and well born, the other the ["turbulent and changing"] mass of the people."

Most of America's early reform movements, including the abolitionists, women's suffrage, environmentalism, civil rights and peace movements grew out of early philanthropic projects, private initiatives for public good. The drastic changes in philanthropic thinking after Carnegie, Ford, and Rockefeller and through to Gates and Zuckerberg, have metamorphosed philanthropy into a true creature of its time, governed by neoliberal principles and the opposite of love for humankind, a postmodern version of Alexander Hamilton's early vision of the control of the "few" over the "many" who, being "turbulent," might be pacified by a few crumbs of magnanimity.

Since their early years, philanthropic foundations like the Rockefeller Foundation and the Ford Foundation have embraced Hamilton's global understanding of American power and become been influential in international politics through strategic use of grants to shape development policies, especially in health and foodstuffs, and expanding their wealth and power in doing so. The Rockefeller Foundation for "promoting the well-being of humanity throughout the world" (a moot point) was set up in 1913 after the Supreme Court ruled in 1911 that Standard Oil was an illegal monopoly. It certainly promoted John D. Rockefeller's well-being as he was then able to protect a great part of his fortune from income and inheritance taxes. After the Crash of 1929, other wealthy individuals responded to high taxes by establishing foundations. Hence, in 1936, Henry Ford and his son Edsel set up the Ford Foundation which was soon to spread its influence around the world. As wealth is increasingly concentrated in the era of globalization and the rise of finance capital, philanthropic foundations have also proliferated, many of them the very embodiment of philanthrocapitalism. While there are philanthropic institutions that really are founded by lovers of mankind—among them Newman's Own food company, founded by Paul Newman who donated some $450 million in after-tax profits to thousands of charities—our concern here is philanthrocapitalism and how it slots into a profoundly unjust world system.

A recent article by Benjamin Soskis[190] in *The Washington Post* a propos of the new "short term" of quick-fix "philanthropy strategy" for the "here and now" proposed by Jeff Bezos (Amazon founder, owner of said newspaper and, hitherto, not especially famed for philanthropic magnanimity) attempts to distinguish between charity and philanthropy. His first stab uses a quote from Michael Zakaras writing for *Forbes*: "The problem with the short-term perspective is that it positions philanthropy as charity rather than a mechanism for shaping a more just, equitable world." So charity and philanthropy are different. Or are they? "Traditional charity" is seen as "operating outside the rules of the marketplace," so "charity can be cast in opposition to capitalism." We beg to differ. Mainstream charity has always operated within and supported "systems." The same goes for philanthropy, especially when presented as the rich saving the world "by channeling market forces toward philanthropic ends." Yet Soskis plows on: "[...] charity's radical possibilities are now coming to the fore. Premised on the proximate encounter with human suffering, staked to the fundamental dignity of those in need and humble in the immediacy of its ambitions, charity stands against the powerful forces of contemporary life that feel distant, hubristic, bureaucratic and unresponsive." But surely respecting the *dignity* of those in need means honoring their capacity to decide and choose, and respecting their freedom. The focus tends, as usual, to be on the intentions of the giver without a thought as to how the receiver is affected and, still less, given that their functions are not so different, how charity or philanthropy fits into the system which creates needy receivers and keeps them in that position. Nothing to do with rights.

In this view charity purports to give immediate relief to a particular problem, while philanthropy supposedly aims to address the cause of the problem. Give a hungry person a fish or teach the person how to fish. According to Soskis, "Philanthropists are supposed to pursue "systems change," long-term impact and the "extirpation of root causes." The example he gives is Mark Zuckerberg's and Priscilla Chan's $3 billion effort to cure "all disease in our children's lifetime." Evidently, Zuckerberg's wealth and way of thinking is not considered as a "root cause" of the political and social problems that give rise to the need for philanthropy in the first place. Philanthropy, Soskis says, "borrowed its logic from the laboratory and the boardroom" and has "technocratic pretensions." It's all about "systems."[191] But doesn't a system of such concentrated wealth and power keep poverty entrenched? The new tool the systems moguls have come up with is "systems entrepreneurship," which doesn't of course include the wretched of the earth. They can't be entrepreneurs. They don't appear in the neat, very manageable little diagram.[192] Especially when the "systems entrepreneurs" are nothing less than the central cog.

The idea boils down to an inane notion: billionaires can solve the world's problems. And the fox should guard the chickens. At the crassest end of the same scale which includes Davos, Bill Gates, and the Clinton Global Initiative, is Donald Trump: I can fix America because I'm rich.[193]

Logically, in this global system, corporate love for humanity is not confined to the western world. Entrepreneurial philanthropy is also taking off in China. But since it is now based on the wealth of a few individuals who became immensely rich after the country's economic liberalization, it is very different from the traditional Confucian philanthropy which combined benevolence (as the highest merit and central to social and political life as love and respect for others) and righteousness (the cultivation of the benevolent mind which then proceeds outwards) and aimed at enabling others to stand on their own feet. The new Chinese philanthropy is an individual matter increasingly taking the form of private foundations. When one corporate leader was asked whether his foundation served private or corporate purposes, he answered, "I am the company."[194]

Arundhati Roy has described a similar process in India where corporations, seeking to seduce the growing middle class, embrace the "exquisite art of Corporate Philanthropy," the "most visionary business of all time." Vedanta, whose corporate slogan is "Mining Happiness," emphasizes sustainable development in a "Creating Happiness" film competition it sponsors. Tata Steel ("Values Stronger than Steel") and Rio Tinto are sponsors of the Jaipur Literary Festival, where Oprah blew in to say how much she loves India. Roy notes how easily corporations can make consumers complicit in their philanthropy-arrayed plunder:

> [...W]hich of us sinners was going to cast the first stone? Not me, who lives off royalties from corporate publishing houses. We all watch Tata Sky, we surf the net with Tata Photon, we ride in Tata taxis, we stay in Tata Hotels, we sip our Tata tea in Tata bone china and stir it with teaspoons

> made of Tata Steel. We buy Tata books in Tata bookshops. Hum Tata ka namak khate hain. We're under siege.
>
> If the sledgehammer of moral purity is to be the criterion for stone-throwing, then the only people who qualify are those who have been silenced already. Those who live outside the system; the outlaws in the forests or those whose protests are never covered by the press, or the well-behaved dispossessed, who go from tribunal to tribunal, bearing witness, giving testimony.[195]

Philanthrocapitalism has five notable disturbing features.[196] First, it uses a business and market-based approach to development and stresses measuring results and impact. In this utilitarian model, results are what count, so it is judged by costs and benefits (to itself). Recipients of this brand of philanthropy must demonstrate achievements as defined by the donor and visible quick fixes are given priority so, for example, mosquito nets might be provided but structural problems like weak public health systems are ignored (or despised in the case of Bill Gates). For billionaires, charity is a sort of privatized taxation, or "self-taxation" where they decide the amount they pay and where the money goes. Rather than going to people in real need, grants are given to those who are more likely to come up with cheaper, quicker results, with a focus more on managing than empowering the poor. This model also creates a problem at source because continuity is by no means guaranteed. Private foundations tend to invest in financial markets so everything depends on the general economic situation. With the onset of the economic crisis, international funding by the biggest 1,300 US foundations dropped by 32 percent between 2008 and 2010.

Second, the who's who of Davos—including Tony Blair, Sir Richard Branson, Bill Clinton, Paulo Coelho, Bill and Melinda Gates, Damien Hirst, Sheikha Al Mayassa bint Hamad bin Khalifa Al-Thani, Jeff Koons, Jet Li, Shimon Peres, and Muhammad Yunus—reveals that philanthropic foundations can have an enormous influence in political agenda setting. Behind this influence lurks a claim to legitimacy, which is none other than an autocratic ideology of meritocracy, as supposedly proven by the personal success of the extremely rich, otherwise nondescript man called Bill Gates. The Bill & Melinda Gates Foundation is second only to the US administration for total contributions to the WHO, and such voluntary contributions prioritize short-term preferences and a political shift to vertical funding in a lax regulatory environment. Pet projects in the domain of health don't include the diseases which most afflict the world's poorest people, according to a 2009 report in *The Lancet*.[197]

The Gates health business also causes distortions in malaria research, *inter alia* by limiting the capacity of low-income countries to carry out their own research.[198] Essentially, it gives priority to methods which rely on developing new (American) technology and drugs. Moreover, Bill Gates is a leading proponent of strong intellectual property protections in international trade agreements, almost amounting to a patent monopoly which makes it more difficult for poorer countries to manufacture cheaper, generic versions of drugs. Then there are, for example, studies funded by Coca-Cola which gets a tax break for its "public health" philanthropy. A recent analysis has shown that these are five times more likely to find no link between sugar-laden drinks and weight gain than other studies whose authors reported no financial conflict of interest.[199] Rarely addressed in the discussion about philanthropic motivations is the fact that they are an unabashed expression of wealth and power. This is politics and especially political economy.

The political economy side of philanthropy is evident in the enormous influence of the Rockefeller and Ford foundations in Green Revolution agricultural policy, which widened the rich-poor gap and aggravated social marginalization, caused about a million human pesticide poisonings per year, rising cancer figures (especially in the Punjab), reduced agricultural biodiversity, brought about the permanent loss of valuable genetic traits in traditional varieties of seeds, with land degradation, soil nutrients depletion, deforestation and increased carbon in the atmosphere. These foundations have pushed American-supplied genetically modified seeds in Africa, despite public concern about their effects. The Gates Foundation simply bulldozes over grassroots approaches based on other kinds of knowledge and husbandry, especially with regard to protecting biodiversity.

The third problem with philanthropy is that global governance is weakened by the antidemocratic influence of entities like the Gates Foundation, the Rockefeller Foundation and the UN Foundation which, as major funders, call the shots in global partnerships and thus devalue the role of public decision-making bodies as well as national-level development strategies tailored for local needs. Another upshot is an institutional weakening of the United Nations and its specialized agencies. For example, the Gates Foundation, criticizing the "fragmentation" (outside its own grip) of the global nutrition system, only made it worse by setting up its own organizations like the Scaling Up Nutrition (SUN) Movement, Global Alliance for Improved Nutrition (GAIN), the Micronutrient Initiative (MI), the Flour Fortification Initiative (FFI), the New Alliance on Food Security and Nutrition and many more, and thereby undermining the UN System Standing Committee on Nutrition, which is supposed to be "the food and nutrition policy harmonization forum of the United Nations." Since all actors in these "multi-stakeholder" partnerships have equal rights, public bodies lose their legitimate political and legal status while the power of transnational corporations, philanthropic foundations, and sometimes even wealthy individuals is undemocratically inflated. Members tend to be non-transparently handpicked and not accountable to public mandates. The widespread belief that philanthropic companies are engaged in virtuous pursuits usually obstructs any project of building a political case for proper regulation.

This is related with the fourth problem: a general absence of transparency and accountability mechanisms. The big philanthropic foundations are certainly not accountable to the so-called beneficiaries. So, if some 200,000 Indian farmers committed suicide between 1997 and 2010 as a result of externally imposed agricultural policy in which control of the seed supply was in the hands of the chemical industry, nobody was responsible to the families, communities or government. These foundations are only answerable to their own boards of trustees whose priorities are unlikely to coincide with those of an impoverished Indian farmer. Annual returns are the only public disclosure philanthropic foundations in the United States must make on a form providing basic information about finance, investments and grants. The much-vaunted impact assessments and project evaluations are rarely publicly available.

Fifth and finally, philanthrocapitalism is a power relationship and the recipients have little or no say in how they are to be "helped," even when they know that the help is actually harmful to them and their way of life. This is a one-way relationship keeping the rich sitting pretty and the poor still poor and humiliated in being able to reciprocate, as most self-respecting humans would like to do: "Philanthropy thrills to begging and tolerates activism, but cannot abide a demand from those it wants to save."[200]

One of the Rockefeller Foundation's strategic documents, dating from 1951, shows how, behind all the fine words about feeding the multitudes, food production was definitely seen as a political arm. "Whether additional millions in Asia and elsewhere will become Communists will depend partly on whether the Communist world or the free world fulfills its promises. Hungry people are lured by promises, but they may be won by deeds. Communism makes attractive promises to underfed peoples; democracy must not only promise as much, but must deliver more."[201] David Rockefeller, the ultimate silver-spoon boy who died recently aged 101, may have been the pal Henry

Kissinger turned to when he needed a banker to help out the brutal junta he had installed in Argentina, and may have been champion of municipal austerity, privatization and deregulation in New York, but he was bid a fulsome farewell from his earthly demesne with a host of unctuous obituaries almost exclusively remembering him for his philanthropy (which is a wonderful thing inasmuch as you can destroy people's lives and still end up revered in your coffin).

In 2006, the Gates Foundation and the Rockefeller Foundation launched the Alliance for a Green Revolution in Africa (AGRA) which, claiming that hunger in the continent is due to a need for technology and functioning markets, builds partnerships with the private sector to boost agricultural productivity. Eventually, the Gates Foundation came to dominate the sector through a new setup called GAIN (Global Alliance for Improved Nutrition), functioning on a top-down basis in which selected farmers merely purchase from corporations lab-developed technologies with a focus on biotechnology and genetically modified organisms (GMOs). There is no support for research or development carried out by smallholder farmers, and neither is safety testing a priority. Would it be fair to ask whether these farmers are being used as guinea pigs?

In this careless setting Nigeria, for instance, introduced transgenic cassava, rice, maize, yam, and sorghum before genetic food biosafety testing was legalized. The Nigerian Minister for Agriculture and Development at the time was Akinwumi Adesina, a GMO enthusiast, a senior official in the Rockefeller Foundation, Vice President of Policy and Partnerships for AGRA and, since 2015, President of the African Development Bank. One Nigerian observer has a different take on Akinwumi Adesina's agricultural philanthropy:[202] "Adesina converted Agriculture into a business. [...] With fertilizer distribution totally privatized and seed sellers a private business controlled by the Bill Gates foundation, Monsanto's and other world producers, farmers cannot simply re-plant seeds from the last harvest but take these bank loan facilities to buy seed from Big corp. under the Adesina legacy." Nigeria has joined Ghana and Haiti in the brave "New World Order" of GMOs, artificial food and artificial pricing of food.

Philanthropy is not unlike the humanitarianism denounced by the surrealists so long ago. "We live in a world where destroying people and their dreams is a business," the rapper will.i.am said. According to its website, the International Rescue Committee (founded in 1933 at the request of Albert Einstein) "responds to the world's worst humanitarian crises and helps people whose lives and livelihoods are shattered by conflict and disaster to survive, recover, and gain control of their future." Its president is David Miliband, former British Labour Party politician and now "charity executive." His new annual salary is some US$600,000 for working 37.5 hours a week. (He also gets US$105,000 a year renting out his home in North London.) Its "Overseers" include Timothy F. Geithner (a Kissinger protégé who presided over the Wall Street bank bailouts), four innocent-until-proven guilty war criminals—Henry Kissinger (praised with faint damnation in *Politico* as "one of the worst people ever to be for good"), Madeleine Albright, Condoleezza Rice, and Colin Powell—magnates from JP Morgan Chase, Bank of America, Goldman Sachs, including Felix Rohatyn (who presided over the dismantling of social services in NYC in the 1970s), and James Wolfensohn (past president of the World Bank who destroyed social services on several continents). And, oh dear, the IRC is not clean. In 2016 it was reported that it had millions of dollars in funding withdrawn because of bid-rigging and bribery, in projects supposedly helping Syrian civilians and refugees.

Quite a lot of people are of the view that nonprofits are the cornerstone of American democracy. Yet heads or former heads of state like Tony Blair, Bill Clinton and Donald Trump have foundations run like fiefdoms, which makes one shudder to think about how they view political office. The Trumps are shameless and often stupid about their charitable pretensions, which may make some people think they are a mere aberration. But they are part of a system, maladroit in their arrogance, maybe, but the system was there for them to exploit.

Donald Trump, who said in Indianapolis on April 28 2016, "We have many, many countries that we give a lot of money to, and we get absolutely nothing in return, and that's going to stop fast," obviously doesn't understand the basic principle of charity, that it's not a gift, yet he claims to be an ardent philanthropist—a description removed from the biography posted on the Trump Organization's website at the end of 2016, just before he was elected president—and that he has personally given more than $100 million to charity over the last five years. Said charity is the Donald J. Trump Foundation, a "private non-operating foundation" which is described as a threadbare operation (like those little offices in Luxembourg) with no paid staffers. And, in fact, Pulitzer Prize winner David Farenthold of *The Washington Post* (who also disclosed the "locker-room banter" pussy-grabbing story) found in his dogged investigation that Trump had not donated a single cent to the Donald J. Trump Foundation since 2008. He had simply solicited money from others, knowing that this was illegal since the foundation was not registered to receive such inputs. This unusual "family" foundation receives nearly all its money from other people. The method was simple. For example, Donald Trump went to the New Jersey charity, the Charles Evans Foundation, asking for a donation for the Palm Beach Police Foundation. The charity complied and gave $150,000 to the Donald J. Trump Foundation which then "donated" the money to the police group in the foundation's name. It gets better because, in 2010, Trump then received an award from the Palm Beach Police Foundation for his "selfless support." The police foundation also held its gala at Trump's Mar-a-Lago Club. By 2014 its tax filings showed that it had paid out $276,463 for rented space in Mar-a-Lago that year alone.

A sizable portion of Trump's charity seems to go to organizations buzzing with celebrities or politicians, for example the former major league baseball manager Joe Torre, Larry King, professional golf legends Arnold Palmer, Jack Nicklaus and Tiger Woods, and Tom Cruise (whose weird New York Rescue Workers Detoxification Project offered free Scientology-based cleansing to rescue workers after the 9/11 attacks). Coffee is very expensive these days. That's if you want to take it with Ivanka Trump who, no slouch and taking a leaf from the Clinton philanthropy book, auctioned on the Charitybuzz website in December 2016 the opportunity to "Enjoy Coffee with Ivanka Trump." Since the bidding started at $50,000 it meant that the takers would want something back, like the investment manager Ozan M. Ozkural who was keen to find out about the then president-elect's plans for Turkey and other countries where he has investments. Yet another example of how the rich understand charity. Ivanka's project was nipped in the bud when the bidding reached $72,000. In any case, the money wasn't intended for the St. Jude Children's Research Hospital, as her website implied. It was for the Eric Trump Foundation.

An Associated Press investigation[203] shows that Eric Trump's foundation benefits other charities connected to the Trump family and members of the board, with payments repeatedly going to one of Donald Trump's private golf clubs and to organizations linked to the Trumps by corporate, family or philanthropic relationships. According to IRS filings, the Eric Trump Foundation has raised $7.3 million supposedly for cancer-stricken children, mainly from donors keen to hang out with the Trumps (like the people who paid $50,000 per foursome to play golf and enjoy a gala dinner at the foundation's fundraiser in 2015).

Needless to say, there are plenty of other irregularities, including failure to report conflicts of interest by board members who are friends, relatives or Trump employees, including senior presidential campaign aides; Eric Trump is chairman and reserves board seats for his future children, as if the charity was a private business; the foundation failed to report to the IRS that it paid $100,000 to a Trump golf club in 2013; Eric Trump sought tax-free status from the IRS on condition that his foundation wouldn't do business with any company whose corporate officers were on the charity's board but Eric Trump is executive vice-president of The Trump Organization, and oversees the Trump Organization's golf operations worldwide; it has given to many Jewish organizations associated with his sister Ivanka and her husband, Jared Kushner; there are links between Eric Trump Foundation board members and Donald Trump's presidential campaign, which paid $14.2 million to the company of board member Christl Mahfouz, for campaign paraphernalia, while another board member, Jerry Kaufman was paid rent. Sick children?

Faith? Enter Tony Blair, armchair Iraq warrior and "philanthropist of the year" for *GQ* men's fashion and style magazine (which recently published an excruciating photoshoot with Brad Pitt adopting the fetal position to talk about becoming a "better man"), another canny philanthropist who understands the word in the entrepreneurial sense. By 2016 he had created a tangle of enterprises, with business contacts in twenty-five nations and charities in twenty. He has been accused by a former employee of using the Tony Blair Faith Foundation as a think-tank for his private office, an allegation serious enough to prompt an inquiry by the Charity Commission, not that the latter is known for strong action.

In fact the Tony Blair Faith Foundation (now the "non-profit" Tony Blair Institute for Global Change) is supposed to be an independent charity with Tony Blair as its non-executive patron. But he was always hanging around as the superstar attraction for potential funders, netting millions of pounds in donations from rich individuals, the US government and even the Swedish lottery. Meanwhile, working for the United Arab Emirates, Blair agreed to advise Egyptian president, Abdel Fattah el-Sisi, whose courts were sentencing hundreds of dissidents to death by hanging, and also the Serbian PM Aleksandar Vucic. Other deep-pocketed advisees include the Kazakh dictator Nursultan Nazarbayev (£5 million a year), the Romanian government, Kuwait, and the Colombian government. Then there's Victor Pinchuk, the art-collecting Ukrainian oligarch who gave the Tony Blair Faith Foundation £320,000, maybe not so much to help "people understand the major role that religion plays within society" as to further Pinchuck's pet project of Ukraine's joining the European Union which, naturally, is faithfully backed by Tony Blair. Pinchuk also extended his largesse to Donald Trump ($150,000 for the Trump Foundation, after which Trump made a video link speech at his 2015 Yalta European Strategy Annual Meeting, saying that the United States needed to take a harder line with Vladimir Putin) and forked out $8.6 million for the Clinton Foundation, after which Secretary of State Hillary Clinton hosted him to dinner.

Another Blair foundation, Africa Governance Initiative (AGI) whose five-year vision is to achieve "a footprint that touches on 15–20 countries" by offering governance and investment advice to heads of state and government ministers, was refused funding by the British Department for International Development, but USAID (perhaps concerned about the fast-expanding presence of its rival AFRICOM, the US Military Command for Africa in at least 35 countries) came to the rescue and rewarded Blair's philanthropic panache with £4.5 million in three grants. And, to gild the lily, also rewarded Cherie Blair ("close friend" of Hillary Clinton) with £405,000 for her foundation. One of USAID's top charities Save the Children gave Tony Blair its global legacy award for AGI's efforts in "alleviating poverty in Africa." Carolyn Miles, American Save the Children CEO, in a joint article with Coca-Cola spin doctor Clyde Tuggle, offers further insight into how these lucrative liaisons with USAID work. "[…] American businesses cannot expand overseas alone. To be successful, Coca-

Cola requires clean water, electricity, and roads—the kind of infrastructure our international affairs programs support in the developing world. That is why [...] Coca-Cola is partnering with USAID to provide access to water for millions in Africa. It's just good for business."[204] Access to water? Coca-Cola is a big-time water depleter, drying up local wells and destroying agriculture in its pursuit of water for its plants (Rajasthan, Uttar Pradesh, Mexico, El Salvador....). The people are thirsty? Let them have Coke.

Tony Blair, Quartet Representative to the Middle East, burden on the public purse—an estimated £3 million per year at the end of 2016—has a narrow mandate of promoting Palestinian economic development. As Middle East Envoy and working with the World Bank, he secured a £1 million private contract with the bank, in addition to personal deals he made with Abu Dhabi while negotiating to obtain funds for the Palestinian Authority. He expects help with his private business from British officials abroad in *inter alia* Canada, Macedonia and Albania and, on private business trips, schmoozes the people he must deal with officially as Quartet envoy. No conflict of interest. Philanthropy is a business. Tony Blair's personal corruption is evident enough but the usually ignored issue is that he operates in a philanthropic system in which the scale of his amorality may be large but in its form and content it is all too well established.

But even Tony Blair can't compete with the sleaze of the America's Philanthropic Family par excellence. The Clinton Foundation, with dozens of partnerships with private companies, governments, and other nonprofits, is a "public charity." It is also, as the economist Michael Hudson points out,[205] a sort of savings account. The money is, he says, "hidden in plain sight," legitimate and tax free. It's so legitimate it never got the attention devoted to Hillary Clinton's emails. Set up in 2001 at the end of Bill Clinton's second term in the White House, the foundation claims, of course, that its mission is to "alleviate poverty, improve global health, strengthen economies, and protect the environment." So far so good. By the end of 2014, its assets totaled $354 million and its staff numbered 486 in some 180 countries where they had little or no background in development work. It is basically a "celebrity foundation," a vanity vehicle where celebrities can show off. If they pay $15,000 they can have their photo taken with Hillary Clinton. It may take pains to adhere to the letter of the law but the Clinton Foundation's activities combine fundraising, influence-peddling, networking, "humanitarian" causes and a constant quest for money and power.

Some of the foundation's donors don't fit well with its stated objectives. These would include Coca-Cola, Verizon, Dow Chemical (producer of napalm and Agent Orange for U.S. troops in Vietnam, of dioxin, defective breast implants and notorious for its refusal to accept responsibility for the thousands of people killed or disabled by a toxic leak in Bhopal at the pesticide plant run by its acquired company Union Carbide in India), Goldman Sachs, military contractors and foreign governments like Saudi Arabia which, prior to 2008 when Clinton was vetted for the post of President Obama's Secretary of State, had given the foundation (which also claims it champions women's rights) donations of $10 million and $25 million. When federal law forbids direct giving to candidates for public office, a philanthropic foundation is handy. One third of all donors giving more than $1 million at a time are foreign governments.

Meanwhile, Hillary Clinton's State Department approved a slew of arms sales to foundation donors, $165 billion worth. Michael Hudson describes how it works:[206]

> Hillary's in a position to go to Raytheon, to Boeing, and say, look, do I have a customer for you. Saudi Arabia would love to buy your arms. [...] By the way, you know, my foundation is—you know, I'm a public-spirited person and I'm trying to help the world. Would you like to make a contribution to my foundation?

> Well, lo and behold, the military-industrial complex is one of the big contributors to the Clinton Foundation, as is Saudi Arabia, and many of the parties who are directly affected by her decisions.

Hence, $29 billion worth of advanced fighter jets were sold to Saudi Arabia's feudal monarchy in 2011. The philanthropists weren't going to lose any sleep over consequences their future use in Yemen (UN: "one of the world's worst humanitarian crises"). In total, it is calculated that Hillary Clinton's State Department approved $165 billion worth of commercial arms sales to twenty nations whose governments had donated to the Clinton Foundation. And this doesn't count the Department's approval of $151 billion in Pentagon-brokered deals to sixteen donor countries.

Then there was the matter of the "very transactional" Douglas J. Band, once Bill Clinton's personal assistant who, while still overseeing the Clinton Global Initiative celebrity hub (where you can buy sponsorships starting at $250,000), started a corporate consulting firm, Teneo, for which Clinton was a paid adviser. Teneo, marketing the Bill-Band relationship, sold the Clinton Foundation ("Bill Clinton Inc.") to new donors and persuaded its clients to hire the former President to give corporate speeches and serve on boards. This pay-to-play politics (in every sense: people paid to play golf with Bill) reaches into the highest levels of US foreign policy and circles of economic power. Band even got Clinton staffers to call British lawmakers "on behalf of President Clinton" asking them to help Dow Chemical when moves were made to scrap a deal in which the company was to fund an "artistic centerpiece" for the 2012 Olympic Games. Eventually—after the collapse of MF Global headed by the international derivatives broker Jon Corzine (former governor of New Jersey and CEO of Goldman Sachs) who was paying up to $125,000 per month for Teneo's public relations work—Bill Clinton ended his advisory role in March 2012. Nonetheless, Teneo clients, including

Alibaba (grabber of intellectual property rights), Dow Chemical and Coca-Cola kept receiving State Department bounty during Hillary's reign.

The most troubling stories of the foundation's initiatives are in the area of disaster capitalism, especially in Haiti after the earthquake in 2010 which killed between 220,000 and 316,000 people, injured 300,000, and displaced 1.5 million. Here it pushed the $300 million Caracol Industrial Park (launched with Sean Penn and Ben Stiller in tow and funded by, among others, USAID) where foreign-owned clothing companies can exploit Haitian labor. Caracol was supposed to provide 60,000 jobs but the net result was 1,500 jobs and hundreds of small farmers left destitute after the project took 600 acres of agricultural land. But, hey, Americans can buy $12.99 six-packs of Hanes T-shirts while the U.S. military gets uniform parts made in Haitian sweatshops.

The Clinton Foundation also set up the Haiti Development Fund, a limited-liability corporation (LLC), with an initial endowment of $20 million from the dodgy Canadian mining mogul Frank Giustra (who travelled to Kazakhstan with Bill Clinton in 2005 and, a few days later, acquired assets worth more than $3 billion in three of the country's state-run uranium mines) and Mexican billionaire Carlos Slim. Since this is a private entity it is not subject to the same disclosure laws as a charity (which are feeble enough) but neither was the fund disclosed in tax filings as an associated entity, as required by the IRS. There is nothing on the public record about what happened to the millions that were supposed to help poor Haitians.

The Clinton Foundation activities in the extraordinarily castigated country of Haiti—the only one in the world where a slave revolt led to the founding of a state, a rebellion which flew in the face of the order of empires built on slavery, colonization, subjugation and dispossession and perhaps at least partially explains why Haiti has been so maltreated, in a kind of historical vengeance—are part of an amalgam of philanthropy, humanitarian disaster relief, charity, and personal, corporate and national interest. After the earthquake the international community pledged $5.35 billion in aid. Nearly half a billion dollars from the US government went to the Defense Department. Less than 1% went to the Haitian government and almost half was not delivered at all. Haiti became a "Republic of NGOs" while versatile Bill Clinton (who ordered the 1994 invasion of Haiti and the following year forced the nation to drop tariffs on rice imported from America from 50% to 3%, thereby destroying Haitian rice farming) co-chaired the Interim Haiti Recovery Commission, a nominally Haitian government agency charged with overseeing the allocation of reconstruction money donated by foreign governments to the World Bank.

One of Clinton's successes was his deal with the Irish cell phone company Digicel which has cornered 80% of Haiti's phone market and is heavily funded by USAID for its "Haiti Mobile Money Initiative" program allowing individuals to send donations directly to friends and relatives in Haiti. Digicel is 94% owned by the Irish billionaire and official (tax-avoiding) resident of Malta, Denis O'Brien, who also happens to be chairman of the Clinton Global Initiative's Haiti Action Network and, of course, donated up to $10 million to the Clinton Foundation between 2010 and 2011, in grants more or less coinciding with speaking gigs that he arranged for his buddy Bill. A couple of months later Digicel received its first grant from USAID, which has directed some $1.3 million to Digicel and even more to the Food for Peace program by means of which the State Department distributed Digicel phones free to Haitians. Digicel then makes make money from both the U.S. taxpayer and Haitians. Predictably, its mobile banking service in Haiti also received US$2.5 million from the Bill & Melinda Gates Foundation. Money is mobile in more ways than one. It really likes revolving doors. The Clinton Foundation calls it "the power of creative collaboration."

In 2015, Bill Clinton went to Haiti for the opening of the Marriott hotel in Port-au-Prince (or "building back better," showing the world that Haiti is ready to do business). After all it was his idea, though the hotel is owned by Denis O'Brien. Digicel invested $45 million in the hotel, which also received $26.5 from the International Finance Corporation, a World Bank affiliate that offers "investment, advisory, and asset management services to encourage private sector development in developing countries." O'Brien happily tells people who ask him why a telecom company is investing in a luxury hotel that the idea came from Bill Clinton: "Let's do this together for Haiti." As the Clinton Foundation website informs the ingenuous reader, it responds "to critical needs in Haiti." One "critical need" it met in Haiti was a cushy job for Hillary's brother Tony Rodham who was appointed—by chance, we are supposed to believe—a director of the company that had acquired a lucrative gold mining contract.

Haiti aid went to foreign enterprises which provided 80% of basic services, making Haiti one of the world's most privatized countries. Private military contractors, strutting around with assault rifles also grabbed their share. The anti-governance repercussions of this are far-reaching, not least because NGOs have appropriated state powers without the slightest capacity to deal with serious problems like nation-wide emergency response, environmental protection and sewage treatment, not to mention a cholera epidemic. In September 2012, the UN Special Envoy reported that only 52.3% of the money pledged had been disbursed (which doesn't mean spent) and much of it has gone to the UN, World Bank or IDB in opaque maneuvers, while most USAID dollars went to Washington-based contractors. Instead of empowering the Haitian government to direct relief and recovery, the US military took over the country in the first weeks after the earthquake. Cheap US-grown food "aid" flooded Haiti's markets, undermining local farmers who end up in shanties that will be destroyed in the next earthquake. Constructing a clean water system, a logical way to start "building back better," was of no interest to the Clinton Foundation. What philanthropic foundations *don't* do is telling, especially when they raise vast sums of money. Worse, they don't do and they don't tell either so some, by commission or omission, get away with murder. A cover-up is a very deliberate way of not telling. Naturally, they get the highest possible rating by charity watchdogs like Charity Navigator and one with the perfect name of "cozy!" which, in 2016, gave the Clinton Foundation four out of four stars.

The kickbacks outlined here show the ways in which money and celebrity benefit from benevolence. Kimberley A. Strassel didn't mince her words when describing the Clinton Foundation as a "Hillary superPac that throws in the occasional good deed," adding that, "The media's focus is on Hillary Clinton's time as secretary of state, and whether she took official actions to benefit her family's global charity. But the mistake is starting from the premise that the Clinton Foundation is a 'charity.' What's clear by now is that this family enterprise was set up as a global shakedown operation, designed to finance and nurture the Clintons' continued political ambitions."[207]

The Clintons' tentacles stretch far and deep into nasty corners of the world's darkest, most inhuman transactions. The fact that, even so, they remain bedizened in their self-endowed probity raises hard questions not just about the nature of charity itself but how it distorts the capacity for self-knowledge, and even suggests a terrible relationship between philanthropy and sociopathy. The Clintons could not have been ignorant of the effects of their work. But Bill Clinton still had the gall to say, "We're trying to do good things…If there's something wrong with creating jobs and saving lives, I don't know what it is. […] I have nothing to say about it except that I'm really proud."[208]

Another Janus-faced philanthropist is Jeffrey Sachs, moralizing development guru, purveyor of poverty porn, superstar economist, constructor of the neoliberal system, shock-therapist destroyer of economies (Latin America, Eastern Europe and Russia), finagler of fluffy factoids (especially about over-population), charity chum of Bono, Bill Gates, Madonna and Angelina Jolie, social-engineer (trying to re-create the neoliberal market society in Africa) and, more recently, the good-guy stalwart supporter of Yanis Varoufakis in his trials with the Troika. Where humanitarianism is being wreaked, he's often in the thick of it, trying to be seen as something nicer than an economic wrecking ball loathed by the working classes of several countries. He has no expertise in medicine, public health, epidemiology, or any other form of medical knowledge. Yet, there he is, one of the supremos sorting out the global health system.

Sachs platitudinously believes in celebrity philanthropy: "In the very noisy and complicated world that we have, people that reach large numbers of people, like Madonna does, have an extraordinarily important role to play. When they're devoting their time, their money, their name, a lot of effort, a lot of organization skill to all of this, it makes a huge difference. The cynics are just wrong. They don't get it."[209]

Apart from Sachs' totalitarian methods in the Millennium Village Project (ably described from first-hand experience by Japhy Wilson in *Jeffrey Sachs: The Strange Case of Dr Shock and Mr Aid*) and his sloppy methodology when assessing his results (no control villages!), his philanthropic populism is perhaps of even more serious concern. Today Sachs is into the "economics of happiness" after discovering it in the Kingdom of Bhutan (which, in the name of an authentic Bhutanese people, expelled thousands of Nepalese who had settled there). He somehow combines market freewheeling with nostalgia for a lost community (but not the Nepalese who had settled in and were ejected from Bhutan). Sachs is not Bill Clinton but his involvement in philanthropy provides another clear illustration of the schizophrenia of doing "good" in a world you are actually making much worse. The three basic concepts of human rights, justice, freedom and human dignity, are absent and the problem with philanthropy where human rights are absent is not this or that person or foundation, but a huge charity-fraud business, influence peddling and image polishing aimed at dispossessing less fortunate humans of their rights and trying to befuddle their wits and everyone else's in a golden glow of goodness.

But, however much philanthropists try to paper over the breech between their ever-expanding wealth and their much-worked-upon generous image, they will never wholly succeed because the poor know what human rights are (in their absence) and they tend to have a better nose for bull(Soros)shit than the people who produce it.

PART 2
A PARTIAL SOLUTION

CHAPTER 9
BASIC INCOME: NOT CHARITY BUT JUSTICE

If charity is such a warped expression of benevolence that benevolence itself (as in benevolent fund or society) can be suspect, should a cash handout to the whole population with the only condition that the recipient must be a citizen or accredited resident also be viewed with a good dose of leeriness? Charity in disguise? The short answer is no. Basic income isn't charity. It's about a right, not a handout. It's concerned with justice.

However people understand it, basic income is more and more widely discussed nowadays. Even the European Parliament has noted in a Briefing of September 2016, that "[...] basic income has been attracting attention in politics, and in public opinion, in Europe and abroad." Moreover, throughout 2016 and 2017, newspapers like *The Guardian, The Wall Street Journal, The Financial Times, The New York Times* and *Le Monde* and magazines including *The Economist, Le Monde Diplomatique* and *Der Spiegel*, to cite a few of the better known sources, have devoted many pages to the subject with quite a variety of opinions. And, after 2016, in South Korea where basic income was previously totally unknown, politicians, academics and the media also began to show considerable interest. One of the candidates in the 2017 presidential elections, Lee Jae-myung, "South Korea's Bernie Sanders," included a basic income for all citizens of South Korea in his electoral platform.

Basic income is certainly a surprising, polemical and even shocking idea. Yet it is no newbie pipe dream but a proposal with a long philosophical and political tradition behind it showing that it is just, with solid economic studies demonstrating that is both attainable and sustainable. It is defined by the Basic Income Earth Network (BIEN)—an association of academics and activists founded in 1986—as a "periodic cash payment unconditionally delivered to all on an individual basis, without means-test or work requirement." It would be paid at regular intervals (for example every month) and not as a one-off grant; in an appropriate medium of exchange, allowing those who receive it to decide what they spend it on and not, therefore, paid either in kind (such as food or services) or in vouchers dedicated to a specific use; on an individual basis and not, for instance, to households; to everyone, without any means test; and without a requirement to work or to demonstrate willingness-to-work. In a nutshell, basic income has five main features. It is periodic, taking the form of a cash payment, individual, universal and unconditional.[210]

The operative word is "unconditional," a really interesting and probably the most controversial aspect of basic income. With the exponentially growing debate between the fors and againsts, the notion of unconditionality tends to polarize between being a great virtue or dangerous defect. This is the big difference with charity where the benefactor offers the recipient something, whatever, wherever, whenever and however and to whomsoever he or she pleases, usually as a one-off sop. All other aspects apart, the relevant point is that only one party, as a matter or relative privilege, arbitrarily gives (or doesn't) to another. By contrast, a basic income is a formally secular, unconditional and universal *right*, independent of all circumstances except for citizenship or resident status. Indeed, Article 1.3 of the Universal Declaration of Emergent Human Rights, Monterrey 2007 unequivocally identifies basic income as a right, "[...] that guarantees to every human being, independently of age, gender, sexual orientation, civil or employment status, the right to live in material conditions of dignity. To this end, a regular cash payment, financed by tax reforms and covered by the state budget, and sufficient to cover his or her basic needs, is recognized as a right of citizenship of every member-resident of the society, whatever his or her other sources of income may be."

As a cash payment, basic income can be disbursed by an appropriate part of the public administration. Ideally, the geographic space would be the whole planet but obviously there are still many places where people have never heard of basic income. If the community wishing to introduce this measure is small—a town for instance—there would be a problem with funding it since towns normally don't have such an abundance of financial resources or the necessary jurisdiction. Hence funding schemes tend to be at the state level because this is the domain of control of the financial resources large enough to pay for a basic income. Or, for example, if the whole of the European Union adopted a fixed basic income, it may sometimes be advisable in different countries to finance it through more than one administration, as might be the case in Germany with both federal government and the Länden contributing.

As for the BIEN definition of basic income and who would receive it, this raises the question of absolutely everyone or just adults? With regard to children receiving a basic income, there are three main answers: "yes," "no," and "yes, but not as much as adults." The first answer evidently gives minors the same status as adults, from birth and with regard to the quantity they receive. The second answer simply excludes all young people, say, under the age of eighteen. The most common answer among basic income supporters is that minors should receive it but a lesser amount than adults. What percentage of the adult payment this should be varies with the person who is answering.

At this point we'd draw attention to an important difference between basic income and conditional benefits, namely that the former is paid to individuals, always to the person and never to families or households, while the latter is nearly always paid to (usually male) household heads because, it is reasoned, the individual cost of living drops as the number of people living under the same roof rises. The cost of living for one person is less than that for five people in the same household, but not five times less. The Organization for Economic Cooperation and Development (OECD) uses an equivalence scale known as the "Oxford Scale" or the (old) OECD Scale which establishes that the first adult household member is assigned a value of 1, each additional adult 0.7, and each child (0 to 14 years) 0.5. The OECD also uses other scales such as the OECD Modified Scale, which assigns a value of 1 to the household head, of 0.5 to each additional adult member, and of 0.3 to each child.

Another concept which needs attention is that of "cash payment." Why does the basic income take this form rather than being a payment in kind? It could be another kind of currency, for example coupons for specific purposes like foodstuffs, clothes, health services or a combination of such items. This question also gives rise to debate about the compatibility or otherwise of basic income with such universal in-kind services as public health or education.

Left-wing basic income supporters tend to argue that basic income is compatible with these services, while conservative proponents of the measure usually see it as a partial or total substitution for universal in-kind services. More specifically, the ever-expanding bibliography in many languages on this issue shows quite clearly that basic income has left-wing, centrist and right-wing supporters. The infallible criterion for situating them on the ideological spectrum is how they propose to finance the basic income. The measures in the area of political economy they believe should go with the basic income are also telling. Right-wing advocates want to dismantle the welfare state (or what is left of it) in "exchange" for the basic income. This is the case with the American libertarian conservative political scientist, author and columnist Charles Murray, who argues the case for (his version of) basic income in a book whose title says it all: *In Our Hands: A*

Plan to Replace the Welfare State (2016). He wants to trim down the state (except for the courts, police and armed forces) and reduce the tax burden. In this situation where important citizen rights are taken away it might be argued that basic income moves closer to the domain of charity, as the idea behind this scheme can be summed up as "we'll keep you alive but ignorant, hogtied and dependent on our not necessarily guaranteed, private—privatized—magnanimity." Left-wing supporters advocate a redistribution of income from the rich to the rest of the population and reinforcement of other welfare provisions. A basic income mustn't entail any undermining or weakening of public services or social rights (education, health, state support for dependents, housing, and so on). On the contrary, the aim is to strengthen all of them.

In principle, a basic income in the form of legal tender offers more freedom than any in-kind payment. If consumption is limited to just a few products, then freedom of choice is evidently more restricted. If the payment is in cash, then the individual can choose whatever in-kind products or services he or she prefers. There is no Big Bro Bill Gates, or oligarchy or big transnational lurking in the background, deciding what is best for "you."

Basic income requires nothing in return unlike many conditional subsidies which stipulate that the recipient must join the job market under this or that condition, or sign an agreement to undertake training or engage in some other kind of prescribed activity. And it is precisely this unconditionality of basic income which has given rise to much criticism along the lines of "it will just encourage layabouts," "the schnorrers won't work" and so on, in the most pedantic style.

Responding to these "cultural" criticisms, the British economist Anthony Atkinson put forth the case for a "participation income," with which the unconditionality characterizing the basic income would be replaced by a flexibly defined condition of participation in certain activities.[211] Practically everyone can receive it, including wage workers, job seekers, people incapacitated by disability or illness, pensioners and retirees, geriatric and child careers, and voluntary workers. The advantage of Atkinson's proposal is that it gets around the criticism about free-loaders or that people won't want to work. But the big disadvantage is that it would need an army of controllers to supervise compliance with the conditions and, if part of the population must be excluded, however small it may be, administrative work and monitoring would be necessary to ascertain whose participation is worthy of being paid this income. The logic of the participation income would encourage small-scale fraud, such as faking engagement in activities like voluntary work, training, domestic tasks, et cetera, which would make the individual eligible for the income. The advantage of avoiding the ants and grasshoppers criticism would be more than cancelled out by a cure that is worse than the original problem.

Another burning issue: what would be a proper amount? The answers to this over the past four decades vary quite widely in accordance with the different kinds of basic income proposal being presented. One amount which has quite a lot (and a considerable variety) of supporters is at least equal to the poverty threshold. In Europe, this is defined on the basis of the median income of the population in each state, which is to say the income calculated for the person who is at the middle point of a hypothetical list of all the members of a population with regard to income. Then, the sector of the population whose income is below 60% of the median is deemed to be at risk of poverty. With the data from 2014, it is calculated that 16.3% of the population of the European Union is at risk of poverty but there are big differences between countries, ranging from between 9% and 11% in Norway, the Czech Republic and the Netherlands, more than 20% in Latvia, Estonia, Bulgaria and Greece, and with the highest percentages in the Kingdom of Spain (28%) and Romania (37.3%). The main point here is that the quantity of the basic income is as important as the way of financing it and the two aspects are inseparable. Depending on the way in which the basic income is financed, smaller quantities, rather than larger amounts, could favor lower-income people.

Some of the main criticisms of basic income are useful inasmuch as they draw attention to some of its most notable features. In the last four decades, criticisms of the measure in both academic and social circles have principally been political, economic, sociological, and philosophical. One of the main bones of contention has been the matter of work, often with arguments demonstrating that the idea of work itself is at best ill-informed and at worst iffy, thus highlighting the crucial need for more analytical, economic, political, and rigor in this domain of academic enquiry, especially now when automatization and new technologies are so drastically affecting this sphere of human existence.

At first glance, the cliché that basic income would favor and even encourage free-loading seems reasonable enough, at least intuitively, since the assumption is, if you have enough to live on, why be a wage worker? In fact, this apparently logical argument makes it essential to think about what work actually is, and to establish, first and foremost, a conceptual framework identifying three basic kinds of work: remunerated, domestic and voluntary.

In the category of remunerated work, the most important kind would certainly be wage labor. But what is this and how does it relate with basic income? In essence, wage labor in itself doesn't seek direct satisfaction of a particular need, like drinking a glass of water when you're thirsty, but it is an instrumental means for satisfying needs that are external to the work being done, things like housing, food and even leisure. Marx wrote in his *Economic and Philosophic Manuscripts* of 1844 that the alien nature of this work "emerges clearly in the fact that as soon as no physical or other compulsion exists, labor is shunned like the plague. External labor, labor in which man alienates himself, is a labor of self-sacrifice, of mortification."[212] Is this some kind of argument for a natural state of idleness in our species? A quick glance might suggest that the answer is affirmative but things are more complex than this. In 1875, in Part I of his *Critique of the Gotha Programme*, Marx elaborated on this idea: "The bourgeois have very good grounds for falsely ascribing *supernatural creative power* to labour; since precisely from the fact that labour depends on nature it follows that the man who possesses no other property than his labour power must, in all conditions of society and culture, be the slave of other men who have made themselves the owners of the material conditions of labour. He can only work with their permission, hence live only with their permission." This is the alienated labor which means that a large part of the population is unfree and has to live with the permission of others because their material existence is not guaranteed. Obviously they would shun it if they could.

Marx, a classics scholar, was well aware of what Aristotle had to say about work. The opposite of forced, external, alienated work is autotelic work, which is a source of satisfaction for the person engaging in it since it is an end or purpose in itself. This doesn't belong in the means-ends framework which is normally used to describe human activity because the reward is part of the means. It is therefore worlds apart from the usual kinds of wage labor which, with just a few exceptions, is instrumental because it is a means to acquiring indispensible resources like food, lodging and clothing and because, for most people, having paid work is the only way they can subsist. Remunerated work is also referred to as "occupation." Beyond the greater or lesser implications of the word, the pertinent point here is that it is used to denominate activity that gives access to a source of income. This source might be a salary if the recipient is engaged in an occupation which depends on another person, a payment or benefit if received from the person who owns the means of production, or a pension for a person who has retired.

In contrast with wage labor, voluntary work is autotelic, as is political participation when it is something more than merely voting for a new government every so often. But here we must distinguish, on the one hand, between bureaucrats and politicians who are paid for engaging in politics and, on the other, the political engagement for its own sake of activists and political party supporters who see this as taking part in the creating of a better society.

In their book *How Much Is Enough? Money and the Good Life*, Robert and Edward Skidelsky probe this distinction and suggest that leisure and inactivity are not only not synonymous but also antithetical. For them, leisure is an activity with no external aim or ends, or "purposiveness without purpose," as Immanuel Kant put it, in relation with his concept of freedom, a "determination of the will by reason alone." Anyone who engages in an activity—research, art, solidary work, and so on—just for the sake of doing it does so because of its own intrinsic value or its appeal to one's own reason. Naturally, research, art and solidary work (such as charitable activity) can also be done instrumentally, to earn money, put a shine on a CV, move up in a university department or enjoy higher social status, in which case the activity ceases to be autotelic. However, Robert and Edward Skidelsky make another distinction when referring to some people doing scientific or artistic work: "such people have no other aim than to do well what they are doing. They may receive an income for their efforts, but that income is not what motivates them. They are engaged in leisure, not toil."[213]

In a social situation where instrumental work preponderates and is frequently thought to be the only kind and a necessary evil, autotelic work has been much neglected as an area of study. Its possibilities for forging stronger social bonds and protecting our seriously threatened planet present a field of enquiry that demands urgent attention. In her momentous *This Changes Everything*, Naomi Klein pulls together many elements which shape the future of the planet. Concluding that there is a desperate need for valuing work we currently don't value, she specifically mentions basic income, saying, "there has to be a stronger social safety net because when people don't have options, they're going to make bad choices." For Klein, the "universal" sense of basic income is that it could help to transform the way we treat and think about our whole (social and physical) environment.[214] There can be little doubt that a basic income would favor a distribution of time in such a way that people who need to look after someone, study, paint, or rest, would have a choice in the range of activities that lie outside the realm of alienated wage labor.

Domestic work, also called "reproductive" or "care" work has a great number of definitions owing to the difficulties of encompassing all the activities entailed and the many different kinds of domestic coexistence. One of the oldest definitions comes from Margaret Reid in her pioneering work *Economics of Household Production* (1934) where she says domestic production means unpaid work carried out by and for members of the family. Interestingly, however, she focuses on activities that can be replaced by products on the market or remunerated services, when factors such as income, the market situation and consumer preferences make it possible to engage the services of others from outside the family. Nonetheless, the various definitions present a series of constants referring to caring for people—the old, the sick, the disabled and the very young—and looking after the home in order to satisfy the needs of the people living therein.

With all these different kinds of work, it is reasonable to draw the conclusion that the typical criticism claiming that nobody would work if there was a basic income usually refers to remunerated work alone. And this raises the question of what is wrong with that if wage labor is so exploitative. If the assertion embraced the three kinds of work, it would be self-contradictory because the other two main categories of work would actually be favored if basic income freed time from paid work. Many studies have shown that a lot of people would gladly do more voluntary work if remunerated work didn't take up so much of their time. This kind of economic criticism holds little water since activity without remuneration is not necessarily non-productive. Indeed, studies that calculate the economic value of domestic and voluntary work make a point of emphasizing their enormous contribution to GDP.

Yet whatever reason and logic demonstrate, and whatever all the different studies and experiments conclude, this criticism still has a powerful influence in a variety of social spheres, from workers themselves to businesspeople, trade unions, political parties and academia. A closer look at this fallacy requires that a number of factors should be taken into account and we would draw attention to three in particular. First, unlike conditional subsidies so far paid out by the different welfare states and generally incompatible with other sources of income and especially remunerated work, basic income is unconditional and hence perfectly in tune with other kinds of income which, however, might be affected by higher tax rates in accordance with the kind of basic income financing and level of income. In any case, this is preferable to the "poverty trap," a term which describes the penalization of recipients of conditional subsidies if they accept paid work, which they actually end up paying for as it means that they lose all their benefits. Despite efforts over a long time, the conditional nature of benefits has so far been a stumbling block in any attempt to solve the poverty trap dilemma. Thanks to its unconditional nature, basic income simply avoids the problem.

Second, people have all sorts of ideas about willingness or unwillingness to work but the results of three surveys conducted in Catalonia, the Basque Country and Europe have put paid to some of the sillier notions. In the Catalan study, carried out between 13 and 17 of July 2015 with 1,600 people, the question was presented as follows: "Basic income is a monthly payment of 650 euros to every member of the population as a right of citizenship and financed by means of tax reform entailing a redistribution of wealth from the richest 20% of society to the rest of the population: do you agree that it should be introduced in our country?" Result: 72.3% more or less agreed, 20.1% more or less disagreed and 7.6% did not answer. More specifically, with regard to the matter of the measure's being a disincentive to work, 86.2% of the respondents said that if they received a basic income they would keep working, the same as always. Among the unemployed respondents, 84.4 answered that they would keep looking for work just as they had been until then. Only 2.9% of all respondents said they would stop working (for a wage), and only 2.2% of the unemployed that they would stop looking for a job.

The second, unpublished, electronic survey, with 3,003 respondents, was carried out by administrative and teaching staff and also students at the University of the Basque Country. This was not a technical study with all the filters applied in the first survey and was only addressed to a very specific group of people. The employed members of that group were asked, "If you received an unconditional monthly basic income of 650 euros, would you leave your job or work fewer hours?" Only 3.5% answered that they would leave their job, a figure that tallies with the answer to the similar question in the first survey. The last, very recent survey covering the 28 states of the European Union establishes that 68% of respondents would vote in favor of a basic income (75% in Italy, 69% in the United Kingdom and Spain, 68% in Germany and 60% in France).[215]

The third and final factor is illustrated by the results of the now-classic study carried out by researchers at the University of Leuven, Axel Marx and Hans Peeters,[216] among 198 winners of the Win for Life lottery prize, consisting of a lifelong monthly payment of 1,000 euros. Their aim was to discover what the winners would do about work. Would they live on a thousand euros a month without working or would they stay in their jobs? Would they reduce their working hours or keep going as before?

In 2004, when the study was published, one of the key conclusions was that this particular kind of "basic income" would have minimal impact on the job market.

It is possible that the arguments about the poverty trap, the results of the surveys and the study about the Belgian lottery won't convince the diehards who "know" that basic income would be a serious disincentive to work. All social innovation entails risks but whether the advantages are much greater than the disadvantages must also be taken into account. In 1928, John Maynard Keynes wrote a short essay taking a long view and titled "Economic Possibilities for Our Grandchildren"[217] in which, among other considerations, he warned against the errors of political pessimism like, on the one hand, "[...] the pessimism of the revolutionaries who think that things are so bad that nothing can save us but violent change" and, on the other, the "pessimism of the reactionaries who consider the balance of our economic and social life so precarious that we must risk no experiment." Almost a century later, his words seem more germane than ever.

The basic income proposal as it is known today only goes back just over forty years but its earliest origins can be traced back to the dawn of democracy in Athens, around the sixth century BCE. One of the most important changes that occurred not long afterwards were the Ephialtes Reforms—named after one of the leaders of the radical democrats—which were introduced in 462–461 BCE. These measures gradually established a system of payment for political tasks like being a jury member in the courts or working on the council which prepared material for the Assembly. Later, in 403 BCE, the citizens of Athens were paid for the mere fact of attending the Assembly and thereby participating in the political life of the city. The payments weren't high—usually less than the salary of a craftsman—but they did mean that the poorer free citizens could have an effective role in politics if they so wished. One of the reforms, which might be seen as a distant ancestor of basic income, was the *misthos* (state salary), introduced with the idea of allowing poor free men to leave their usual work on a temporary basis in order to occupy public positions or engage in other political work. Without the *misthos*, this wouldn't have been possible and political positions would only have been open to the city's few property owners. Although the *misthos* and today's basic income are very different, in particular because the former was conceded with a view to making it possible to carry out a limited number of tasks, the similarities of their basic democratic principles are important.

Centuries later, ideas that were more or less related with that of basic income may be found in Thomas More's *Utopia* (1516), and also in the work of his contemporary, the Valencian philosopher Joan Lluís Vives (1493–1540), although their proposals clearly concerned payment linked with the requirement of some kind of activity in return rather than advocating an unconditional cash payment. More recently, and coming closer to today's concept of basic income, is the proposal of Thomas Paine, corset-maker by trade, and activist, political philosopher, and revolutionary by inclination, in his pamphlet *Agrarian Justice* (1797) where he states that poverty "is a thing created by that which is called civilized life" and in particular that, "It is a position not to be controverted that the earth, in its natural uncultivated state was, and ever would have continued to be, the common property of the human race." Accordingly, he proposed that, a National Fund should be created "[...] out of which there shall be paid to every person, when arrived at the age of twentyone years, the sum of fifteen pounds sterling, as a compensation in part, for the loss of his or her natural inheritance, by the introduction of the system of landed property: And also, the sum of ten pounds per annum, during life, to every person now living, of the age of fifty years, and to all others as they shall arrive at that age." He concluded that, "it is justice, and not charity, that is the principle of the plan."[218]

Authors who came after Paine and who are also, in one way or another, pioneers of basic income, include Thomas Spence (1750–1814), Charles Fourier (1772–1837), Herbert Spencer (1820–1903), Henry George (1839–1897) and, in the twentieth century, Bertrand Russell (1872–1970), followed in the 1960s by the British and American economists James Meade (1907–1995) and James Tobin (1918–2002), both of them Nobel laureates in Economics, in 1977 and 1981, respectively. However, none of these thinkers advocated basic income as we understand it today, even though there are evident precedents.

The 1970s and early 1980s saw more contributions, usually independent of each other. A turning point in the history, study, and popularizing of the idea of basic income came in 1986 when, two years after a group of trade unionists and researchers of Charles Fourier Collective based in the University of Louvain presented a study titled "L'allocation universelle," the university organized a congress bringing together researchers from different countries who then decided to create the Basic Income European Network (BIEN). This was a major advance. Even since then, the BIEN congress has been held every two years in different countries. The Barcelona congress in 2004 was also important for the expansion of the Network from a European to a global organization whereupon the name was changed to Basic Income Earth Network. The next congress in 2006, the first to be held outside Europe, was in Cape Town. BIEN's basic income proposal was starting to shine brighter and brighter in a dismal academic scene of anemic shopworn ideas.

It was a great idea but one that also seemed crazy or impossible to attain. Yet it is now being taken seriously by increasing numbers of academic, political and social institutions. It is still shocking for supporters or uncritical parroters of the dominant neoliberal dogma but, be this as it may, basic income has long roots in the deepest origins of Enlightenment thought and, in most cases, the reasons given for its implementation are founded in a wide range of theories of justice.

Besides the normative explanation as to why basic income is just (as we shall detail in the next chapter) and other instrumental justifications referring to the measure as a means for avoiding the poverty trap, the social, political and economic realities of these early years of the twenty-first century have now given new grounds for supporting and stressing the urgency of introducing basic income. Hence, a growing number of eminent economists, among them the former Greek Minister of Finance Yanis Varoufakis, and Robert Skidelsky, professor of Political Economy at the University of Warwick, are now saying that, given the present situation of most societies after the Great Recession of 2008, basic income should be put into effect in the very near future.

Of course, poverty is nothing new or specific to contemporary societies. In fact, it can be shown that its incidence is now less in some aspects than in previous epochs but there are also variants today which, as some experts have noted, constitute a good reason for introducing a basic income. To begin with, it is necessary to distinguish between normative and descriptive factors. The former refer to connotations of justice arising from the condition of being poor so, for example, in republican conceptions of justice a poor person who does not have guaranteed means of existence is subjugated, living in a state of dependence on others, and often relying on charity, which means that he or she is not and cannot be free. The descriptive variant requires an account of what is understood by "poverty" as the concept is used with more than one sense and, in particular, depending on the organisms which define it. So, the United Nations and the World Bank have different though not necessarily conflicting conceptions.

With regards to the effect basic income might have on poverty, there is one particularly pertinent situation, namely that of the working poor, which is to say the population that may be employed but also considered to be poor. After the industrial deregulation and destruction of the system of production of extensive geographic zones mainly in the wake of the Great Recession of 2008, combined with economic policies of cuts and austerity imposed more in the European Union than in the United States, poverty has spread into new sectors of the population, affecting people who had mostly enjoyed a relatively well-off economic position in the thirty years following the Second World War, the halcyon days of the welfare state in Europe.

At the end of the second decade of the twenty-first century, the working poor are deemed to be those people who, although they have a contract (or more than one) are still below the poverty threshold of their particular geographic area. These workers were not a very unusual phenomenon in the labor market of the United States in the last couple of decades of the twentieth century but they were not common in Europe. Things changed with the turn of the century and the data are very significant. According to Eurostat, 13.2% of workers in the EU were poor in 2015 but, only six years earlier when the crisis and the economic policies applied at the time had not yet shown their effects on the population, the figure was 8.4%. Furthermore, it must be noted that this 2015 percentage of poor workers, to which must be added self-employed people, hides big differences among the EU states. Hence, the figure for Finland, Belgium, the Czech Republic, and the Netherlands is around or below 5%, while in Greece it is above 15% and, in Romania, almost 20%.

Growing poverty in countries which are considered to be rich, as would be the case with Europe, and the particular phenomenon of the working poor, have swelled the ranks of basic income supporters, for two basic reasons. First, they argue that an income more or less the same as the amount established as the poverty threshold would automatically put an end to poverty (statistically, at least) from the moment of implementation. In other words, basic income wouldn't only be an anti-poverty measure but it would also be much more effective than conditional and targeted benefits which (supposedly) combat poverty directly. In any case, decades of experience with these benefits show that, in the best of cases, they are insufficient for the reality they are dealing with and, in the worst of cases, they accumulate insurmountable shortcomings. At this point, basic income gathers support. At the end of 2016, Yanis Varoufakis, wrote with a markedly democratic republican emphasis that, with a basic income "[...] the poor would be liberated from vicious welfare-state means testing, and a safety net that can entangle people in permanent poverty would be replaced by a platform on which they could stand before reaching out for something better. Young people would gain the freedom to experiment with different careers and to study topics that are not considered lucrative."[219]

Second, with regard to the specific reality of the working poor, a basic income of an amount more or less equal to the poverty threshold would eliminate the social stigma of targeted handouts and also permit people who presently feel obliged to accept any job under any conditions to say no. The Polish economist Michał Kalecki (1899–1970) made a major contribution to business cycle theory, in particular the concept of the "disciplinary effect" of unemployment, which has now been revived as an argument in favor of basic income. The greater the vulnerability of workers and precariousness of the job market, the greater is the inclination to accept worsening working conditions.

In the twenty-first century so far inequality has grown at a dizzying pace. In the case of income or wealth, the situation can be measured in the difference between several countries, or the inhabitants of any one country, or the richest group and the rest of the world taken as a whole. When analyzing the suitability of basic income, these three ways of measuring inequality are of interest, although the second and third are more relevant. In its 2015 report on worldwide wealth, *Global Wealth Databook*, the Credit Suisse bank noted that the richest 1% of people in the world had amassed as much wealth as the other 99%. More recently, in June 2017, Paul Buchheit wrote, "Last year it was 8 men, then down to 6, and now almost 5" who own as much wealth as half the world's population.[220]

What is the cause of these enormous inequalities? Of course, there are many factors involved but some are especially important and have more weight in the political and legal design of markets. Today's inequalities are the result of this shaping of the markets and of the economic policy implemented in recent decades. As John Kenneth Galbraith (1908–2006) pointed out in *A History of Economics: The Past as the Present* (1987), economics does not exist in isolation from politics and it is to be expected that this will continue to be the case in future. Economic policy is, first of all, political and then economic. No economic policy is neutral. It will benefit some at the expense of others. The examples are innumerable: raising or lowering taxes, freezing or increasing pensions, passing laws that ease or hinder layoffs and redundancy, imposing tariffs on imported goods, raising or lowering wages of workers in the public sector, allocating more or fewer resources to education, introducing copayment for health care, or dreaming up national budgets based on austerity in a time of galloping recession, to mention just a few. In the words of Joseph Stiglitz, the government has the power to "[...] to move money from the bottom and middle to the top, but the system is so inefficient that the gains to the top are far less than the losses to the middle and bottom."[221]

If there is confusion as to what an economic policy actually is, the same applies to "the market" and both concepts are certainly related. First of all, there is no such thing as "the" market in singular. There are many markets with very different characteristics. A flea market has little if anything to do with the finance market where debt, currency and shares are traded. What markets do have in common, however, is that they are shaped politically and are the product of state intervention through laws, rules, regulations, institutional designs and decrees. The financial markets operating in the United States under the Glass-Steagall Act which was in force from 1933 to 1999, with provisions separating commercial and investment banking, was very different from those shaped by the Gramm-Leach-Bliley (Financial Services Modernization) Act of 1999 which greatly liberalized the banking sector and was a major contributing factor in the subprime mortgage meltdown.

As Linda McQuaig and Neil Brooks point out, the market is as much a child of the state as the taxation system is, adding that, "The market is nothing but a complex web of government interventions."[222] So, the political shaping of the job market, for example, will determine whether there will or will not be a minimum wage, free dismissal and other more or less harsh stipulations. Similarly, political preference can, by means of passing and applying a law, allow or not allow monopolies or oligopolies to exist in certain markets.

It's interesting to see that the people who justify the existence of today's huge inequalities say they are worth it because they make possible all kinds of contributions and innovations that are beneficial to "society." If people are very rich, it's because they deserve to be because of their efforts, talents, and originality and, so the argument goes, their skills and creativity change the lives of many people for the better and they should therefore be paid sums of money way above the norm. It's all about merit. The idea of the so-called self-made (wo)man becomes more and more commanding as extreme inequality becomes even more extreme in rich societies.

McQuaig and Brooks note that, "In fact, entrepreneurs make up a very small proportion of today's top earners, estimated at less than 4 per cent. Today's super-rich elite is composed mostly of corporate and financial professionals, who account for some 60 percent of those in the top-earning 0.1 per cent (with lawyers and real-estate developers accounting for another 10 per cent)."[223] And, rather than being earned through innovation or benefitting society, this incredible wealth comes from rent-seeking and parasitic rentierism. Rent-seeking money-grubbing produces no additional wealth since it is a mechanism by means of which money simply changes hands, which can be done through laws and other facilities conceded by governments.

The rich have grabbed a lot of income from the rest of the population thanks to laws that they have managed to push through, at least in part by means of countless lobbyists who work closely with legislators to this end. For example, the banking sector earmarks about $1,200 million a year for an army of 1,700 lobbyists to pressure EU legislators in Brussels to look after their interests. A machine that can exert pressure in order to ensure that legislation of financial markets will be as beneficial as possible for them is very powerful indeed, and certainly a lot more influential than pensioners queuing at the bank to get their money at the end the month. The present political configuration of the markets clearly explains why the rich get richer, even more than they did before the onset of the Great Recession of 2008, while most of the population gets poorer.

With a basic income financed by way of a tax reform that would entail a redistribution of wealth from the richest segment to the rest of the population the levels of inequality would be reduced, as indicators like the Gini coefficient show. Nevertheless, the basic income would be an element of economic policy but not economic policy in itself. There are other factors which would have to be dealt with by any economic policy aiming to reduce inequality, among them tax havens, tax evasion and fraud.

When thinking about the future, we have to consider another urgent matter, namely automatization of work, which also involves the issues of wage labor and the meaning of leisure in present-day societies. And then there are the standpoints of feminism, unionism and ecology. It's also essential to examine both right and left political positions in defense of basic income and whether they have anything in common because, while they may sound similar, they can be very different from both the economic and political points of view. And with people like Elon Musk and Mark Zuckerberg suddenly discovering the potential of basic income (this being hailed by many mindless, blinded-by-celebrity supporters as a good thing) the distinction is increasingly important. How is it possible that upholders of neoliberal economic policy like Milton Friedman and declared adversaries of the same policies support basic income? Is that really the case?

The future augurs an imminent overwhelming presence of driverless cars and trucks, 3D printing, nanotechnology and biotechnology, artificial intelligence, and the ascendancy of digitalization in almost every sphere of everyday life. In 2016, Yanis Varoufakis wrote that this means "[...] the rise of machines that, for the first time since the start of industrialization, threaten to destroy more jobs than technological innovation creates—and to pull the rug out from under the feet of white-collar professionals."[224] His is just one of the many warnings from eminent economists about the effects of automatization. The World Economic Forum is also "concerned" (from its Davos perspective), as reflected in its 2016 report titled *The Future of Jobs* where it discussed the social impact of the "Fourth Industrial Revolution" in which millions of jobs will be made redundant by the new technology. And then there's Mark Zuckerberg, whose Facebook takes aggressive measures to minimize its tax burdens. He sees basic income as an entrepreneurial thing and a replacement for public services: "It comes from conservative principles of smaller government, rather than progressive principles of a larger safety net."[225] There are rumors abounding that he has his sights set on the White House. May we be spared from his version of "basic income."

More and more people are considering basic income as a measure that will make it possible to confront not only the imminent automatization of many jobs but also how to deal with the free time liberated by this and its consequences. Automatization could very well become either hell on earth for millions of people losing their means of existence, or a chance to live more freely and much more creatively if a basic income guaranteed the material existence of the whole population. As Aristotle put it, "[...] no man can live well, or indeed live at all, unless he is provided with necessaries."[226] These words have taken on tremendous urgency in this second decade of the twenty-first century. In 1930, John Maynard Keynes predicted that a century later, thanks to increased productivity and all the benefits that would bring for our species, the working week would be cut to fifteen hours. Little could he imagine that, since then, the working week has been reduced by twenty percent, at most.

The future of basic income depends, to a great extent, on how it is accepted and supported by individuals and groups like trade unions, social movements, feminism and ecologists. The more it is advocated by people from these sectors, the closer it will be to the majority of the rest of the population who will also support it. But basic income has not been very well accepted by trade unionists, except for a few notable exceptions like Unite, Britain's biggest trade union, some leaders of the biggest American federation of trade unions AFL-CIO, the Basque union Ezker Sindikalaren Konbergentzia, and others. The main objection is based on a fear that most union members, consisting of workers with stable contracts for full-time jobs and relatively well paid (or less badly paid than the average worker, to be more exact) will end up losing economically because of the tax reforms required to finance a basic income. It is also argued that union power will be undermined because a basic income would strengthen individual bargaining power at the expense of collective action, and some keep chewing the old chestnut that all versions of basic income are a pretext to dismantle the welfare state, especially in the areas of education and public health. Another claim is that a basic income will partially cover pay, so employers will try to cut workers' salaries, an argument which, oddly enough, has been wielded against the national minimum wage in countries like Italy, Cyprus, Denmark and Sweden where it has not been introduced. However, this view is not only *not* shared by unionists in states where this does exist but is fiercely rebutted. The underlying contention (situation X will automatically get worse if remedy Y is introduced) simply doesn't hold empirical water.

Basically, the notion that basic income is hostile to the culture of employment has predominated in trade union circles where rights are seen as derived directly or indirectly from a working life. Related with this is the assertion that basic income uncouples material existence from employment and all its associated rights. Philippe Martínez, Secretary-General of the French Confédération Générale du Travail (CGT) puts this clearly enough:[227] "We believe that work structures life, that it's a place of socialization, of social relations and something which saves people from being isolated or disappearing, as long as the working conditions are decent. This is why we have some doubts about Basic Income."

The logical response to such arguments is that the number of wage workers without full-time or stable contracts is rising all the time. Worse, the stable contract, once called a "permanent contract," is now a more or less token arrangement between employer and worker. Except for some civil servants, hardly anyone has a "permanent" contract, understood as "secure." Opposition to basic income by the few workers who enjoy relatively well-paid contracts shouldn't distract from the huge numbers of people with precarious contracts or zero job security who would undoubtedly benefit from the measure. Then again, it is true that with a basic income the individual worker's bargaining power would be stronger, making it possible to leave the job market when working conditions are deemed to be abusive. But the enhanced individual negotiating power doesn't mean that collective bargaining power would be undermined. As more than a few unions have seen, in an extended strike a basic income could act as a kind of resistance fund.

To sum up, basic income is neither incompatible nor opposed to employment since it holds out a flexible way of sharing work and for wage workers putting in long hours it would hold out better chances of having an easier timetable. As Philippe van Parijs points out:[228]

> [Basic Income] provides a flexible, intelligent form of job sharing. It makes it easier for people who work too much to reduce their working time or take a career break. It enables the jobless to pick up the employment thereby freed, the more easily as they can do so on a part-time basis, since their earnings are being added to their basic income. And the firm floor provided by the basic income makes for a more fluid back and forth between employment, training and family that should reduce the occurrence of burnout and early retirement, thus enabling people to spread employment over a longer portion of their lives.

Another highly significant area of the basic income debate is feminism, in all its variations, where a wide range of philosophical and political ideas are expressed in pro and con positions. One often heard objection is that basic income would once again confine many women to the home since, if a woman has money in this form, she would no longer need to look for work outside the domestic sphere and would therefore be under pressure to become a housewife. Other feminists assert that women would gain more than men given that, on average, they are paid less for doing the same work. Indeed, they would enjoy freedom they don't have now in being freed from economic dependence on their menfolk.

Furthermore, many women who are victims of domestic violence are economically dependent on the men who abuse them: in fact, twice as many women who don't go out to work compared with women who do. These women usually can't make the decision to separate because of their dependence on men. Aware of this injustice, some feminist scholars have recalled the argument of Mary Wollstonecraft more than two centuries ago, in her *A Vindication of the Rights of Women* (1792), pointing out that rights, citizenship and a better status for women, both married and single, required their economic independence, and they see basic income as a way of ensuring this often life-saving independence.

Basic income is also a good answer to the need for social policy to adapt to changes in types of cohabitation and especially single-parent families headed by women. Since it is an individual payment, basic income would improve the economic situation, and therefore independence, of a lot of married women or those who are cohabiting in the poorer sectors of society. Nowadays, a good part of conditional benefits are paid out to the family as the unit of allocation. The veteran British feminist Carole Pateman[229] is clear on this point: "A basic income is important for feminism and democratization precisely because it is paid not to households but individuals as citizens." The economic independence afforded by basic income would mean that it would be a kind of domestic counter-power working against gender-based relations of domination and giving women a stronger negotiating status, especially those receiving very low wages or depending on a male partner. And, as many feminists have shown in recent decades, the social security systems constructed in the wealthier countries after World War II were designed in keeping with the assumption that women were economically dependent on their husbands, which meant that any benefits they received from the system were thanks to their husbands and unrelated with their position as citizens. In the situation where the stereotype of the man as the head of the household is increasingly challenged, it wouldn't be rash to imagine that, with a basic income, the distribution of domestic work could be much more democratic than it has been hitherto.

Basic income has always been positively received by ecologists who are well known for their rejection of the establishment notion of "growth" as an adequate response to the poverty and unemployment which are now afflicting people all over the world. Since, by definition, basic income uncouples the notions of income and employment, environmentalists see it as a possible way of countering uncontrolled destructive growth. Philippe van Parijs and Yannick Vanderborght, both ecologically sensitive basic income theorists, write that, "Basic income would make it possible to prevent never-ending productivity from essentially bringing about a widening of consumption or from creating involuntary unemployment on an enormous scale which, ecologist or not, no party that calls itself progressive can accept. The fact that basic income would operate as a mechanism for flexible distribution of available employment would allow us to nourish some hopes here."[230]

Along similar lines, the ecologist Florent Marcellesi, member of the European Parliament from the Group of the Greens, wrote an article with the significant title "Una renta básica de ciudadanía para vivir mejor con menos" (Basic Income of Citizenship to Live Better with Less)[231] in which he says, "Basic income can be understood as one of the engines of improved social and environmental justice, an ecological restructuring of the economy, and promotion of the autonomous sphere." In brief, a good part of ecological thinking sees basic income as a tool for opting for non-material wealth since wellbeing is not conceived as being synonymous with consumerism, which is how it is presented by productivism. For many ecologists like Marcellesi, basic income is a "[...] direct allowance to foster activities that, once deemed to be non-productive or as not belonging to the heteronomous sector, are essential sources of social and ecological wealth. By means of basic income political ecology would construct a plural economy, leaving more and more space for non-commercial, social and ecologically useful production, for cooperation instead of competition, for free, non-instrumental activity, a reduction of working time, and care of the environment, which is to say, an economy on the human scale and respectful of the biosphere."

Although basic income has been welcomed by activists from the different social movements, this doesn't mean that acceptance has been unanimous or even majority. Perhaps the best known case in international terms is Spain's 15-M anti-austerity movement which, in 2011, saw hundreds of thousands of people occupying the streets and squares of many cities around the country. On the first anniversary of the movement, five essential demands were made and basic income was one of them. Consequently, basic income attracted the attention of a great number of people who, previously, never knew it existed.

This generalized interest in the measure has highlighted a situation that seems to have been ignored when basic income was striving to gain support and was not so carefully scrutinized. We refer to the fact that there are notions and versions of basic income which not only differ considerably but also clash. Schematically, some are on the political and economic right, some occupy some kind of middle ground, and others are clearly left, and easily distinguished, as we have noted, by the way they propose to finance the basic income. So Milton Friedman, Nobel laureate and one of the world's most influential economists in the last three decades of the twentieth century wanted to dismantle the welfare system by way of a negative income tax (NIT) whereby people earning below a certain amount would receive a supplemental payment from the government instead of paying taxes. His idea was the NIT could replace the usual benefits offered by the welfare state. The NIT had been formulated by other economists but Friedman and James Tobin were the ones who pushed it beyond the confines of academia.

Some neoliberal economists are beginning to accept that, given the gigantic structural changes occurring in the present-day economic model, basic income might be inevitable. They are therefore pushing a project consisting of two fronts. First, they would link the introduction of basic income with tax exemption and dismantling the welfare state, so that basic income would be reduced to a kind of universal check for buying on the market the former, newly privatized public services. Second, they want labor deregulation which would make the general employment scene even more precarious than it already is.

The left-wing concept of basic income aims at a redistribution of income from the richest members of society to the rest of the population and maintaining and, indeed, strengthening the welfare state. Basic income would then be of real benefit to citizens who have least. It would not be—as it is in the right-wing version—merely a cheaper, economically streamlined welfare system (though, with a different emphasis, it could be cheaper and more efficient in the left-wing version). Besides a financing policy that, with a highly progressive redistribution of income, clearly favors the less affluent citizens, left-wing supporters envisage a sweeping package of measures including a reduction in working hours, decent wages and working conditions in all sectors, active policies and support for additional selected kinds of employment for disadvantaged groups, better distribution between genders, and generation of all kinds of work. These are by no means Luddite positions, and neither are they against technological advances as long as they respect the planet, with growth and degrowth where appropriate. Hence, production growth rates and costs would no longer be standard indicators of wellbeing.

It is significant that the evident tension between the very different basic income proposals should have reached such an extreme that, at the last BIEN Congress, held in Seoul in June 2016, the organization which brings together scholars and activists of a wide variety of ideological hues, decided with a comfortable majority that so much ambiguity was no longer acceptable. Where the original definition described basic income as "an income unconditionally granted to all on an individual basis, without means test or work requirement," the addition in the new, ambitious version in the amended statutes reads, "[...] stable in size and frequency and high enough to be, in combination with other social services, part of a policy strategy to eliminate material poverty and enable the social and cultural participation of every individual. We oppose the replacement of social services or entitlements, if that replacement worsens the situation of relatively disadvantaged, vulnerable, or lower-income people."

Arthur C. Clarke once wrote,[232] "Every revolutionary idea seems to evoke three stages of reaction. They may be summed up by the phrases: (1) It's completely impossible. (2) It's possible, but it's not worth doing. (3) I said it was a good idea all along." Maybe basic income has already entered the third stage. In any case, history shows that the idea of justice is embedded in human DNA. Most people know what it is in the pain of its absence and they are the ones constantly seeking it. Basic income is the best chance they have today. But, knowing the revolutionary potential of the quest for justice, the Davos people will be doing their best to smother it with their own distorted, counterrevolutionary "charitable" version.

CHAPTER 10
JUSTICE AND HOW TO FINANCE IT

In any normative discussion about basic income, the key word is justice, which then signals that charity, as an unequal relationship by definition, is a bedfellow of injustice. This first, rudimentary, approximation to the different realms inhabited by charity and basic income is especially important when some of basic income's newer extremely wealthy enthusiasts like Mark Zuckerberg and Sir Richard Branson now seem to be promoting it (both with pronouncements about how tech will replace jobs) as a way of conserving the unjust status quo, just as charity, humanitarianism and philanthropy have been used through the ages to do the same. This confuses the basic income debate even more, because their newfound enthusiasm for basic income leads some people on the left to think that basic income is just a "philanthropic" way of underpinning the most rampant capitalism, while others use such celebrities to justify their right-wing versions. Very rich people tend to push the notion of meritocracy as deservingness, which they equate with justice so, therefore, there is nothing unjust about their wealth, even while they are constantly flaunting their bloated Ayn-Randian sense of entitlement in their lifestyle, political power and high-handed pronouncements, which often take a philanthropic form.

Since justice is so central to our democratic republican conception of basic income, then some—albeit far too brief because this would be a book in itself—discussion of the concept is required, starting with theories of justice and, in particular, those of the academic liberal ilk which are also the basis of the academic fad of altruism. The word "liberalism" opens the way to a great number of distinctions, divisions and subdivisions but the fundamental one and most pertinent here is that between political and academic liberalism. The former, mythology aside, is just over two centuries old, having existed through the nineteenth and twentieth centuries and thus far into the twenty-first. As for the latter, rather than being any clear kind of discipline, it is a hotchpotch embracing hard, center and moderate left authors, including libertarians, egalitarians and propietarians, *inter alia*.[233] What they have in common, according to Philippe Van Parijs, is "nondiscrimination among conceptions of the good life."[234]

For historical republicanism this point—and, in particular, the allied notion of state "neutrality"—is and always has been fundamental. For a liberal, this means that the state doesn't favor certain conceptions of the good life, which must be a matter of personal choice.[235] Hence, academic liberal theories of justice are considered to be neutral in this regard. Any theory of justice that opted for and rewarded a specific form of the good life would be "perfectionist." We don't think this is very helpful except in a few secondary matters. For the historical republican tradition, the really interesting point is different. To begin with, state neutrality is a very old idea: "[...] a characteristically republican invention at least as old as Pericles,"[236] but the truly far-reaching aspect is that while the state must respect whatever different conceptions of the good life the citizens may embrace, it is also *obliged* to interfere in order to destroy or limit the economic or institutional base of any person, corporation or private group that threatens to successfully dispute the republican state's right to determine what is in the public interest.

If a private power is so influential that it can impose its will (its conception of private good) on the state, it would mean that the state has *de facto* been stripped of its neutrality. Then a large part of the population (obviously depending on the case in question) is willy-nilly affected by this conception of private good. The republican conception of state neutrality consists precisely in the state's being able to intervene to prevent such an imposition. Two examples offered by Bertomeu and Domènech are sufficient to make this point clear. "[T]he Weimar Republic was fighting for the neutrality of the state when it fought, and eventually succumbed to, the great *Kartells* of German industry that financed Hitler's rise to power; the North-American republic was fighting—without success—for the neutrality of the state when it tried to rein in what Roosevelt called the "economic monarchs" with the Antitrust Laws of 1937 [...]."[237]

The problem of state neutrality for the republican tradition is not whether one should respect a conception of the good life which, for example, might consider that it consists in repeated reading of H. P. Lovecraft's novels combined with almost uninterrupted listening to John Lennon, and whether such a conception should be protected by the state. It should, of course, be respected. The problem is whether, for example, the material existence of an individual or group of people depends on the investment plans of a transnational company; or whether the energy resources of a whole country should be at the disposition of the boards of directors in a handful of powerful companies; or whether the dogmas of some religions can lead to the expropriation of the conditions of material existence of any particular group of people.

In the strict historical sense, political liberalism was born in the Cadiz Cortes (1812),[238] the first national assembly to claim sovereignty in Spain, after which it spread around the world. Since it is just over two centuries old, it is not exactly accurate to present as liberals John Locke (d. 1704), Adam Smith (d. 1790) and Immanuel Kant (d. 1804)—and some would even include Maximilien Robespierre (d. 1794)—who could hardly be proponents of something that hadn't been invented in their lifetimes. Taking, outside any temporal context, the vague definition, "A liberal is a man who believes in liberty," those who would dub these four thinkers as liberals would seem to be more interested in shackling radical republican liberty in liberal chains than in historical veracity. Analyzing the historical role of political liberalism and its enmity toward democracy, freedom and equality is an important and still pending task for historians.

Republicanism is our main concern here, though, and we'll limit our discussion to two variants coming under the heading of historical republicanism: oligarchic and democratic.[239] To be fair, we should also mention, at least in passing, the fairly influential version known as academic neorepublicanism, with Philip Pettit, Quentin Skinner, and J. G. A. Pocock as its outstanding theorists, but this lies beyond the scope of our present concerns.[240]

Republicanism goes back more than 2,000 years. In its democratic plebeian version, it is associated with names like Ephialtes (?–461 BCE), Pericles (495–429 BCE), Protagoras (485–411 BCE) and Democritus (470/460–370/360 BCE) and, in the antidemocratic kind, with Aristotle (384–322 BCE) and the emphatically oligarchic Cicero (106–43 BCE). One way or another, both variants have endured until today. The democratic type aspires to the universalization of republican freedom with the consequent inclusion as citizens of the poor majority and even government by them, while antidemocratic republicanism seeks to protect the monopoly of power of the rich and to exclude poor, non-proprietor workers from political and civil life. Names that can be related with the modern renaissance of republicanism include Marsiglio da Padova (?–1342), Machiavelli (1469–1527), Montesquieu (1689–1755), Locke (1632–1704), Rousseau (1712–1778), Kant (1724–1804), Smith (1723–1790), Jefferson (1743–1826), Madison (1751–1836), Robespierre (1758–1794), and Marx (1818–1883).

Athens in the year 461 BCE was not only a forum in which the politics and philosophy of democratic republicanism was discussed but also a testing ground for its principles in the form of a program that included redistribution of land, suppression of debt slavery, and (male) universal suffrage with sufficient remuneration (*misthos*) for elected office-holders. For the Greeks at the time, democracy meant government by poor (free) men, as

Aristotle clearly describes in *Politics* and, moreover, after 461 BCE women and slaves enjoyed the right of free speech in the agora.

Whatever the differences expressed by republican thinkers over time, they agree on at least two principles. First, that being free means not having to ask the permission of another person to live, survive or exist socially. Any person who depends on another in this regard is subject to arbitrary interference and is therefore not free. And a person who doesn't have this "right of existence" guaranteed because of lack of property is not a citizen in his or her own right—*sui iuris*—but lives at the mercy of others and is not capable of cultivating and, still less, exercising civic virtue because this dependence on another party subjects him or her to an alien regime—*alieni iuris*—thus making of him or her, to all intents and purposes, an "alien."

Second, republican freedom can extend to the many (the plebeian democracy advocated by democratic republicans) or the few (the plutocratic form of the oligarchic republicans) but it is always based on property and the material independence deriving from that. This freedom can't be sustained if property ownership is so unequal and so polarized in its distribution that only a handful of individuals is in a position to challenge the republic, successfully overcoming any opposition from the citizenry so as to impose its own conception of the public good. As Machiavelli pointed out, when most property is held by a clique of *gentilhuomini* there is no space left for establishing any kind of republic, and the only hope in political life remains at the discretion of some absolutist prince.

Like democratic republicanism, the oligarchic (antidemocratic) republican tradition recognized that property is the condition of freedom but opposed universalizing property. Accordingly, it claims that non-proprietors can't be citizens, while democratic republicanism insists that every person should have the means to be materially independent and thus to be able to participate as citizens. Property, then, is essential in both main variants of the republican tradition. The definition of property which has triumphed today and has served as the foundation on which many liberal and libertarian philosophers have constructed their doctrinal corpus, is that offered by William Blackstone (1723–1780), for whom it was "that sole and despotic dominion which one man claims and exercises over the external things of the world, in total exclusion of the right of any other individual in the universe."[241] This is the concept liberalism has embraced.

This may be only one of the historical concepts of property but it is very important since it constitutes the basis of a good part of present-day civil law,[242] although it can also be traced back to Roman civil law. Yet, as we say, it's not the only kind of property. Another kind is property understood as "control" over a resource, thus conferring material independence, and this is the kind that interests republicanism because the independence bestowed by property is not merely a private matter but one of great political importance because having an assured material base is indispensable for both one's own independence and the exercise of political power.

There is a sharp, not to say shocking, contrast between Blackstone's "sole and despotic dominion" and property as understood by Maximilien Robespierre[243] who, in a speech before the Convention on 24 April 1793 summarizes what property should be in the following articles:

> Article 1. Property is the right of every citizen to enjoy and dispose of the portion of goods that is guaranteed by law.
>
> Article 2. The right to property is limited, as are all other rights, by the obligation of respecting the rights of others.
>
> Article 3. Property cannot jeopardize the security, liberty, existence or property of others.
>
> Article 4. Any possession or any kind of commerce that violates this principle is illicit and immoral.

Compare this way of understanding property with that of his contemporary, Dupont de Nemours (1739–1817): "It is evident that the proprietors, without whose permission nobody could find lodgings and maintenance in all the country, are citizens *par excellence*. They are the sovereigns by the grace of God and nature, their work, their investments and the work and investments of their forbears."[244] Dupont de Nemours was a famous Thermidorian who founded the company that would bear his name to the present day, now as a giant chemicals and "healthcare" multinational.

The relationship between property and freedom in this tradition revolves around the central thesis that individuals can't be free if their material existence is not politically guaranteed. So, the problem of freedom can be synthesized as we'll now outline. X is free in social life if (a) he or she does not depend on any other person in order to live, which is the same as saying that X's social life is guaranteed if he or she has some kind of property that furnishes a reasonable level of subsistence; (b) nobody can arbitrarily (in other words, illicitly or illegally) interfere in the autonomous sphere of social existence (in the property) of X. This also means (c) that the republic can lawfully interfere in X's sphere of autonomous social existence as long as the republican citizen is in a political relationship of equality with all the other free citizens of the republic and is therefore equal before the law being applied, which he or she has equally codetermined with the other citizens, with equal possibilities of protesting against it and of codetermining a different law that abolishes the one presently being enforced by the government; (d) that any interference (from an individual, several people or the republic as a whole) in the sphere of X's private social existence that damages it to the point of making X lose his or her social autonomy, leaving him or her at the mercy of other parties, is illicit; (e) that the republic is obliged to interfere in the sphere of X's private social existence if this private sphere enables X to successfully dispute with the republic the right to define the public good, which is to say, the guarantee of republican freedom to all members of the polity; and, finally, (f) that X is secure in his or her civic-political freedom because of a—more or less extensive—hard core of *constitutive* (and not purely instrumental)[245] rights that nobody can appropriate. Any attempt by X willingly to alienate (sell or give away) these rights would mean losing his or her condition as a free citizen.[246]

To sum up, if oligarchic and democratic republicanism coincide in their conception of freedom, namely that individuals can't be free if their material existence is not assured, they differ over what portion of the population can enjoy this guarantee. For the oligarchic variety, the fortunate free individuals are those who possess some kind of property, some set of resources, which allows them to be independent while, for democratic republicans, all men and women in the community must enjoy freedom and must therefore have their material existence politically guaranteed.

Republicanism doesn't understand equality as equality of resources but, rather, as reciprocal freedom. Hence, equality or reciprocity in the exercise of freedom appears in a society whose political institutions recognize the civil equality of all its members and thus confers on everyone the status of a materially independent social actor. Individual freedom is limited by arbitrary interference, but it's evident that some kinds of interference are normatively more relevant than others when it comes to understanding how present-day social institutions act and attempting to prescribe how they should act. Some kinds but not others are intimately linked with basic mechanisms that govern the dynamics of human societies. Class struggle is one example. Or lies or scams are arbitrary interferences that can have negative effects in the lives of people affected by them, but the structure of contemporary societies is not based on lies and scams (though in the form of fake news it could be argued they are playing a more important role these days) but on property rights. So we would venture that the main distinction that should be made in any effort to understand society today is that between rich and poor and this, in the republican tradition, has been understood since Aristotle's times, as "independent people" of guaranteed material existence and "dependent (on others) people" who don't have a guaranteed material existence. And this is where charity comes in, shoring up the idea that it's okay for people to be dependent as long as the rich give them a few crumbs from their table from time to time. In normative terms, the distinction between independent and dependent people is more relevant for calibrating the scope of freedom than, for example, using income levels to talk about the differences between rich and poor.

Nowadays, in order to survive, poor people usually have to sell themselves, five days a week or more, to owners of material resources in order to receive some kind of salary. In today's capitalist societies, individuals or groups—especially transnational companies and their owners—possessing vast material resources are therefore able to interfere arbitrarily with the set of opportunities of millions of people. They can shape the structure of markets and condition the nature of entire economies. They can impose in productive units the working conditions of people who depend on them in order to live. They can dispossess millions of people in both rich and poor countries of the means necessary to sustain traditional forms of life or alternative ways of managing the productive sphere. And, finally, they can influence the political agenda and decision making. In his 1935 State of the Union Address, none other than President Franklin Delano Roosevelt gave an unambiguous modern-day version of what Aristotle, Cicero and Robespierre had taught: "[...] Americans must forswear that conception of the acquisition of wealth which, through excessive profits, creates undue private power over private affairs and, to our misfortune, over public affairs as well." Or as Louis D. Brandeis, associate justice of the

U.S. Supreme Court, reputedly noted about a hundred years ago: "We must make our choice. We may have democracy, or we may have wealth concentrated in the hands of a few, but we can't have both."[247]

Since basic income is universal and unconditional in its conception, then democratic republicanism is the logical framework for its normative justification. No other measure in modern times has pondered guaranteeing the material existence of entire populations. As we have said, the independence, material existence or autonomous base—straightforwardly interchangeable terms—conferred by property is the indispensable condition for the exercise of freedom, which is why republican supporters of basic income speak metaphorically of "universalizing property." With this it is understood that a basic income at or above the poverty line is a way of universalizing property in order to guarantee the material existence of everyone. The socioeconomic independence this would give to all individuals is a guarantee that they will be free of the humiliations of public and private charity and the arbitrary power of employers, which is to say property owners.

As we have described in Chapter 9, among the groups that would most benefit from the freedom opened up by basic income are women, for whom a basic income would represent a kind of domestic counter-power; young people who are often obliged to accept insulting wages and terrible working conditions; people who wish to engage in voluntary, non-remunerated work; workers subjected to conditions of semi-slavery thanks to what Michał Kalecki called the "disciplinary effect" of unemployment (which is now so crushing that some establishment economists are smugly decreeing "better a bad job than none at all"); strikers who would have a sort of fallback position or resistance fund; and people who feel stigmatized by welfare system benefits (where they exist). Self-fulfillment could come hand in hand with improved social relations, because, in the absence of domination in so many spheres of existence, opportunities for community endeavors and social activity would expand.

Security of economic resources would empower individuals to reject, in certain circumstances and in keeping with their own desires, certain conditions of work. It is usually considered desirable to have a contract of employment, but this still denotes, in both inception and operation, a relationship of economic dependence and social subordination because inequality of bargaining power is built into the relationship, however much the contract devised by legal minds contrives to conceal this fact. In Roman law the *locatio conductio operarum* was a contract of service in which the parties had to agree that services would be rendered (*operae*) and the remuneration to be paid. Another kind of contract, the *locatio conductio operis*, means that a person (the *operis*, say a silversmith) undertakes to perform or execute a particular piece of work. The former, then, means that one person engages another for an indeterminate period of time during which the contracted person must do any job he or she is ordered to do, a degrading situation because it undermines freedom, while the *locatio conductio operis* better respects the worker's dignity because it concerns a specific service supplied by someone in a certain category (let's say a dyer or a tanner).

It's important, in this regard, to highlight the fact that, in the words of Antoni Domènech, "The relevant sphere of interference is *institutionally* characterized (not only psychologically) and is related with the material and moral bases of X's autonomous social existence and also the material and moral bases of his or her possible dominators. Any arbitrary interference by Z in the set of X's opportunities which have nothing to do with the bases of his autonomous social existence can be aesthetically lamentable, or morally reprehensible but it is *politically* irrelevant. [...] It is not irrelevant if Z can dispose of X at whim, even if only for some hours a day because X is *institutionally* obliged to accept this in order to subsist because of lacking his or her own means of existence that would guarantee a separate, autonomous social life which does not crucially depend on other individuals."[248] For Cicero, in his *De Officiis* (*On Obligations*), making one's labor power available for exploitation on such general terms in exchange for a salary is the same as entering into a bond of servitude, and this is almost identical to what Aristotle had called "limited slavery" two centuries earlier.

It's interesting to see that, on this point, the staunch oligarchic republican Cicero affirms in his *De Officiis*, that the general availability of an individual to work for another for a wage is servitude, and that another unquestionable republican, John Locke, noted in his *Second Treatise on Government* that "[...] a free man makes himself a servant to another by selling him for a certain time the service he undertakes to do in exchange for wages he is to receive [...]."[249]

The true political sense of a measure like basic income lies in its recognition of the power relations which pervade social life. These are the relations that explain the "decision" of a worker to sign "service contracts" (although the widespread more accurate expression nowadays is "shit contract"). In an article defending basic income, Philip Pettit puts it neatly and we couldn't agree more:

> Suppose there are just a few employers and many available employees, and that times are hard. In those conditions I and those who like me will not be able to command a decent wage: a wage that will enable us to function properly in society. And in those conditions it will be equally true that we would be defenseless against our employers' petty abuse or their power to arbitrarily dismiss us. Other protections, such as those that strong trade unions might provide, are possible against such alien control. But the most effective of all protections, and one that should complement other measures available, would be one's ability to leave employment and fall back on a basic wage available unconditionally from the state.[250]

If we have shown in normative terms that basic income is a just measure, the next step is the practical one of demonstrating that it is financially feasible. It wouldn't be very helpful to prove that a measure is impeccably just if it was impossible to implement it in practice. Fortunately, this isn't the case. Then again, given the technocratic, quick-fix mindset of late capitalist society, this aspect has received a great amount of attention by critics and supporters alike, so it's also necessary to separate the chaff from the grain. The last three decades have seen several different proposals for financing basic income. Over time, they have become more sophisticated, to such an extent that, in retrospect and with the knowledge we have now, some of the early efforts look quite shoddy, either because they are incompetent in technical terms or because they belong in the realm of cloud-cuckoo-land. However, some very sound schemes have appeared in recent years, most of them considering a system of financing in which a country or a larger geographic area is the unit of operation.

One example dates from the 1990s and suggests a basic income of some €1,500 per year on the European scale by means of a tax, also European-wide, on polluting sources of energy—mainly fossil fuels—after a study assessing the costs to the environment of their use. This suprastate basic income would then be combined with the welfare services offered by the different European states. Another financing scheme has been put forth by Philippe Van Parijs, who calls it the "eurodividend." This consists of a basic income introduced for the European Union as a whole but adjusted to the cost of living in the various states. The exact amount to be paid has changed over time but Van Parijs suggests approximately €200 per month in the richer states and a smaller quantity in those that are less rich, to be financed by part of the VAT collected in them European Union.

Both these Europe-wide proposals specify quantities that are significantly below the poverty threshold, even in the poorer countries. Their supporters therefore speak of a "partial basic income" because it can't be expected to achieve the benefits that are envisaged with a complete basic income, which is to say one that is at least at the level of the poverty threshold. Some authors see this incomplete version as a possible first step towards a full basic income.

The proposals for a state-level basic income take into account the characteristics of the taxation system and the social policy of conditional cash transfers involved in each case. They differ somewhat from state to state, although in more or less uniform areas like the European Union they have some aspects in common. Studies along these lines have been carried out for the Czech Republic, Finland, Italy, Germany and the United Kingdom, to give a few recent examples. They differ in some regards but all of them aim to show how a basic income (in some cases with modifications) would work, and then to compare the results with present schemes of conditional cash transfers in each state.

To a large extent, the present economic crisis explains why basic income, now defined as an unconditional cash payment to all members of the population of an amount above the poverty line, is being discussed more than ever before in rich and poor countries alike, and why some experiments or pilot projects are being carried out.[251] When any political proposal enters the public arena, criticisms are normally voiced from across the spectrum, some of them downright bizarre. Basic income is no exception. A lot of dissenting voices claim it can't be financed. However, it has been demonstrated using an immense database on personal income tax in Spain (IRPF) that it is possible to finance a basic income equal to the poverty threshold for all people residing in the country. Moreover, this example would be easily transferable to other states with similar taxation systems. The database would obviously vary and in each country the financing proposal would require relevant but not difficult adjustments. After detailing how the scheme works, we will also address some of the common criticisms.[252]

THE DATABASE

The study is based on data ceded by the Institute of Fiscal Studies, and consists of a sample of almost two million personal income tax declarations throughout Spain except the Autonomous Communities of Navarre and the Basque Country.[253] It opted for 2010 in order to use data reflecting one of the worst years of the crisis. Work with more recent data, and specifically from 2016, validates the calculations from 2010, showing little variation in the results.

The IRPF data revealed an almost total allocation of the taxpayer's gross and net income flows, covering salary, capital gains, property, economic activities, equity profit and loss, as well as identifying, in individual and joint declarations, the declarant's social and family situation with details of age, marital status, number of children, progenitors, and so on. Of the 43.7 million people who would receive a basic income, 34.3 million are detected in the IRPF data, while 9.4 million (8.2 million adults and 1.2 million minors) do not figure.

A considerable degree of income inequality was clear from the beginning. Hence the Gini coefficient for gross income (from nearly all sources including salary, wages, tips, capital gains, property, dividends, interest, rents, pensions and alimony, but not including offsets) before the IRPF declaration is 0.4114. Afterwards (gross income minus taxable income), it is 0.3664. Hence, personal income tax only makes the Gini index more equal by less than 5% (0.4114 - 0.3664 = 0.045). This is because a good part of the IRPF reductions and deductions are regressive, for example exemptions for pension plans, alimony and property losses.

TABLE 1.

	Declarants Pensioners	Declarants Waged	Declarants Business	Declarants Farming	Other	Total (millions)
Declarants	3.91	14.55	1.30	0.25	1.92	21.93
GROSS INCOME (€)	65,518.30	359,335.94	26,357.67	3,309.22	50,572.98	505,094.12
General tax base	58,561.81	348,356.88	23,959.72	2,799.15	42,796.79	476,474.35
Savings tax base	6,956.49	10,979.06	2,397.95	510.07	7,776.20	28,619.77
Earned income	53,625.63	340,217.21	1,770.30	271.77	34,646.02	430,530.93
Company earnings	169.29	1,926.57	20,691.70	583.53	315.86	23,686.96
Farming income	333.46	416.51	0.00	1,661.79	90.75	2,502.51
Other income	4,365.07	5,070.93	1,429.57	270.51	7,662.97	18,799.05
Tax due	5,299.24	49,061.40	4,340.49	339.39	8,767.00	67,807.53
EX ANTE INCOME	60,219.05	310,274.54	22,017.18	2,969.83	41,805.99	437,286.60

Table 1 shows that average gross income for wage workers is about €24,700 per year and, surprisingly, for businesspeople €20,275. Hence the latter declare an average of 17.7% less income. Income shown in the general tax base reveals that this figure rises to 22.8%, yet the savings tax base shows that the average income of businesspeople is 45.2% higher. Finally, the average tax due is almost the same for both groups, with figures of around €3,372 and €3,349, respectively, per annum.

THE BASIC INCOME TO BE FINANCED

The study inquired into the possibility of financing a basic income paid to the whole population, including accredited residents, and of a quantity that is equal to the poverty line (specified below). The basic income itself would be non-taxable, although any earnings in addition to it would be subject to income tax. A further, very important, condition—and one that, as we have said, constitutes an essential difference from right-wing proposals—is that the basic income would not entail subtraction by means of income tax from any pre-existing state benefits. Accordingly, the study incorporates what is already paid for in the public domain by present IRPF revenue as well as the amount necessary to finance a basic income.

The basic income would only replace other cash benefits, including allowances, grants, and pensions. If the benefits are of a lesser amount than the basic income, they would be eliminated as they are (more than) covered by the basic income. If they are of a greater amount, any quantity exceeding that of the basic income would still be granted, under the present conditions. Hence, people receiving less than the amount offered by the basic income end up gaining, while those receiving more neither win nor lose.

The criterion for calculating the quantity of the basic income was that it should be at least equal to the poverty line, which is defined by the European Union as earnings totaling 60% of the median income for the whole population. In Spain, with the exception of Navarre and the Basque Country, this was calculated to be €7,471 (€622.50 in twelve monthly payments) for people over the age of 18. The basic income amount the study adopted for minors is €1,494 per year, a fifth of that for adults.[254] With an individual basic income, a household with one adult and three minors would receive €11,952 per year, while one with three adults and one minor would receive €23,907. However, using the poverty risk threshold presents the problem that it might drop in a recession while objective basic needs remain the same. Hence, further work is being done to refine this proposal.

SAVINGS AND COSTS OF A BASIC INCOME

First, we shall examine the savings produced by a basic income, in accordance with the criteria we have specified, in particular the proviso that it will replace any cash benefits of a quantity below and up to that of the basic income.

TABLE 2. SAVINGS ON BENEFITS (€ MILLION)

Family	3,661.68
Housing	2,164.76
Social exclusion	1,957.84
Pensions	54,023.56
Unemployment	21,405.84
Grants	1,917.07
State pensioners	3,815.71
Non-deployed reservists	258.95
Catholic priests (granted by government)	126.50
Prisoners (BI suspended)	533.57
50% administration expenditure	2,356.80
TOTAL	**92,222.29**

Table 2 shows savings of €92,222.29 million.

For evident and purely analytical reasons, it is assumed that there are two distinct populations, people who are identified in IRPF data and those who are not. The cost of a basic income for the population not identified in IRPF data is detailed in Table 3, while the cost for that which is identified is shown in Table 4.

TABLE 3. POPULATION NOT IDENTIFIED IN IRPF DATA

	National Statistics Institute (INE)	IRPF	Difference	Cost (millions of €)
Population under 18 years	7,819,887	6,515,781	1,304,106	1,948.59
Adult population	35,926,543	27,774,210	8,152,333	60,906.08
TOTAL	**43,746,430**	**34,289,991**	**9,456,439**	**62,854.67**

Note that the €92,222.29 million, the total savings[255] represented by a basic income, is €29,367.62 more than the cost (€62,854.67 million) of a basic income for the population not detected in IRPF data. This balance would help to finance the basic income paid to the population which does appear in IRPF data.

TABLE 4. POPULATION IDENTIFIED IN IRPF DATA

	Population detected in IRPF data	Cost (millions of €)
Under 18s	6,515,781	9,735.88
Adults	27,774,210	207,501.12
Total	34,289,991	217,237.01
		Millions of euros
Total tax collected under present IRPF		**67,807.53**
Total cost of basic income for population detected in IRPF data		**285,044.53**

The characteristics of the tax reform proposed in the study are as follows:

1) Inclusion of the savings tax base in the general tax base.
2) Elimination of trade-offs between sources of income.
3) Elimination of non-taxable family and personal income.
4) Elimination of all reductions in taxable income (pension plans, personal circumstances, employment income, etc.).
5) Elimination of all tax deductions (housing, incentives, etc.).
6) Flat tax rate combined with basic income payment.[256]

RESULTS OF THE TAX REFORM

The micro-simulation model designed by Jordi Arcarons, which is only applicable to the population identified in IRPF data, allows us to come to several conclusions once all the data has been introduced.

A flat tax rate of 49% can finance a basic income for about 34.3 million people, almost 28 million adults and just over 6.5 million minors, while guaranteeing pre-existing levels of tax revenue. Moreover it embraces the 9.4 million not detected in IRPF data which means that 43.7 million citizens and accredited residents in Spain could receive a basic income.

A total of 61.7% of declarants would be better-off with a basic income. They would pay more tax for any income in addition to the basic income, but the latter would exceed the increased tax. This figure rises to 75% when each taxpayer's dependents are included because the basic income is paid to individuals. Accordingly, the figures for those who lose are 38.3% and 25% respectively.

The result is achieved with external financing to an amount of €51,102 million which can be broken down into the sum of the difference between the cost of financing a basic income for population not detected in the IRPF data and savings in benefits that would be abolished (€29,367.62 million), and applying the flat rate to those who are not obliged to declare (€21,734.38 million).

The first 70%, from lowest to highest income, would increase their participation in *ex post* (after the proposed reform) income by a total of 9.3% more than their *ex ante* (pre-reform) income. This is the amount that the 30% richest segment would lose. In other words, a transfer of €32,000 million would be made from the top 30% to the bottom 70%.

In the *ex ante* situation, the first 70% would contribute 17% of tax revenue, while the richest 10% would contribute 53.7%. In the *ex post* situation, the first 40% are net beneficiaries (the basic income is higher than amount of tax paid) and the richest 10% contributes almost 64% of the new tax revenue.

The following graph and related table show clearly who gains and who loses.

GRAPH 1. THOSE WHO GAIN AND THOSE WHO LOSE

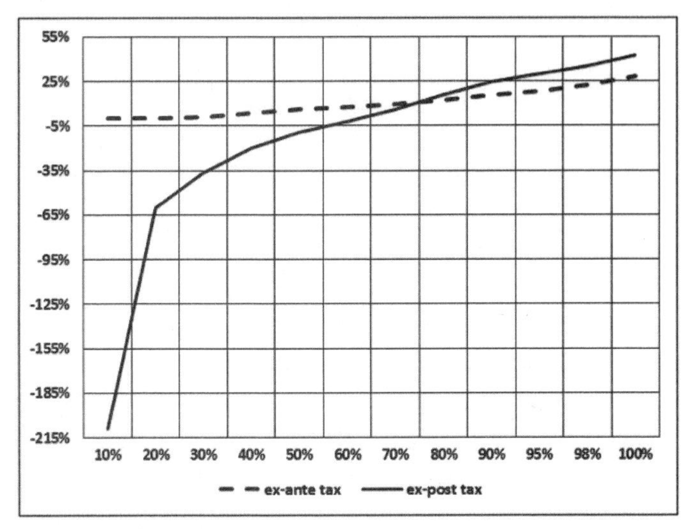

Source: Jordi Arcarons

TABLE 5. *EX ANTE* AND *EX POST* QUOTA BY DECILE

Income deciles	*Ex ante* quota on gross income	*Ex post* quota on gross income
10%	0.15%	-209.23%
20%	0.35%	-59.43%
30%	0.86%	-36.77%
40%	3.28%	-19.95%
50%	6.04%	-9.38%
60%	7.86%	-1.72%
70%	9.84%	6.23%
80%	12.53%	15.56%
90%	15.29%	24.32%
95%	18.38%	29.98%
98%	22.07%	35.02%
100%	28.03%	42.56%

In this table a subdivision has also been made within the top decile to show the richest 5% and 2%. The figures are revealing as they show who gains and who loses by comparison with the starting point (*ex ante*) situation. The poorest seven deciles gain. Take the second decile, for example. The present real interest rate is 0.35%. With a tax-exempt basic income and a flat interest rate, the tax quota is -59.42%. The negative quota denotes a net transfer. In the seventh decile, the real interest rate *ex ante* is 9.84% and the *ex post* quota is 6.23%, signifying another net transfer. However, the ninth decile loses by comparison with the *ex ante* situation because the quota rises from 15.29% to 24.32%. As Graph 1 and Table 6 show, 70% of the population detected in the IRPF data gains by comparison with the present situation, although, in some cases, there are still losers in the 70% that, in general, gains. Nevertheless, this situation can easily be rectified with refinements to the simulation model.

Then, of course, the richest 30% loses. And the population not detected in the IRPF data also gains, for obvious reasons. If these people are not declarants it is because their income is so low that they are not obliged to file. There could be a few odd exceptions but most of the population not detected in the IRPF data receives income below the filing threshold. The basic income, clearly a redistribution of wealth from the richest 20% to the remaining 80%,[257] entails a significant reduction of the Gini coefficient. If, as we have noted, this stands at 0.3664 before the present IRPF is applied, and rises to 0.4114 after IRPF, it drops to 0.2502 after the tax reform we suggest. It is now more than 11 points lower.[258]

Here is a brief summary of the main results and data arising from this model of financing a basic income.

1) It is possible to finance a basic income equal to the poverty line without touching a single cent of tax revenue preceding the reform we propose, which means that social spending

presently financed by IRPF, basically health and education, remains intact.

2) From the moment the basic income is introduced, poverty will be eradicated, at least at the statistical level, as every citizen or accredited resident receives an amount equivalent to the poverty line.
3) Although every citizen or accredited resident receives a basic income, not everyone gains in net terms. The richest 20% will receive the basic income but will lose by comparison with the previous situation. The remaining 80% starting with the poorest person, will gain with a basic income financed as we suggest.
4) Several indicators and, in particular, the Gini coefficient, show that the resulting redistribution of income will be much less unequal than it is at present.

CRITICISMS

Since December 2014, when the first report on the financing method described above was presented, there has been some critical feedback, which we believe we should note here, even if only briefly.

Some commentators assert that, among the richest 20%, there are people who can in no way be described as "rich." This emotionally loaded, often demagogically wielded opinion is weak from the substantive point of view. According to IRPF data from 2010 (and, in the 2015 data, the figures are actually lower), the central value of median gross income is €16,080, while average income is €23,000. The difference between the two values clearly shows a concentration of high values in the top tail of distribution. A tax filer with a declared total income of more than €42,000 will be situated among the richest 10%. Another person who declares more than €55,000 will be among the richest 5%.

How is this possible? In 2015 Spain's 20 richest people amassed a total fortune of €115.10 billion—the same amount as that held by the country's poorest 30% (15 million) combined. What if we contrast this with the IRPF data? Clearly, there is massive tax evasion and fraud by the richest group. If their fortunes were duly declared in their tax returns, there is no doubt that it would be even easier to finance a basic income, and the necessary tax rate (or rates) could be much lower than what we propose here.

Another, reasonable, criticism is that any proposal for financing a basic income based solely on personal income tax (IRPF) reform is incomplete and additional financing sources should be included. The reason why this method was chosen is that it offered a huge amount of detailed data which couldn't be obtained with other kinds of tax. However, there is no problem about using other sources of tax revenue to finance a basic income. These might include:

- reviewing calculation of IRPF tax bases (modules);
- additional taxes: financial transactions, luxury goods, environmental and property taxes;
- new VAT rules: elimination of reduced rates and compensation by means of a basic income;
- elimination of social security contributions ceilings;
- harmonization of inheritance, estate and gift taxes;
- elimination of corporate tax deductions, and international corporate tax harmonization in favor of taxing in accordance with the business turnover in each country;
- A tougher government stance against tax evasion and measures to prevent fraud.

As we have mentioned some critics make claims like, "people wouldn't agree with a basic income," or "society isn't ready" (sic), or "people wouldn't want to work," or "women would be housebound." These views have been amply refuted in many surveys and academic, social and political debates about basic income over the last two decades.

When Andrew Carnegie published his "Gospel of Wealth" essay in 1889,[259] suggesting not only that that private philanthropy would solve the problem of rich and poor, but "hasten the coming brotherhood of man, and at last to make our earth a heaven," William Jewett Tucker, liberal theologian and subsequently president of Dartmouth College, in a critique published by *Andover Review* in June 1891, retorted that the problem of the age was not how to administer wealth but its accumulation in a few hands. "I can conceive of no greater mistake, more disastrous in the end to religion if not to society, than that of trying to make charity do the work of justice." To judge by the extent to which charity, humanitarianism and philanthropy are presented as a way of solving the world's problems today, it wouldn't be farfetched to say that his warning went unheeded.

Andrew Carnegie, the "father of philanthropy," whose motto was "the man who dies rich dies disgraced," died rich and was a ruthless exploiter who resorted to violence against refractory workers who didn't appreciate his way of loving humanity. However, the problem is infinitely worse now than exploitation alone because neoliberalism, which is to say, the oligarchy of the tiny minority of the very rich, contemplates and is working to normalize the idea of human redundancy and hence the exclusion of enormous numbers of people from public life, and even life itself, because they are overwhelmed by the struggle to survive.

This so-called "market," which views entire populations as either a commodity or "surplus," caters to antihuman individualism (hence the Australian Prime Minister Malcolm Turnbull referred to refugees as a "product" when discussing a "deal" concerning them with Donald Trump), and encourages rejection and reviling of human rights, community spirit and social bonds.

The suffering of others, if recognized at all, is usually seen as their own fault and, if there are any qualms on that matter, charity can dispense with them. Disabling citizens makes it easier to gut the social state, but it's not just gutted. Social services and facilities are being replaced by security, surveillance and armed enforcers. Politics is no longer about serving the people but state violence against them. Fear is cultivated to justify and drive authoritarianism and redundancy. People who speak out about human rights are suspect.

If we are not already living in a dystopia, it's just around the corner. The state flexes its muscle by clamping down on people who don't fit its mold so kids are expelled from school for the way they do their hair or dress, immigrants are bad hombres, Muslims are terrorists, beggars and people forced to sleep rough are felons, and journalists are traitors. People are killed, and stripped of their freedom, dignity and rights but, since they are excluded from the sphere of things that are supposed to matter (like Trump's latest tweet or Brad Pitt's divorce-or-not-divorce), few people notice. Extreme injustice and cruelty, for example in the treatment of refugees, is now normal. This is how the rich protect their wealth and power. The planet itself is threatened and governments and big business are continuing with its despoliation and funding climate deniers. Greed is rewarded with celebrity.

Freedom is touted as freedom from government regulation in the marketplace and freedom from taxes for the rich—who, as we have described, have found that charity is the perfect vehicle for this goal—while they wait for new laws to be passed in their favor. Freedom is not for the *hoi polloi* but a very personal thing for them, even at trivial levels like philanthropic George Clooney and his human rights lawyer wife getting their privacy protected at their Lake Como mansion with the help of fines of up to €500 imposed by the mayor of Laglio on anyone who leaves a car or boat within a 100m of their two villas. They are suing paparazzi who dared to take blurry photos of their baby twins. Citing security concerns. This kind of freedom belongs in a glitzy vacuum, totally estranged from the realm of social and economic rights. Far from Lake Como, a lot of other baby twins die for lack of food and water. And who gives a damn about their security?

This is just one of many examples we could give to symbolize what we want to say. This kind of exercise of rarefied privilege symbolizes an attack on the freedom of the majority. It's not just that these displays of wealth and privilege are an insult to the intelligence—not to mention aesthetics—of most people, but they represent a serious problem of freedom: the threat posed by the rich minority to the freedom of the rest of humanity.

Any struggle against the present awful situation humanity is in, now with pundits even talking about a third world war, will require a political economy aiming at guaranteeing the right of existence for all citizens, and a decent standard of living in every sense (housing, education, health, culture and so on). Nobel Prize laureate Herbert Simon estimates that a flat tax of 90% is justifiable because social capital accounts for some 90% of income in developed countries.[260] It is social capital that terrifies antisocial (sociopathic, more like it, in a lot of cases) capitalists since, in fact, a producer's output depends on it, on shared values, shared knowledge, trust and ethics. So "social," "sharing," "trusting," and "ethical" must be stripped from capital, turning it into a cold, hard instrument to be used against the very people who create it. If Thomas Paine argued for everyone's ownership of the land and its bounty, Herbert Simon writes that social capital belongs jointly to all members of society, so the end producer should get only a small share of the profits and the rest should be taxed and redistributed as a basic income to everyone. Yanis Varoufakis expresses a similar view when he points out that the official narrative is that wealth production is private but taken by state for social purposes. But wealth production is, in fact, social and privately appropriated. No economic system could accurately estimate all the value generated by these common elements, because they are historical to begin with (which means taking into account slavery and colonial dispossession, for example), and reallocate it fairly, especially as we collectively generate things outside the monetary system which, in turn, enable market production. This understanding of the social and political aspects of economics requires recognition of social and universal rights. In this framework, basic income would not just be a crutch to prop up moribund industrialism but a universal right.

Basic income is possible. It can be financed. But financing it is not the real obstacle. It's a problem not of economics but of politics. Yet, basic income is so far by far the best mechanism that has tried to come to grips with the three great concerns of universal human rights—justice, freedom and human dignity—as well as holding out a viable means for attaining them. So the question is, do we care enough to try?

ENDNOTES

1 The blog by Elizabeth Lunday, 2012, "The Milk of Human Kindness! As in Literal Milk. Of Kindness," May 14, offers some fine images and a droll text. Online at https://www.goodreads.com/author_blog_posts/2452930-the-milk-of-human-kindness-as-in-literal-milk-of-kindness (Last accessed 10 October 10 2017).

2 See the website http://milkydreams.com/roman_charity/paintings-roman-charity-daughter-breastfeeding-her-father-starving-prison (Last accessed January 2017).

3 See http://www.culture24.org.uk/art/painting-and-drawing/art520935-ten-artists-exploring-the-legacy-of-world-war-two-in-russian-art (Last accessed January 2012).

4 See, for example https://www.asianart.com/articles/husain/figure3.html (Last accessed 28 February 2016).

5 See http://bestiary.ca/beasts/beast244.htm (Last accessed 10 February 2016).

6 Feifei Sun, 2012, "Behind the Cover: Are You Mom Enough?" 10 May 2012. Online at http://time.com/3450144/#1 (Last accessed 5 April 2015).

7 Online at http://mujeresycaridad.umwblogs.org/goya-caridad/ (Last accessed 10 February 2016).

8 Online at http://www.metmuseum.org/collection/the-collection-online/search/333963 (Last accessed, 10 February 2016).

9 Marcel Mauss, 1990, *The Gift: The Form and Reason for Exchange in Archaic Societies*, New York, London, W. W. Norton (translated by W. D. Halls).

10 See http://www.legislation.gov.uk/ukpga/2011/25 (Last accessed 10 February 2016).

11 See Rowena Mason, 2016, "David Cameron Boasts of 'Brilliant' UK Arms Exports to Saudi Arabia," *The Guardian*, February 25, Online at http://www.theguardian.com/world/2016/feb/25/david-cameron-brilliant-uk-arms-exports-saudi-arabia-bae (Last accessed February 2016).

12 See Ewen MacAskill, 2016, "UN report into Saudi-led Strikes in Yemen Raises Questions over UK Role," *The Guardian*, January 27. Online at http://www.theguardian.com/world/2016/jan/27/un-report-into-saudi-led-strikes-in-yemen-raises-questions-over-uk-role (Last accessed February 2016).

13 Oscar Wilde, 1900, *The Soul of Man*, London, Arthur L. Humphreys, p. 9. Online at http://www.gutenberg.org/files/1017/1017-h/1017-h.htm (Last accessed 3 April 2015).

14 Thomas Szasz, 1973, *The Second Sin*, New York, Anchor Press, p.64. Online at http://es.scribd.com/doc/142558436/Thomas-Szasz-The-Second-Sin#scribd (Last accessed 3 April 2015).

15 Chinua Achebe, 1988, *Anthills of the Savannah*, Heinemann, p. 155.

16 Thomas Browne, 1645, *Religio Medici*, p. 130. Online at http://penelope.uchicago.edu/relmed/relmed1645.pdf (Last accessed May 2017).

17 Op. cit. footnote 9, Chapter 1.

18 "Top Ten Charities That Should Raise a Red Flag for Donors," Online at http://give.org/news-updates/news/2016/08/top-10-charities-that-should-raise-a-red-flag-for-donors/ (Last accessed January 2016).

19 See Jonathan Parry, 1986, "The Gift, the Indian Gift and the 'Indian Gift'," *Man*, 21 (3), pp. 453–473.

20 Peter Singer, 2014, "Best Charities for 2015," online at http://www.thelifeyoucansave.org/Blog/ID/139/Best-Charities-for-2015 (Last accessed 2016).

21 *Irin News*, July 1, 2015, "Where Is All the Money Going: The Humanitarian Economy," online at http://newirin.irinnews.org/the-humanitarian-economy/ (Last accessed August 2017).

22 Chris Gregory, 1982, Chapter 1, "The Competing Theories," *Gifts and Commodities*, London, Academic Press, online at http://haubooks.org/viewbook/gifts-and-commodities/08_ch01 (Last accessed August 2016).

23 Bronislaw Malinowski, 2014 [1922], *Argonauts of the Western Pacific*, London, Routledge.

24 Annette Weiner, (1992). *Inalienable Possessions: The Paradox of Keeping-while-Giving*. Berkeley: University of California Press.

25 Chris Gregory, 1982, op.cit. footnote 22, Chapter One.

26 Karl Marx 1859, *Critique of Political Economy*, Part I, "The Commodity," online at https://www.marxists.org/archive/marx/works/1859/critique-pol-economy/ch01.htm (Last accessed August 2016).

27 Karl Marx, *Capital*, Volume 1, "Exchange," Chapter 2, online at https://www.marxists.org/archive/marx/works/1867-c1/ch02.htm (Last accessed August 2016).

28 Eric Curren, 2012, "Charles Eisenstein Wants to Devalue Your Money to Save the Economy," *Transition Voice*, August, online at: http://transition-voice.com/2012/08/charles-eisenstein-wants-to-devalue-your-money-to-save-the-economy/ (Last accessed August 23, 2016).

29 Raymond Williams, 1975, *The Country and the City* (New York: Oxford University Press) p. 30.

30 John Locke, 1689, Two Treatises of Government (Second Treatise), Chapter 5, "of Property," paragraphs 26 and 27. Online at http://press-pubs.uchicago.edu/founders/documents/v1ch16s3.html (Last accessed November 2017).

31 Carlos Delclós, Rosemary Bechler and Alex Sakalis, 2016, "What Kind of Hope Is a Promise?," *openDemocracy*, February, online at https://www.*openDemocracy*.net/can-europe-make-it/carlos-delcl-s-rosemary-bechler-alex-sakalis/what-kind-of-hope-is-promise (Last accessed August 2016).

32 The threefold punishment was that her suffering in childbearing would be greatly multiplied; that she would still lust for her husband; and that she must submit to her husband (Genesis 3:16).

33 John C. Cumbler, 1980, "The Politics of Charity: Gender and Class in Late 19th Century Charity Policy," *Journal of Social History*, Vol. 14 (1), Autumn, pp. 99–111.

34 Friedrich Engels, *Origin of the Family, Private Propery and the State*, pp. 95–96. Online at https://www.marxists.org/archive/marx/works/download/pdf/origin_family.pdf (Last accessed January 2017).

35 See *Chuang Tzu*, in the section "Nature and Government." Online at http://www.humanistictexts.org/chuang.htm (Last accessed January 2017).

36 See *Chuang Tzu*, Chapter 14. Online at http://www.universal-tao-eproducts.com/taoism-resources/ChuangTzu14UTEP.html (Last accessed January 2017).

37 Marcus Tullius Cicero, *De Legibus*, Book 2, Section 11 (translation by C. W. Keyes)

38 Marcus Tullius Cicero, *De Oficiis*, 1:43. See *Complete Works of Cicero*, 2014, Delhi Classics (translated by C. D. Yonge). Online at https://books.google.es/books?id=lSONAgAAQBAJ&pg=PT3077&lpg=PT3077&dq=Cicero+%22generous%22+benefactors&source=bl&ots=3VirBfHSaC&sig=zYzlvKNQM6NydIcVolHa_9Zuwfo&hl=es&sa=X&ved=0ahUKEwjqld3gl-PRAhVBuhQKHah3CxcQ6AEIGjAA#v=onepage&q=Cicero%20%22generous%22%20benefactors&f=false (Last accessed January 2017).

39 Online at http://www.thenagain.info/Classes/Sources/Julian.html (Last accessed January 2017).

40 Plato, *The Republic*, Book II, Cambridge, Massachusetts, Harvard University Press, p. 185 (translation by Paul Shorey).

41 Aristotle, 1999, Politics, Batoche Books, Book VI, Part 3 (translation by Benjamin Jowett), p. 143.

42 G. E. M. Ste. Croix, 1981, *The Class Struggle in the Ancient Greek World: From the Archaic Age to the Arab Conquests*, Cornell University Press, p. 306. Online at https://es.scribd.com/document/145580446/Class-Struggle-in-the-Ancient-Greek-World-St-Croix (Last accessed February 2017).

43 Ibid., pp. 433–434.

44 Quoted by Brian Tierney, 1959, *Medieval Poor Law: A Sketch of Canonical Theory and Its Application in England*, University of California Press, p. 56.

45 Bronislaw Geremek, 1994, *Poverty a History*, Blackwell, p. 21.

46 Maimomedes, 1170–1180, *Mishneh Torah* (Laws on Gifts to the Poor 10:7–14). See Marc Lee Raphael, 2003, *Gifts for the Poor: Moses Maimomedes Treatise on Tzedakah* (Introduction and translation by Joseph B. Meszler), online at http://rabbimeszler.com/yahoo_site_admin/assets/docs/Gifts_for_the_Poor.27084324.pdf (Last accessed January 2017).

47 Cited by Ste Croix https://es.scribd.com/document/145580446/Class-Struggle-in-the-Ancient-Greek-World-St-Croix p. 435

48 See "Tzedakah and Sadaqah: The Laws of Charity in Islam and Judaism." Online at http://www.judaism-islam.com/tzedakah-zakah-sadaqah-the-laws-of-charity-in-islam-and-judaism/ (Last accessed January 2017).

49 David Nasaw, 2006, *Andrew Carnegie*, Penguin Books, pp. xii–xiii.

50 Thorstein Veblen, *The Theory of the Leisure Class*, p. 36. Online at: http://moglen.law.columbia.edu/LCS/theoryleisureclass.pdf (Last accessed February 2017).

51 Patrick West, 2004. Online at http://www.cis.org.au/app/uploads/2016/09/Conspicuous-Compassion.pdf (Last accessed February 2017)

52 Elizabeth Anderson, 2015, "How Rich Are the Beckhams? Wealthier Than the Queen," *The Telegraph*, 22 September. Online at http://www.telegraph.co.uk/finance/enterprise/11882076/How-rich-are-the-Beckhams-Wealthier-than-the-Queen.html (Last accessed January 2017).

53 Vanessa Thorpe, 2017, "Me, Marriage and a Big Regret: David Tells All for Desert Island Discs," *The Guardian*, 29 January. Online at https://www.theguardian.com/tv-and-radio/2017/jan/29/david-beckham-desert-island-discs-75th-anniversary (Last accessed January 2017).

54 See, for example, Robert Booth and Jamie Grierson, 2017, "Publication of Hacked David Beckham Emails Renders Injunction Worthless," *The Guardian*, February 6.

55 See, for example, Shana Lebowitz, 2016, "Scientists Say This Behavior Can Make Men More Attractive to Women," *Business Insider*, February 14.

56 Pat Barclay, 2011, "The Evolution of Charitable Behaviour and the Power of Reputation," *Applied Evolutionary Psychology*, November.

57 Charles Darwin, 1871, *The Descent of Man and Selection in Relation to Sex*, New York: Appleton, p. 163.

58 Jorge Moll and Jordan Grafman, 2006, "Human fronto-mesolimbic networks guide decisions about charitable donation," *Proceedings of the National Academy of Sciences*: 103 (42); 15623–15628.

59 Donald W. Pfaff, 2015, *The Altruistic Brain: How We Are Naturally Good*, Oxford University Press.

60 Wilhelm von Humboldt, (1792) 1851, *Ideen zu einem Versuch, die Gränzen der Wirksamkeit des Staats zu bestimmen* (On the Limits of State Action), Breslau, Verlag von Eduard Trewendt. (Original work published 1792).

61 David Sloan Wilson, 2015, *Does Altruism Exist? Culture, Genes, and the Welfare of Others*, Yale University Press/Templeton Press.

62 See for example the report by Queen Mary University of London, 2015, "Campaigns of Violence towards Rohingya Are Highly Organised and Genocidal in Intent," October. Online at http://www.qmul.ac.uk/media/news/items/hss/165941.html (Last accessed February 2015). See also, Allard K. Lowenstein, 2015 "Persecution of the Rohingya Muslims: Is Genocide Occurring in Rakhine State? A Legal Analysis," Human Rights Clinic, Yale Law School. October. Online at http://www.fortifyrights.org/downloads/Yale_Persecution_of_the_Rohingya_October_2015.pdf (Last accessed February 2017).

63 Timothy B. Smith, 2001, "Charity and Poor Relief: The Modern Period," *Encyclopedia of European Social History*, The Gale Group, Inc. Online at http://www.encyclopedia.com/international/encyclopedias-almanacs-transcripts-and-maps/charity-and-poor-relief-modern-period (Last accessed February 2017).

64 Comte, August, 1852, *Catéchisme positiviste* (1852) or *Catechism of Positivism*, 1891, London, Kegan Paul (translated by R. Congreve), p. 332.

65 Peter Singer, 1972, "Fame, Affluence, and Morality," *Philosophy and Public Affairs*, Vol. I, Nº 1 (Spring).

66 Interview for London Weekend Television, *Weekend World* (6 January, 1980).

67 Op. cit., footnote 65.

68 Steven W. Mosher, 2015, "Zombie Charities Push Population Control," *The Washington Times*, June 22. Online at http://www.washingtontimes.com/news/2015/jun/22/steven-mosher-zombie-charities-push-population-con/ (Last accessed February 2017).

69 See Samuel Osborne, 2017, "African Refugee Drowns in Venice As Tourists Film on Phones while Laughing and Making Racist Remarks," *The Independent*, January 26. Online at http://www.independent.co.uk/news/world/europe/african-man-drowns-venice-grand-canal-video-onlookers-italy-racism-he-is-stupid-migrant-a7546806.html. And then there are the approximately 5,000 excluded, criminalized refugees who drowned in the Mediterranean in 2016, and so many other human beings "drowning" one way or another in cruelty and contempt. See http://www.unhcr.org/news/briefing/2016/12/585ce804105/mediterranean-sea-100-people-reported-dead-yesterday-bringing-year-total.html (both links Last accessed February 2017).

70 Mengzi 2A6.1–6.3; Mengzi zhengyi, 7.232–233. We are indebted to Albert Galvany for his translation and discussion of this text and the fragment of the *Lüshi chunquiu* which follows.

71 Chen Qiyou 陳奇猷 (annot.), *Lüshi chunqiu xin jiao shi* 呂氏春秋新校釋 (Shanghai: Shanghai guji chubanshe, 2002), 16.6.1013.

72 Paul Gomberg, 2002, "The Fallacy of Philanthropy," *Canadian Journal of Philosophy*, 32:1, pp. 29–65.

73 Cited by Mathew Snow, "Against Charity," *Jacobin*, August 25, 2015

74 Peter Unger, 1996, *Living High and Letting Die: Our Illusion of Innocence*, New York, Oxford University Press.

75 Dylan Matthews, 2013, "Join Wall Street. Save the World," *The Washington Post*, 31 May.

76 For example, Ken Stern, 2013, "Why the Rich Don't Give to Charity," *The Atlantic*, April. Online at https://www.theatlantic.com/magazine/archive/2013/04/why-the-rich-dont-give/309254/ (Last accessed February 2017).

77 Daisy Grewal, 2012, "How Wealth Reduces Compassion," *Scientific American*, April 10. Online at https://www.scientificamerican.com/article/how-wealth-reduces-compassion/ (Last accessed May 2017).

78 Peter Singer, "The Why and How of Effective Altruism." Online at http://www.ted.com/talks/peter_singer_the_why_and_how_of_effective_altruism/transcript?language=en (Last accessed February 2017).

79 Melody Y. Guan, 2015, "The New Social Movement of Our Generation: Effective Altruism," *The Huffington Post*, 19 April.

80 Paul Bloom, 2014 "Against Empathy," *Boston Review*, 10 September. Online at http://bostonreview.net/forum/paul-bloom-against-empathy (Last accessed February 2017).

81 Barack Obama, 2009, Remarks in a Discussion with Students in Istanbul, Turkey, Tophane Cultural Center, April 7.

82 Ann Deslandes, 2016, "Against Empathy," *Overland*, October 31. Online at https://overland.org.au/2016/10/against-empathy/ (Last accessed August 2017).

83 Roman Krznarik, 2015, "Welcome to the Empathy Wars," *openDemocracy*, June 29, Online at https://www.*openDemocracy*.net/transformation/roman-krznaric/welcome-to-empathy-wars (Last accessed February 2017).

84 The Editorial Board, "The Pope on Panhandling: Give without Worrying," *The New York Times*, March 3, 2017. Online at https://www.nytimes.com/2017/03/03/opinion/the-pope-on-panhandling-give-without-worry.html?smid=tw-share&_r=0 (Last accessed March 2017).

85 Online at http://www3.weforum.org/docs/Media/TheGlobalRisksReport2016.pdf (Last accessed February 2017).

86 Sir Richard loves hanging out with wonderful folks. He's also invited "wonderfully interesting people"—like Kate Winslett, Kate Moss, Mick Jagger, Princess Diana, Sarah Ferguson and daughters, Kate Middleton, Prince Harry, Nelson Mandela (in a group to discuss poverty, climate change and AIDS), Kofi Annan (in said group), Jimmy Carter, and Tony Blair (using the place as an "environmental war room")—to his wonderful PR asset.

87 See Richard Murphy, 2012, "Microsoft's Tax Avoidance Represents 3.5% of the World's Aid Budget," *Tax Research UK*. Online at http://www.taxresearch.org.uk/Blog/2012/12/10/microsofts-tax-avoidance-represents-3-5-of-the-world-aid-budget/ (Last accessed April 2017).

88 Barrie Gunter, 2014, *Celebrity Capital: Assessing the Value of Fame*, Bloomsbury, p. 196.

89 Christopher Lasch, 1979, *The Culture of Narcissism: American Life in an Age of Diminishing Expectations*, W. W. Norton and Company, p. 22.

90 But let us never forget James Baldwin: "It is the innocence which constitutes the crime."

91 See, The University of Manchester, 2014, "Celebrity Promotion of Charities 'Is Largely Ineffective.'" Online at http://www.manchester.ac.uk/discover/news/article/?id=12611 (Last accessed April 2017).

92 "Celebrity Power and Its Influence on Global Consumer Behaviour," 2014, *Euromonitor International*, Strategy Briefing, March. Online at http://www.euromonitor.com/celebrity-power-and-its-influence-on-global-consumer-behaviour/report (Last accessed March 2017).

93 Angela Sokolovska, 2016, "Impact of Celebrity Endorsement on Consumer Buying Behavior," *Guided Selling*, October 4. Online at http://www.guided-selling.org/impact-of-celebrity-endorsement-on-consumer-buying-behavior/ (Last accessed March 2017).

94 Jo Littler, 2008, "I feel Your Pain: Cosmopolitan Charity and the Public Fashioning of the Celebrity Soul," *Social Semiotics*, Vol. 8, Nº 2. Online at http://www.academia.edu/2546349/_I_feel_your_pain_cosmopolitan_charity_and_the_public_fashioning_of_the_celebrity_soul (Last accessed April 2017).

95 See https://en.wikipedia.org/wiki/List_of_UNICEF_Goodwill_Ambassadors (Last accessed February 2017).

96 Jasmin Malik Chua, 2016, "Report: Prada, Gucci Fail to Address Sweatshop Labor in Their Supply Chains, December 16, 2016. Online at http://www.ecouterre.com/report-prada-gucci-fail-to-address-sweatshop-labor-in-their-supply-chains/ (Last accessed February 2017).

97 Ian Birrell, 2015, "Spare us the Toe-Curling Stunts of Celebrities on Foreign Aid Ego trips," *The Daily Mail*, December 30. Online at http://www.dailymail.co.uk/news/article-3378341/IAN-BIRRELL-Spare-toe-curling-stunts-celebrities-foreign-aid-ego-trips.html#ixzz4Z09y8Y6f (Last accessed April 2017).

98 Dan McDougall, 2006, "Now Charity Staff Hit at Cult of Celebrity," *The Guardian*, November 26. Online at https://www.theguardian.com/society/2006/nov/26/internationalaidanddevelopment.internationalnews (Last accessed February 2017).

99 See https://amalalamuddinstyle.wordpress.com/tag/gucci-dress/ (Last accessed February 2017).

100 Adam Smith, 1759, *The Theory of Moral Sentiments*, I.III.28–34. Online at http://www.econlib.org/cgi-bin/searchbooks.pl?searchtype=BookSearchPara&id=smMS&query=disposition+to+admire (Last accessed February 2017).

101 Chuck Collins and Josh Hoxie, 2015, "The Forbes 400 and the Rest of Us," Institute for Policy Studies, http://www.ips-dc.org/wp-content/uploads/2015/12/Billionaire-Bonanza-The-Forbes-400-and-the-Rest-of-Us-Dec1.pdf (Last accessed April 2017).

102 OXFAM International, 2017, "Just 8 Men Own Same Wealth as Half the World," January 16, online at https://www.oxfam.org/en/pressroom/pressreleases/2017-01-16/just-8-men-own-same-wealth-half-world (Last accessed February 2017).

103 Jerome Phelps, 2017, *OpenDemocracy*, May 17. Online at https://www.*openDemocracy*.net/5050/jerome-phelps/refugee-crisis-art-weiwei (Last accessed May 2017).

104 This paragraph is basically a summary of a part of lecture, "Humanitats en transició" given by the Catalan philosopher Marina Garcés at the Centre of Contemporary Culture of Barcelona, October 18, 2016.

105 Cited by Mark O'Connell, 2017, "'Your Animal Life Is over. Machine Life Has Begun.' The Road to Immortality," *The Guardian*, March 25. Online at https://www.theguardian.com/science/2017/mar/25/animal-life-is-over-machine-life-has-begun-road-to-immortality?CMP=soc_568 (Last accessed March 2017).

106 *The Guardian* staff and agencies, 2017, "Elon Musk Wants to Connect brains with Computers with New Company," March 28. Online at https://www.theguardian.com/technology/2017/mar/28/elon-musk-merge-brains-computers-neuralink?CMP=soc_568 (Last accessed March 2017).

107 This "simple" project seems to have ethical and operational problems. See https://www.youtube.com/watch?v=RqgDqSVu1HU (Last accessed March 2017).

108 See https://www.ted.com/talks/bill_gates_unplugged#t-28694 (Last accessed March 2017).

109 Thomas C. Mountain, 2011, "Bill Gates and His $10 Billion Vaccine Scam," *Foreign Policy Journal*, August 2. Online at https://www.foreign-policy journal.com/2011/08/02/bill-gates-and-his-10-billion-vaccine-scam/ (Last accessed May 2017).

110 Cited by Linsey McGoey, "The Philanthropic State: Market-State Hybrids in the Philanthrocapitalist Turn" in Lisa Ann Richey andStefano Ponte (eds.), 2015, *New Actors and Alliances in Development*, Routledge, p. 112.

111 Jens Martens and Karolin Seitz, 2015, *Philanthropic Power and Development: Who Shapes the Agenda,* Bischöfliches Hilfswerk MISEREOR, Evangelisches Werk für Diakonie und Entwicklung Brot für die Welt – Evangelischer Entwicklungsdienst, and Global Policy Forum. P.31. Online at https://www.globalpolicy.org/images/pdfs/GPFEurope/Philanthropic_Power_online.pdf (Last accessed May 2017).

112 Ibid., p. 38.

113 Ibid., p. 35.

114 See Yuval Noah Harari, 2016, *Homo Deus: A Brief History of Tomorrow, Harvill Secker.*

115 Su Holmes and Sean Redmond, 2010, "Editorial," *Journal of celebrity Studies*, Vol. 1, nº 1, March. Online at http://www.tandfonline.com/doi/full/10.1080/19392390903519016 (Last accessed March 2017).

116 "Beckham in Degree Course," 2000, *BBC News*, March 29, http://news.bbc.co.uk/2/hi/uk_news/education/694451.stm (Last accessed February 2017).

117 Elizabeth Tippens, 1992, "Mastering Madonna," *Rolling Stone*, http://www.rollingstone.com/culture/features/mastering-madonna-19920917 (Last accessed February 2017).

118 Ibid.

119 Marja Mills, 2001, "Influence of Oprah, the College Course," *Los Angeles Times*, February 21 http://articles.latimes.com/2001/feb/21/entertainment/ca-27886 (Last accessed February 2017).

120 BBC News, US and Canada, "Oprah Winfrey for President? 'Now I'm thinking,'" http://www.bbc.com/news/world-us-canada-39136132?ocid=socialflow_twitter (Last accessed March 2017).

121 Zoe Williams, 2017, "Filthy Rich: Our Tortured Love Affair with Wealth Porn," *The Guardian*, March 6. Online at https://www.theguardian.com/tv-and-radio/2017/mar/06/big-little-lies-fifty-shades-grey-darker-billions-wealth-porn (Last accessed April 2017). On the other hand, those like Donald Trump with a thing about gold seem to be giving the message that they have no conscience to salve. Then there is golden girl Ivanka, his "hot" (daddy's word) daughter and self-proclaimed "feminist" who thinks that being complicit with daddy's pussy-grabbing and nepotism is being a "force for good."

122 As Christopher Hitchens put it in his article of 2003, "Mommie Dearest," *Slate*, October 20. Online at http://www.slate.com/articles/news_and_politics/fighting_words/2003/10/mommie_dearest.html (Last accessed May 2017).

123 See, for one example among many, Penny Green, 2015, "Aung San Suu Kyi's Silence on the Genocide of Rohingya Muslims is Tantamount to Complicity," *The Independent*, May 20. Online at http://www.independent.co.uk/voices/comment/aung-san-suu-kyis-silence-on-the-genocide-of-rohingya-muslims-is-tantamount-to-complicity-10264497.html (Last accessed April 2017).

124 A small homage to Patty Cundy who has as fine an eye for fakery as anyone ever did.

125 Evan Osnos, 2017, "Doomsday Prep for the Super-Rich," *Vanity Fair*, January 30. Online at http://www.newyorker.com/magazine/2017/01/30/doomsday-prep-for-the-super-rich (Last accessed April 2017).

126 Guy Debord, 1967, "Society of the Spectacle," Sections 29 and 27. Online at https://www.marxists.org/reference/archive/debord/society.htm (Last accessed April 2017).

127 The term "nonprofit organization" covers a range of entities including credit unions, sports clubs, political parties and religious groups, depending on a country's laws and tax regime. We are concerned here with those that are set up as charities, foundations or NGOs in the philanthropic sector.

128 Justin Elliot and Laura Sullivan, 2015, "How the Red Cross Raised Half a Billion Dollars for Haiti and Built Six Homes," *ProPublica*, June 3. Online at https://www.*ProPublica*.org/article/how-the-red-cross-raised-half-a-billion-dollars-for-haiti-and-built-6-homes (Last accessed May 2017).

129 See United States Senate, 2016, "Investigation of the American Red Cross," June 15. Online at https://www.grassley.senate.gov/sites/default/files/constituents/2016-06-15%20Senator%20Grassley%20Red%20Cross%20Inquiry.pdf (Last accessed May 2017).

130 Op. cit. footnote 128.

131 Vijaya Ramachandran and Julie Walz, 2013, "Haiti's Earthquake Generated a $9bn Response. Where Did the Money Go?," *The Guardian*, January 14. Online at https://www.theguardian.com/global-development/poverty-matters/2013/jan/14/haiti-earthquake-where-did-money-go (Last accessed May 2017). This regular Poverty Matters blog ("Transparency") has a prominent note at the beginning: "Global development is supported by Bill & Melinda Gates Foundation" (notable for transparency?).

132 See USAID, 2013, "Financial Audits of USAID Contractors, Recipients, and Host Government Entities," p.9. Online at https://www.usaid.gov/sites/default/files/documents/1868/591.pdf (Last accessed May 2017).

133 Alan Yuhas, 2015, "The Red Cross, Haiti and the 'Black Hole' of Accountability for International Aid," *The Guardian*, June 15. Online at https://www.theguardian.com/world/2015/jun/05/red-cross-haiti-black-hole-accountability-international-aid (Last accessed May 2017).

134 Vijay Prashad, 2012, "Mother Teresa as the Mirror of Bourgeois Guilt," in Najmi, Samina; Srikanth, Rajini (eds.), *White Women in Racialized Spaces: Imaginative Transformation and Ethical Action in Literature*, State University of New York Press, pp. 67–68.

135 Saimi Jeong and Michael Safi, 2014, "Global Fundraising Company Keeps $7 Million of $12.2 Million Raised for Special Olympics," *The Guardian*, June 19. Online at https://www.theguardian.com/society/2014/jun/19/global-fundraising-company-keeps-96-of-122m-raised-for-special-olympics (Last accessed May 2017).

136 Polly Curtis, 2012, "Can George Osborne Really Be 'Shocked' That the Richest People Avoid Tax?" *The Guardian*, April 10. Online at https://www.theguardian.com/politics/reality-check-with-polly-curtis/2012/apr/10/george-osborne-richest-avoid-tax (Last accessed May 2017).

137 Kris Hundley and Kendall Taggart, 2013, "Above the Law: America's Worst Charities," *CNN*, June 13. Online at http://edition.cnn.com/2013/06/13/us/worst-charities/ (Last accessed May 2017).

138 See Richard Murphy, 2013, "Can Charities Be Used for Tax Avoidance? It Seems So." Blog, "Tax Research UK." Online at http://www.taxresearch.org.uk/Blog/2013/02/01/can-charities-be-used-for-tax-avoidance-it-seems-so/ (Last accessed May 2017).

139 See Linsey McGoey, 2015, *No Such Thing As a Free Gift*, Verso, p. 232.

140 Ashlea Ebeling, 2016, "The $80 Billion Charity Stash: Donor-Advised Funds Reach Record Highs," Forbes, November 15. Online at https://www.forbes.com/sites/ashleaebeling/2016/11/15/the-80-billion-charity-stash-donor-advised-funds-reach-record-highs/#13ad847c56a2 (Last accessed May 2017).

141 Op. cit., footnote 139. p. 243.

142 Ken Stern, 2013, "Why Don't Corporations Give to Charity?," *Slate*, August 8. Online at http://www.slate.com/articles/business/moneybox/2013/08/corporations_don_t_give_to_charity_why_the_most_profitable_companies_are.html (Last accessed May 2017).

143 "Gates Foundation Awards $11 Million for Financial Inclusion in Africa," 2014, *Philanthropy News Digest*, December 8. Online at http://philanthropynewsdigest.org/news/gates-foundation-awards-11-million-for-financial-inclusion-in-africa (Last accessed May 2017).

144 Buffett, Warren E., 2011, "Stop Coddling the Super-Rich," *New York Times*, August 14. Online at http://www.nytimes.com/2011/08/15/opinion/stop-coddling-the-super-rich.html?mtrref=undefined&gwh=FFB2B912341239D912DD3F4A2B4E0E39&gwt=pay&assetType=opinion (Last accessed May 2017).

145 John Naughton, 2017, "Mark Zuckerberg Should Try Living in the Real World," *The Guardian*, May 7. Online at https://www.theguardian.com/commentisfree/2017/may/07/mark-zuckerberg-should-try-living-in-real-world-facebook?CMP=soc_568 (Last accessed May 2017).

146 Nicholas Carr, 2017, "Zuckerberg's World," February 18. Online at http://www.roughtype.com/?p=7651 (Last accessed May 2017).

147 See (last updated 2016), https://www.charitywatch.org/charitywatch-articles/charitywatch-hall-of-shame/63 (Last accessed May 2017).

148 Nicholas Carlson, 2012, "The Dwarf-Throwing Billionaire Who's Buying up America: Tales of the Mysterious Saudi Prince Alwaleed," *Business Insider*, June 12. Online at http://www.businessinsider.com/prince-alwaleed-2012-1 (Last accessed May 2017).

149 Ibid.

150 SustainAbility et al, *The 21st-Century NGO in the Market for Change*, p. 11. Online at file:///E:/Users/HOME/Downloads/The+21st+Century+NGO+-+In+the+market+for+change.pdf (Last accessed June 2017).

151 To paraphrase Antoine de Saint-Exupery 1969, *Flight to Arras*, Harcourt Brace, p. 148: "The dignity of the individual demands that he be not reduced to vassalage by the largesse of others."

152 Teju Cole 2012, "The White-Savior Industrial Complex," *The Atlantic*, March 21. Online at https://www.theatlantic.com/international/archive/2012/03/the-white-savior-industrial-complex/254843/ (Last accessed May 2017).

153 Henry Shue, 1996, *Basic Rights: Subsistence, Affluence and U.S. Foreign Policy*, Princeton University Press, p. 53.

154 Translated into English by Samuel Beckett and published in Nancy Cunard, 1934, *The Negro Anthology Made by Nancy Cunard 1931–1933*, Wishart and Co.

155 Cited by Annie Slemrod, 2017, "Princes and Bankers and Aid: Oh My!: Humanitarians at the World Economic Forum," *Irin*, May 26. https://www.irinnews.org/analysis/2017/05/26/princes-and-bankers-and-aid-oh-my (Last accessed May 2017).

156 David Kennedy, 2005, "Reassessing International Humanitarianism: The Dark Sides." Online at http://www.law.harvard.edu/faculty/dkennedy/speeches/TheDarkSides.pdf (Last accessed May 2017).

157 Antonio Donini, 2016, "The Crisis of Multilateralism and the Future of Humanitarian Action," *Irin*, November 30. Online at https://www.irinnews.org/opinion/2016/11/30/crisis-multilateralism-and-future-humanitarian-action (Last accessed May 2017).

158 Robert Block, 1994, "Hutus Keep on Killing Tutsis in Goma Camp," *Independent*, July 26. Online at http://www.independent.co.uk/news/world/hutus-keep-on-killing-tutsis-in-goma-camp-robert-block-in-goma-finds-rwandas-genocidal-conflict-is-1416473.html (Last accessed May 2017).

159 See reports cited in footnote 62.

160 Cited by Qaabata Boru, 2013, "Life in the Kakuma Refugee Camp," *Fair Observer*, June 22. Online at https://www.fairobserver.com/region/africa/life-kakuma-refugee-camp/

161 Rosa Freedman has given a clear, detailed and compelling account of why this is the case in her book *Failing to Protect: the UN and the Politicisation of Human Rights*, Hurst & Company, London, 2014.

162 Thomas Pogge, 2006, "Poverty and Human Rights," *Ethics & International Affairs*, August. Online at file:///E:/Users/HOME/Downloads/World_Poverty_and_Human_Rights.pdf (Last accessed May 2017).

163 Malachy Postlethwayt, 2010 [1745], *The African Trade, The Great Pillar and Support of the British Plantation Trade in America*, Gale ECCO.

164 David Kennedy, 2004, "International Humanitarianism: The Dark Sides," *The International Journal of Not-for-Profit Law*, Vol.6, Issue 3, June.

165 Op. cit footnote 2.

166 Arundhati Roy, 2014, "The NGOization of Resistance," *Pambazuka.org*, Issue 695, September 23. Online at https://revolutionaryfrontlines.wordpress.com/2014/09/25/ngoisation-of-resistance-arundhati-roy/ (Last accessed May 2017).

167 Cited by Japhry Wilson, 2014, *Jeffrey Sachs: The Strange Case of Dr Shock and Mr Aid*, Verso, p. 106.

168 L. David Brown et al., 2000, "Globalization, NGOs and Multi-Sectoral Relations," Hauser Center Working Paper N°1, July.

169 "Misplaced Charity," *The Economist*, June 11, 2016. Online at http://www.economist.com/news/international/21700323-development-aid-best-spent-poor-well-governed-countries-isnt-where-it?fsrc=scn/tw_ec/foreign_aid_is_a_shambles_in_almost_every_way (Last accessed May 2017).

170 Bernard Kouchner, 2004, "The Future of Humanitarianism," 23rd Annual Morgenthau Memorial Lecture on Ethics and Foreign Policy, March 2. Online at http://archive.li/loXgh#selection-927.0-947.125 (Last accessed May 2017).

171 Report of the Secretary General pursuant to the statement adopted by the Summit Meeting of the Security Council on January 31, 1992. Online at http://www.un-documents.net/a47-277.htm (Last accessed May 2017).

172 1994. Online at https://www.icrc.org/eng/assets/files/publications/icrc-002-1067.pdf (Last accessed May 2017).

173 Bertrand Russell, 1995 [1946], *History of Western Philosophy,* Routledge, p. 488.

174 Ibid, p. 94.

175 Linsey McGoey, 2016, "Does Philanthrocapitalism Make the Rich Richer and the Poor Poorer?" *Evonomics*, February 23. Online at http://evonomics.com/does-philanthropy-actually-make-the-rich-richer-and-the-poor/ (Last accessed June 2017).

176 Cited by Gabriel Winant, 2014, "American Philanthropy and Its Discontents," *Jacobin*, May 8. Online at https://www.*Jacobin*mag.com/2014/05/american-philanthropy-and-its-discontents/ (Last accessed July 2017).

177 Thanks, for this and other insights, to Tim Scott, 2017, "Impact Investing and Venture Philanthropy's Role in Sowing the Seeds of Financial Opportunity," *Truthout*, June 10. Online at http://www.truth-out.org/news/item/40860-impact-investing-and-venture-philanthropy-s-role-in-sowing-the-seeds-of-financial-opportunity (Last accessed July 2017).

178 Cited by Maria Hengeveld, 2015, "The Anti-Poverty Swindle," *Jacobin*, November 15. https://www.*Jacobin*mag.com/2015/11/united-nations-nike-walmart-sustainable-development-ngo/ (Last accessed July 2017).

179 A majority of conservative judges in the Supreme Court threw out the case in 2011, on the technicality that the million plaintiffs had not been discriminated against in the same way.

180 Matthew Bishop and Michael Green, 2008, *Philanthrocapitalism: How the Rich Can Save the World*, Bloomsbury (USA).

181 Joel Fleishman, 2009, "The New Noblesse Oblige," *Stanford Social Innovation Review*, winter. (Online at https://ssir.org/book_reviews/entry/philanthrocapitalism_how_rich_can_save_world_mattew_bishop_michael_green (Last accessed June 2017).

182 See Kelly Riddell, 2015, "Ideological Billionaires Sway Universities' Agendas with Big Bucks," *The Washington Times*, August 26. Online at http://www.washingtontimes.com/news/2015/aug/26/george-soros-tom-steyer-michael-bloomberg-koch-bro/ (Last accessed June 2017).

183 Cited in an article titled "The Birth of Philanthrocapitalism," *The Economist*, February 23, 2006. Online at http://www.economist.com/node/5517656 (Last accessed July 2017).

184 Adam Meyerson, 2013 "President's Note: Misconceptions about "Dark Money," *Philanthropy* magazine, Fall Issue. Online at http://www.philanthropyroundtable.org/topic/philanthropic_freedom/presidents_note (Last accessed July 2017).

185 Friedrich von Hayek, 1941, "Planning, Science and Freedom," *Nature 148*, November 15.

186 Paul Krugman, 2011, "Things That never Happened in the History of Macroeconomics," *The New York Times*, December 5. Online at https://krugman.blogs.nytimes.com/2011/12/05/things-that-never-happened-in-the-history-of-macroeconomics/ (Last accessed June 2017).

187 Fergal Byrne, 2006, "Dinner with the FT: Auction Man," *Financial Times*, March 24. Online at https://www.ft.com/content/25bcd80c-b967-11da-9d02-0000779e2340 (Last accessed June 2017).

188 Antoni Domènech, 2010, Preface to David Casassas, 2010, *La ciudad en llamas. La vigencia del repubicanismo comercial de Adam Smith*, Montesinos.

189 Adam Smith, *The Wealth of Nations*, 1776, William Strahan, Thomas Cadell, II, 2, p. 94.

190 Benjamin Soskis, 2017, "What If Philanthropy Isn't the Best Way for Rich People to Help Others?," *The Washington Post*, June 30. Online at https://www.washingtonpost.com/outlook/what-if-philanthropy-isnt-the-best-way-for-rich-people-to-help-others/2017/06/30/88afcb6e-5d15-11e7-9fc6-c7ef4bc58d13_story.html?utm_term=.35ba6400a7f0 (Last accessed July 2017).

191 Dan Vexler, 2017, "What Exactly Do We Mean by Systems?," *Stanford Social Innovation Review*, June 22. Online at https://ssir.org/articles/entry/what_exactly_do_we_mean_by_systems (Last accessed July 2017).

192 Ibid.

193 See Anna Marie Cox, 2017, "Naomi Klein Is Sick of Benevolent Billionaires," *The New York Times Magazine*, June 14. Online at https://www.nytimes.com/2017/06/14/magazine/naomi-klein-is-sick-of-benevolent-billionaires.html?_r=1 (Last accessed July 2017).

194 Anna-Marie Harling and Christina Tung, 2017, "Seven Things You Probably Didn't Know about Chinese Philanthropy," *The Guardian*, June 28. Online at https://www.theguardian.com/global-development-professionals-network/2017/jun/28/seven-things-you-probably-didnt-know-about-chinese-philanthropy?CMP=soc_568 (Last accessed July 2017).

195 Arundhati Roy, 2012, "Capitalism: A Ghost Story, *Dawn*, March 18. Online at https://www.dawn.com/news/703595/capitalism-a-ghost-story-2 (Last accessed July 2017).

196 For this summary we are indebted to Jens Martens and Karolin Seitz, 2015, op. cit. footnote 111.

197 David McCoy, Gayatri Kembhavi, Jinesh Patel, and Akish Luintel, 2009, "The Bill & Melinda Gates Foundation's Grant-Making Programme for Global Health," *The Lancet*, May 9. Online at http://www.thelancet.com/journals/lancet/article/PIIS0140-6736%2809%2960571-7/abstract (Last accessed July 2017).

198 For a detailed, depressing account see Sophie Harman, 2016, "The Bill and Melinda Gates Foundation and Legitimacy in Global Health Governance," http://www.academia.edu/27618803/The_Bill_and_Melinda_Gates_Foundation_and_Legitimacy_in_Global_Health_Governance (Last accessed July 2017).

199 Stefanie Garden, 2015, "From Coca-Cola, a Reminder about Corporate Philanthropy's Dark Side," *Inside Philanthropy*, August 11. Online at https://www.insidephilanthropy.com/home/2015/8/11/from-coca-cola-a-reminder-about-corporate-philanthropys-dark.html (Last accessed July 2017).

200 See Winant 2014, op. cit, footnote 176.

201 Cited by Raj Patel, 2012, "The Long Green Revolution," *The Journal of Peasant Studies*, published online November 16. Available at http://www.tandfonline.com/doi/full/10.1080/03066150.2012.719224 (Last accessed July 2017).

202 Peregrino Brimah, 2015, "Goodbye Akinwumi Adesina, Goodbye GMO, Goodbye NWO," *NewsRescue*, April 23. Online at http://newsrescue.com/goodbye-akinwumi-adesina-goodbye-gmo-goodbye-nwo/#ixzz4mGyzqcjI (Last accessed July 2017).

203 Jeff Donn, 2016, "Eric Trump Foundation Flouts Charity Standards," *Associated Press*, December 23. (Online at https://www.msn.com/en-us/news/politics/ap-eric-trump-foundation-flouts-charity-standards/ar-BBxsRwW (Last accessed July 2017).

204 Carolyn Miles and Clyde Tuggle, 2012, "The Business of Doing Good Is Good Business," *The Hill*, July 17. Online at http://thehill.com/blogs/congress-blog/foreign-policy/238299-the-business-of-doing-good-is-good-business (Last accessed November 2017).

205 Michael Hudson and Paul Jay, 2016, "Is the Real Scandal the Clinton Foundation?," *CounterPunch*, July 11. Online at https://www.counterpunch.org/2016/07/11/is-the-real-scandal-the-clinton-foundation/ (Last accessed July 2017).

206 Ibid.

207 Kimberley A. Strassel, 2015, "The Clinton 'Charity' Begins at Home," *The Wall Street Journal*, June 4.

208 Tribune News Services, 2016, "Bill Clinton Defends Clinton Foundation, Says It Creates Jobs, Saves Lives," *Chicago Tribune*, August 24. Online at http://www.chicagotribune.com/news/nationworld/politics/ct-bill-clinton-foundation-20160824-story.html (Last accessed July 2016).

209 Cited by Belinda Luscombe, 2006, "Exclusive: Madonna Speaks about Her 'Big, Big Project,'" *Time,* August 3. Online at http://content.time.com/time/world/article/0,8599,1222449,00.html (Last accessed July 2017).

210 See "About Basic Income," BIEN website, online at http://basicincome.org/basic-income/ (Last accessed July 2017).

211 See A. B. Atkinson, 1996, "The Case for a Participation Income," *The Political Quarterly,* 67(1): 67–70.

212 Karl Marx, 1959, *Economic and Philosophic Manuscripts of 1844*, Moscow, Progress Publishers, p. 30. Online at https://www.marxists.org/archive/marx/works/download/pdf/Economic-Philosophic-Manuscripts-1844.pdf (Last accessed August 2017).

213 Robert and Edward Skidelsky, 2013, *How Much is Enough?: Money and the Good Life*, Other Press, p.9.

214 See Sarah Jaffe, 2014, "Naomi Klein on Cause of Climate Crisis: 'Capitalism Is Stupid,'" *Truthout*, September 24. Online at http://www.truth-out.org/news/item/26369-naomi-klein-on-cause-of-climate-crisis-capitalism-is-stupid (Last accessed August 2017).

215 http://basicincome.org/wp-content/uploads/2017/05/DR-2017-survey.pdf

216 Axel Marx and Hans Peeters, (first published in) 2004, "An Unconditional Basic Income and Labor Supply: Results from a Survey of Lottery Winners." Online at http://www.usbig.net/papers/106-Peters-Marx--LaborSupply.pdf (Last accessed July 2017).

217 See John Maynard Keynes, 1963, *Essays in Persuasion*, New York: W. W. Norton & Co., pp. 358–373

218 Thomas Paine, 1999 (digital edition), *Agrarian Justice*, p. 16. Online at http://piketty.pse.ens.fr/files/Paine1795.pdf (Last accessed August 2017).

219 Yanis Varoufakis, 2016, "The Universal Right to Capital Income," *Project Syndicate*, October 31. Online at https://www.project-syndicate.org/commentary/basic-income-funded-by-capital-income-by-yanis-varoufakis-2016-10?barrier=accessreg (Last accessed July 2017).

220 Paul Buchheit, 2017, "Now Just Five Men Own Almost As Much Wealth As Half the World's Population," *CommonDreams*, June 12. Online at https://www.commondreams.org/views/2017/06/12/now-just-five-men-own-almost-much-wealth-half-worlds-population (Last accessed July 2017).

221 Joseph Stiglitz, 2012, *The Price of Inequality: How Today's Divided Society Endangers Our Future*, W. W. Norton and Company, p. liii

222 Linda McQuaig and Neil Brooks, 2011, *The Trouble with Billionaires: Why Too Much Money at the Top is bad for Everyone*, Penguin Canada, p.49.

223 Ibid., p. 34.

224 Op. cit. See footnote 219.

225 Sonia Sodha, "Mark Zuckerberg Has Some Cheek Advocating a Basic Income," *The Guardian* July 17. Online at https://www.theguardian.com/commentisfree/2017/jul/10/mark-zuckerberg-universal-basic-income-facebook-tax (Last accessed August 2017).

226 Aristotle, *Politics*, Book One, Part IV. Online at http://classics.mit.edu/Aristotle/politics.mb.txt (Last accessed July 2017).

227 Rafael Poch, 2016, "Estamos preparados para una nueva confrontación," *La Vanguardia*, December 12. Online at http://www.lavanguardia.com/internacional/20161212/412546895096/entrevista-philippe-martinez-estamos-preparados-nueva-confrontacion.html (Last accessed July 2017)

228 Philippe van Parijs, 2016, "Basic Income and Social Democracy," *Social Europe*, 11 April. Online at https://www.socialeurope.eu/44878 (Last accessed August 2017).

229 Carole Pateman, "Democratizing Citizenship: Some Advantages of a Basic Income," in Bruce Ackerman, Anne Alstott, and Philippe van Parijs, 2003, *Redesigning Distribution*: p. 95. Online at https://www.ssc.wisc.edu/~wright/Redesigning%20Distribution%20v1.pdf (Last accessed August 2017).

230 Yannick Vanderborght and Philippe van Parijs, 2006, *La renta básica. Una medida eficaz para luchar contra la pobreza*, Paidós, p. 109.

231 Florent Marcellesi. 2011, "Una renta básica de ciudadanía para vivir mejor con menos," *Ecología Política*, N° 40. Online at http://florentmarcellesi.eu/2011/02/15/una-renta-basica-de-ciudadania-para-vivir-mejor-con-menos/ (Last accessed August 2017).

232 Arthur C. Clarke, 1985, *The Promise of Space*, Berkeley Publishing Group, p. xii.

233 See Daniel Raventós, 2007, *Basic Income: The Material Conditions of Freedom*, Pluto Press, for a review of liberal academic theories justifying basic income.

234 Philippe Van Parijs, 1991, "Why Surfers Should Be Fed: The Liberal Case for a Universal basic Income," *Philosophy and Public Affairs*, Vol. 20, N° 2, p. 102. Online at https://cdn.uclouvain.be/public/Exports%20reddot/etes/documents/1991l.Surfers.pdf (Last accessed August 2017).

235 The following discussion of state neutrality is taken from Daniel Raventós 2007, op. cit. footnote 233. See Chapter 3.

236 M. J. Bertomeu and Antoni Domènech (2006): "El republicanismo y la crisis del rawlsismo metodológico (Nota sobre método y substancia normativa en el debate republicano)," *Isegoría*, N° 33, pp. 51–75.

237 Ibid.

238 See the interview by Carlos Abel Suárez with Antoni Domènech where he emphasizes this fact in *El periodista de Chile*, N°. 64, 2004. Available online at http://www.sinpermiso.info/textos/entrevista-poltica-a-antoni-domnech (Last accessed August 2017).

239 We are indebted in much of the following discussion to work, first of all, by Antoni Domènech but also by María Julia Bertomeu, David Casassas and Jordi Mundó.

240 For a discussion of neorepublicanism, see Antoni Domènech and Daniel Raventós, 2008, "Property and Republican Freedom: An Institutional Approach to Basic Income," *Basic Income Studies*, Vol. 2 (2).

241 See Rose, Carol M., 1999 "Canons of Property Talk, or, Blackstone's Anxiety," Yale Law School, p.601. Online at http://digitalcommons.law.yale.edu/cgi/viewcontent.cgi?article=2801&context=fss_papers (Last accessed August 2017).

242 As María Julia Bertomeu specifies, "From the legal standpoint, the liberal concept of property has been developed in the Napoleonic Code which, in Article 544 is defined as the "right of enjoying and disposing of things in the most absolute manner, provided they are not used in a way prohibited by the laws or statutes." This means that it embraces the following basic rights: enjoying, which means using something (*jus utendi*), receiving its fruits (*jus fruendi*) and disposing of it (*jus abutendi*) or, in other words, transferring ownership of it to another person. See, María Julia Bertomeu, 2005, "Republicanismo y propiedad," *Sin Permiso*, July 5. Online at http://www.sinpermiso.info/textos/republicanismo-y-propiedad (Last accessed August 2017).

243 That this eminent republican thinker should have been maligned and derided by right-wing intellectuals, politicians and propagandists since his death at the age of 36 is hardly surprising but the fact that the majority of left-wing thinkers have shown little interest in his ideas is lamentable.

244 Cited by Daniel Raventós 2007, op. cit. footnote 233, p. 62.

245 Non-constitutive or instrumental rights are alienable. Public law does not allow us to sell our citizenship, or to enter into private contracts of voluntary slavery, even though some liberal-libertarian philosophers would have no problem with the latter.

246 See M. J. Bertomeu, M.J. and Antoni Domènech (2006), op. cit., footnote 236.

247 Cited, for example, by Ralph Nader in his acceptance statement for the Green Party presidential nomination, June 25, 2000, this very popular quote may be apocryphal as it seems impossible to trace the exact source but whether Brandeis actually said the words or not, it is difficult to dispute their truth. And anyway, "If it is not a Brandeis quote, it is at least a Brandeisian one." See http://greenbag.org/v16n3/v16n3_articles_campbell.pdf (Last accessed August 2017).

248 Antoni Domènech (2005), "El socialismo y la herencia de la democracia republicana fraternal," *El Viejo Topo*, Nº. 205.

249 John Locke, 1690, *Second Treatise on Government*, VII, 85.

250 Philip Pettit, 2007, "A Republican Right to Basic Income?" *Basic Income Studies*, Vol 2 (2), p.5.

251 See, for example, the recent books, Guy Standing, 2017, *Basic Income: And How We Can Make It Happen*, Pelican; and Philippe Van Parijs and Yannick Vanderborght, 2017, *Basic Income: A Radical Proposal for a Free Society and a Sane Economy*, Harvard University Press.

252 In this account we have mainly drawn on two studies based on earlier surveys carried out for Catalonia and Spain, the more recent one containing changes made thanks to new data and feedback from colleagues. The studies are, Jordi Arcarons, Antoni Domènech, Daniel Raventós and Lluís Torrens, 2014, "Un modelo de financiación de la Renta Básica para el conjunto de España: sí, se puede y es racional," *Sin Permiso*, December 7, online at http://www.sinpermiso.info/textos/un-modelo-de-financiacin-de-la-renta-bsica-para-el-conjunto-del-reino-de-espaa-s-se-puede-y-es (Last accessed August 2017); and, in English, Jordi Arcarons, Daniel Raventós and Lluís Torrens, 2014, "Feasibility of Financing a Basic Income," *Basic Income Studies* Vol. 9 (1-1) pp. 79–93.

253 The reasons for this exclusion are technical: since these two regions are not part of the "common system," including them could result in data distortion. However, both communities have a higher average income than the rest of Spain so their inclusion would only bolster our argument. In fact, one year before the Spanish study, Arcarons, Raventós and Torrens, using data ceded by the provincial government, demonstrated that a basic income could be financed in the Basque province of Guipúzcoa at a lower cost than for Spain. This time, it was not just a sample but all the province's personal income tax declarations.

254 This figure of one fifth of the amount set for adults requires explanation. It is indisputable that the living costs for one person are less than those for five people, even if they all share the same home. But not five times less. As we have noted above, the OECD uses the Oxford Scale, which calculates that one adult in the family has a weighting of 100%, other adults 70%, and under-fourteens 50%, although it also applies another related OECD-modified scale, where the first adult has a weighting of 100%, other adults 50%, and under-fourteens 30%. The number of consumption units (c.u.) in a household is calculated using the formula: N° of c.u. = 1 + (a-1) x 0.7 + b x 0.5 (where a is the number of adults and b is the number of minors). In a household with three adults and one minor, the total amount received in the form of a basic income would be €23,907 or, applying the Oxford scale, €21,664 (although there is some small distortion as our age limit for minors is 18 and the OECD's is 14). However, the poverty line is still a convention (as noted above, 60% of the median income of inhabitants of a geographic zone) which is more related with inequality than with any objective indicator of poverty or material need. The choice of an individual basic income rather than one based on a family unit is guided more by democratic than technical questions because it is paid to individuals as citizens.

255 By "savings" we refer to amounts presently paid by the state which would be abolished if a basic income were introduced.

256 This idea of a flat tax rate has alarmed more than one critic of this model. Indeed, a flat tax rate without a basic income could be very regressive. As we shall demonstrate, a flat tax rate combined with a tax-exempt basic income is highly progressive. Moreover, the simulation model we use allows us to introduce different tax brackets and rates for financing a basic income. We refer only to a flat tax rate here for reasons of simplification.

257 These are figures for the population as a whole. In terms of the IRPF population, they are 30% and 70%.

258 The Kakwani and Suits indices, for example, also confirm the high degree of progressivity of the tax reform we propose, thus eliminating any doubts about the combination of a flat rate and a basic income in terms of progressiveness and redistribution.

259 See "Carnegie Speaks: A Recording of the Gospel of Wealth," *History Matters*. Online at http://historymatters.gmu.edu/d/5766/ (Last accessed August 2017).

260 Herbert A. Simon, 2000, "A Basic Income for All," *Boston Review*, October 1. Online at http://bostonreview.net/forum/basic-income-all/herbert-simon-ubi-and-flat-tax (Last accessed August 2017).

INDEX